JUSTIN FASHANU

The Biography

JIM READ

First published in Great Britain in 2012 by The Derby Books Publishing Company Limited, 3 The Parker Centre, Derby, DE21 4SZ.

Paperback edition published in Great Britain in 2012 by The Derby Books Publishing Company Limited, 3 The Parker Centre, Derby, DE21 4SZ.

ISBN 978-1-78091-228-8
Printed and bound by Copytech (UK) Limited, Peterborough.

JUSTIN FASHANU
The Biography

Contents

Acknowledgements

Special thanks to Malcolm Black and Vroni Dewan. Without their encouragement and practical help throughout I could not have written this book.

I have depended on the generosity and contributions of: Maria Sol Acuña, Sue Anderson, Thurstine Basset, Rachel Blundy, Charles Briody, Ronnie Brooks, Peter Campbell, Terry Carpenter, Glenn Case, Matthew Clark, Les Cleevely, Rob Crane, Graham Daniels, Mike Davage, Malcolm Doney, Tim Edwards, Roger Haywood, Chris Fairclough, Troy Andrew Fairclough, Rachel Gerlis, John Gibson, Katherine Haywood, Matthew Hodson, Gordon Homes, Nick House, Dorothy Howes, Clare Hynes, Edward Jackson, Jemima Jackson, Rachel Jackson, George Kimm, Joanne Ireland, James Ledward, Mick Leonard, Peter Mendham, Angus McAlpine, Graham Mitchell, Peter Pinizzotto, Kevan Platt, Goff Powell, John Price, John Punshon, Alan Quick, John Samways, Neil Slawson, Bee Springwood, Gary Stewart, Richard Stevenson, Peter Tatchell, David Thomas, Kevin Thompson, Veronica Toner, Dawn Viveash, Derek John Walker, Andrew Wenley, Michael West, Terry Wing, Michele Wolton, Lonny Wortham.

Thanks to people who responded to my posts on message boards at the following websites: Forest Forum, Knees Up Mother Brown, North Stand Chat, Notts County Mad, The Pink'un, The Stomp, Torquay Fans Forum, Voyageurs Forum, Yellow Fever.

Thanks also to staff at the British Film Institute, British Library, British Newspaper Library, National Library of Scotland; libraries at the following locations: Brighton, Edinburgh, Manchester, Norwich, Nottingham, Southampton, Thetford, Torquay and the London Boroughs of Ealing, Haringey, Newham and Walthamstow, and the Nottingham Post library. Staff at Barnardo's and the *Who Cares?* Trust were most helpful. I appreciate the enthusiasm and expertise of the staff at DB publishing.

Permission to use lyrics and cover art from *Do It 'Cos You Like It* courtesy of Roger Haywood, business manager of Justin Fashanu at the time.

Chapter 1

Barnardo's Boy

Justin Fashanu's mother, Pearl, is visiting him in the USA and they go out for a meal. As they drive back to his apartment, he asks 'Why did you send the two of us away?' She tries to explain why she put Justin and his younger brother, John, into care and why she did not take them back when she married and had another child. But for Justin the story never adds up and so he keeps asking, 'Why?'

It is the last time he sees his mother. A few months later, back in London, in a lock-up garage three miles from Hackney Hospital where he was born, he hangs himself.

The feeling of being rejected by your mother is as raw and basic as it gets. But perhaps the emotional pain can be eased by explanation of the circumstances and intentions. In the direst of situations, giving her child away could be the most loving action a mother can take. To the end of his 37 years of life, Justin was still seeking an explanation that satisfied him.

Justin Fashanu led a life of spectacular highs and lows. His destiny was determined by his skin colour, sexuality, religious beliefs and sporting talent; his charm, warmth and exuberance; his desperate desire for celebrity and material wealth; and some disastrous decision making. And it was overshadowed by his experiences of first being abandoned by his father and then put into care by his mother.

He never did get over it.

JUSTIN FASHANU

*　*　*

Pearl Lawrence was from British Guiana (now Guyana). Growing up as a subject of the British Empire she would have thought of Britain as the Mother Country and, like many people from the Caribbean in the 1950s, answered the call to move there and work in the National Health Service. She found somewhere to live in Hackney in London's East End and a job as a nurse. Her first child, Dawn, was born in 1956.

Patrick Fashanu's presence in London was also a consequence of his home country's status as a British colony. He was from Nigeria and in London studying to be a lawyer. Pearl and Patrick had three sons together: Phillip was born in 1959, Justin (Justinus Soni on his birth certificate) on 19 February 1961 and John 19 months later. Then things began to fall apart. There are conflicting accounts of the timing and detail of events but this is broadly what happened.

First, Patrick left the family, later claiming he felt he had no choice, having been instructed to return to Nigeria by his grandfather. Shortly after, he married and started a new family. Justin did not see him again until he was 21 years old. After Patrick left, Pearl's children were taken into care. Some of the time the three brothers were together, possibly in foster care. Later, Dawn and Phillip were fostered while Justin and John were placed in a children's home. Meanwhile, Pearl started a relationship with Walter Gopaul, a shoe machinist, and they married in 1964. According to a family friend, Pearl did not tell Walter about her children until after the wedding. Dawn and Phillip were taken back to live with their mother and stepfather; Justin and John were left in a home run by Dr Barnardo's, a charity set up in Victorian times by an evangelical Christian, Thomas Barnardo. So synonymous is the name 'Barnardo's' with the care of orphans and abandoned children that Justin and John were forever after referred to as 'Barnardo's boys'.

It was a traumatic time for Justin. Separated from his parents, sister and older brother and sent to live in an institution, sharing a dormitory with children he had never met, his parents replaced by paid carers, his sense of security was further undermined by staff teasing him about why he had been left there. As well as coping with his own feelings, this young child had to assume the role of protector. John became dependent on Justin, following him everywhere, holding on to his shirt tails or pullover, and developed a speech defect so severe that only Justin could understand him. Speaking in a TV documentary, *Fallen Hero*, John said: 'Justin was my shining light. He was my life. He was the one who I saw as my mother and my father as I was growing up. He was strength. He was my inspiration. He was what I idolised.'

The Biography

Justin seldom spoke of this period of his life and was most revealing when, aged 30, he was interviewed by three teenage boys from a care home in Plymouth for the magazine, *Who Cares?*. He always tended to look for the positives in any situation and when they asked him what it was like being in care he replied that he had thought it was great, a new adventure with plenty of toys and open space, before adding that it was no substitute for being in a family. They asked him if he could have changed anything about being in care and he spoke about his struggles: 'I think I probably would have been a little bit more open to people, let people help me and talk to me. I had to close up and it's taken me 29 years to start to deal with all the things that happened in my youth though it wasn't that bad. People tell me I'm a good communicator when it comes to dealing with other people's problems or business, but when it comes to me being able to express my own feelings – it's difficult. It's a great question. To change the past, probably I would have learned to trust people earlier.'

* * *

Betty and Alf Jackson and their children, Susan and Edward – a white family – lived in Kensal Rise, north-west London, where Alf ran a small engineering business making wheels for Hornby model trains. But he was expecting to lose the lease on his workshop. The Jacksons had taken holidays in Norfolk and decided to move there, swapping their city life for the quiet of rural England. Their new home, known as Flint House, was in the small village of Shropham, 20 miles south-west of the city of Norwich.

Alf continued his business – building a workshop in the back garden and taking on five or six staff – and Betty played the organ in her local church and gave piano lessons. But it was not enough to keep her fully occupied. Susan and Edward had grown up and when Alf was not working late he was often in the pub. Their large home felt empty. So, aged 46, she decided to foster children and approached Dr Barnardo's.

In recent times there has been a debate about black children being placed with white parents, with white prospective parents complaining that social workers are reluctant to let them adopt or foster black children, and people who have been 'transracially placed' saying they have grown up with a fractured sense of identity. In the 1960s these tensions were less understood and acknowledged. Agencies had not yet adapted to engaging with the black community and were eager for white people to adopt and foster black children but expected them to be reluctant. Notes on children of mixed heritage invariably focused on their light skin, straight hair or other features which would allow them to pass as white.

The Fashanu boys were undoubtedly black – 'coloured' to use the language of the day – and such was Barnardo's difficulty finding foster parents for them it was looking as if it would be necessary to split them up, which would have been devastating for them. They were saved from this fate by Betty Jackson.

She recalled that when she first met Justin and John she did not see them as black but just as two children with runny noses who needed a home. And, although she had only intended to foster one child, was persuaded to take them both. She realised that raising them in a white rural community would not be straightforward and it was her own children who persuaded her to take the plunge. Even so, the original arrangement was only short-term, and she found them so troubled and troublesome that she seriously considered handing them back before eventually agreeing to keep them.

Justin and John arrived in Norfolk in the summer of 1965. Justin was four years old and John two. Meanwhile their mother was expecting her fifth child. Nicklaus was born to Pearl and Walter Gopaul in October of that year. It is not hard to understand her initial decision to put her children into care, especially as there was more prejudice against single mothers then, and less practical and financial help. Why she did not take back Justin and John, along with Dawn and Phillip, when she married is less obvious.

It is easy to condemn without complete knowledge of the choices Justin's mother really had and to focus on the mother rather than the father, who seems to have felt no responsibility towards his three sons at all. Her own explanation, given in a TV documentary made after Justin's death, was that once Justin and John were with the Jacksons she felt they had a better life there than she could offer them. Speaking in the formal English she had learned in British Guiana, she revealed what she told Justin that last time she saw him: 'Every time I had the same answer for him, feeling they were being looked after so well. They were well treated as part of the family and where would I be able to render that sort of treatment and facilities to them? I couldn't have done it.'

People who knew Justin and John when they were growing up in Norfolk tend to assume they were adopted by the Jacksons. They were not; they remained fostered, an arrangement that lasted until they were 18 after which they had no formal ties with the Jackson family. They retained the Fashanu name throughout. Fostering made it easier for them to stay in touch with their family of origin and have a sense of their heritage. They at least knew where they came from even if they were confronted with the painful reality of no longer being there.

Adoption would have given them a different set of experiences. They would probably have lost touch with their birth family, leaving them with a weaker sense of identity and more scope for fantasy, for believing their parents must have loved them deeply and only been parted from them by tragic circumstances beyond their control. As fostered children they were confronted with reality. Pearl occasionally visited the Jacksons with her family and it must have been difficult for Justin to see Dawn and Phillip reunited with their mother, and with a new father and baby brother.

Fortunately, in many respects, Betty was the perfect foster mother, warm and loving. John remembers her as 'a big round woman'. She would squeeze him into her breasts and he would feel that nothing could get to him. It took John a year to wean himself away from Justin and go round holding on to Betty instead and several more years to overcome his speech defect. Alf was a more distant figure than Betty and 10 years older, the age of a grandfather. John remembers him always surrounded by tobacco smoke. The boys were at last receiving the mothering they had missed but they had to wait for an influential father figure to enter their lives.

Stories of fostering and adoption are the stuff of myth and fable. It is easy to romanticise the story of the young Fashanu boys, abandoned amid the smoke and slums of London's East End and whisked away to the warm embrace of the Jackson family in their rural idyll; the black boys taken into the hearts of the good country folk of East Anglia. It is a lovely story and there's an element of truth in it. But it is not the whole story.

Justin and John were by no means the first black people to live in Norfolk. In fact Thetford, just down the road from Shropham, was the first town in Britain to elect a black mayor. Dr Allan Glaisyer Minns was born and brought up in The Bahamas before moving to London and studying to become a doctor. He took up the post of Medical Officer of Thetford Workhouse and became mayor in 1904. But the Fashanu boys were the first black people most local residents had encountered. As such they were objects of curiosity. Children are generally uncomfortable when they stand out as different. Justin and John had no choice, with their skin and their hair fascinating to the other children. There was the obvious difference in appearance from their foster parents and the name, Fashanu, an unfamiliar one in that part of the world although in years to come it would be chanted by thousands on the Carrow Road terraces and resound throughout the county.

For the interview with *Who Cares?* Justin was asked if he ever found himself picked on or victimised at school. He replied: 'I didn't, but I felt that I had to fight to establish myself…When you're probably the only one at school from care and the others find out about it, it can be hard. The way I look at it is, although it is unfortunate and you don't want it to happen, the positive side of being picked on is that if you can overcome it, still do your work, enjoy it as much as you can and win them over, you'll find it's a good training for life.'

It is a typical Justin Fashanu quote with his determination to find a positive angle on every challenge, and he was similarly upbeat when, aged 20, he was interviewed by Ernest Cashmore for a book, *Black Sportsmen*. By this time he was already a successful professional footballer, about to leave Norwich City in a £1 million transfer to Nottingham Forest. He told Cashmore: 'The thing with me and Crooksy [Garth Crooks, another black footballer] as well is that, if you're black in a small community where there aren't too many blacks and you've got a little bit of style, then you cannot go wrong. If you can be just a little bit clued-up and not be Rastafarian with dreadlocks, you cannot fail. The jet setters like novelty and things like that. As long as you hold yourself well and don't embarrass people by letting them think, "Oh he's so thick" or "his ways are so silly", you're all right. You have to have a little presence about you; and that's what made me here. I'm not the kind of fellow that's going to creep to anybody, but I didn't cause aggravation unless I had to. I didn't give anybody a chance to hate me.'

Somehow skin colour became a sufficient issue for the Fashanu boys for Betty Jackson to refer, in a TV interview, to 'when they were young and wanted to be white'. Her response was to tell them, 'You're black, you're going to stay black and you're to be proud of being black'; this coupled with a declaration that they had to be better than anyone else, which both took to heart. But Betty Jackson didn't always know how to help them. Justin told his friend and business manager, Roger Haywood, about a problem he had as a child with flaky skin, severe enough for the pain to keep him awake at night. The GP thought it might be eczema but it did not respond to treatment. Eventually, Justin was taken to a specialist in London. His condition turned out to be no more than the dry skin many black people experience and which can easily be kept moist with the right creams, which a black parent would have known about. Betty was distraught to learn that the daily baths she had given Justin had only made the condition worse.

There were centres in Norfolk, and neighbouring counties, where black people lived and where there was knowledge and understanding not only of the care of black skin but also the culture and heritage of black people. But they were also places where racial tensions could simmer and occasionally erupt. They were US airbases, scattered around the region of East Anglia but almost completely cut off from local life. One base was at Lakenheath, 20 miles west of Shropham where around a sixth of the personnel were black.

The Biography

Fast forward to spring 1977 and the 16-year-old Justin is perusing his local paper, the *Thetford and Walton Times*, for its coverage of his exploits as a teenage boxer. But his attention is taken by a front page report of an incident at Lakenheath where some white servicemen had taken exception to the organisation of a Black History Month. As a protest they had erected a Klu Klux Klan-style cross on a football pitch in the local countryside before setting it ablaze. One had followed up by calling the security office at the base and warning: 'This is just the start for niggers.' A court martial was held resulting in six servicemen being discharged.

Justin and John rarely, if ever, met other black people until they started travelling further afield. Speaking on a radio programme about transracial fostering and adoption, John said the only other black people he saw were on television, 'Michael Jackson and Quincy Jones – people like that'. It was not until he started visiting London that he actually met and related to black people other than his brother and thought: 'I'm a zebra being brought up as a lion. Hang on. There are other zebras out there. That's interesting.'

Justin was born into one culture and raised in another. Moving from life in a family of black immigrants in a big city via Dr Barnardo's to a white family in the countryside was an abrupt shift. He was unlikely to feel as comfortable and secure as a black man as he would have done if he had stayed with his family of birth. His early upbringing, people's reactions to his skin colour, and his working class London accent would ensure that he could never feel completely at home in Norfolk. This experience left him with a particular set of attributes and insecurities familiar to people who grow up with a dual identity, under the influence of more than one set of values, beliefs and lifestyles. He was adept at moving between different worlds. When he played football for Nottingham Forest, he would go from practicing his passing at the training ground to praising the Lord at the evangelical Christian Centre. On another evening, he would be off to the Part II club to be with other gay men before going home to his fiancé. But this versatility came at a price. Wherever he was, part of him was somewhere else.

Chapter 2

Choirboy, Boxer, Footballer

Despite his troubles, Justin settled into his new life and was able to enjoy growing up in the countryside. Norfolk is a place of open fields, big skies and long beaches. The family photograph album shows him and John enjoying it to the full. A favourite pastime was piloting a plastic dingy down the local river.

He attended primary and then high school at nearby Attleborough. He later recalled his first day at school: 'All the other kids were crying and it was no outward deal for me whatsoever because I had been through things before.' Justin settled in well. When he was six years old his class teacher wrote in a school report: 'Justin is a lively member of the class. In a general discussion he shows keen interest and an enquiring mind and makes one feel teaching is worthwhile. He is capable of appreciating adult humour and has a good sense of humour himself. He is a very helpful child and can be relied upon. He is very well-spoken and well-mannered. Sometimes Justin's work is good and careful. At other times it is sloppy and full of careless mistakes which I think are due to lack of concentration. This is a set-back to his progress although not too serious. Justin has been a great asset to the class and is very popular.' It was a remarkable achievement by Justin and his foster parents for him to be showing so few signs of the behavioural problems that might have been expected following his early experiences of rejection and disruption.

As he got older Justin developed an interest in singing and joined the choir of East Harling Church, run by Betty and Alf Jackson's son, Edward. He took it seriously enough to attend a residential choristers' course at Addington Palace, near London and also joined the Norwich Boys' Choir. With his fellow choristers, he played an urchin in a production of *Carmen* at the Theatre Royal in Norwich. Edward remembers he was 'good average, if slightly husky'.

By the time Justin started secondary school his talent and interest in sport, especially football was apparent to all and it was through sport that he found the father figures who had been missing all his life. Through his relationships with these robust, extrovert and caring men a more confident, dynamic, determined and outspoken Justin Fashanu emerged. This began with his PE teacher, Chris Allen. Speaking about his time at Attleborough High School for the book, *Black Sportsmen*, Justin recalled: 'Everybody was there to be academically acknowledged at the highest level they could and sport was just something that came as well. So everybody bar the PE teacher hated me playing football and everything they could do to stop me playing football they did. If they needed a punishment to hurt me, they'd stop me playing. They put as many blocks in my path as they could. But the PE teacher was strong willed and I associated myself with him more than anybody else.' Chris Allen was in no doubt of his ability: 'He had a talent that you saw maybe once in 30 years in a school.' Justin was turning out for local boys' teams, as well as the school, sometimes playing in four matches over a weekend.

At least Justin's teachers did not stereotype him in the way that was common at the time, by assuming this black pupil would only excel at sports. In the month of Justin's 14th birthday his form teacher wrote: 'Justin is without doubt a strong social leader, and remarkably mature and competent in most forms of social intercourse. My advice would be to use this well-developed expertise to raise his academic standards.' He was losing interest in his studies. In Justin's interview for *Who Cares?* he explained why: 'I didn't have a great schooling because the teachers said, "If you don't work hard you'll end up a barman, but if you do work at school, you'll end up like me, a teacher". I used to think, "Well I don't want to end up like you", so I didn't work much'. School records show that, aged 15, he was given three strokes of the cane for 'deliberately disobeying a member of staff' but he was never in serious trouble at school.

Justin's nearest professional football club was Norwich City, nicknamed the Canaries. Their distinctive yellow and green strip was chosen because of the city's trade in breeding pet birds. Under manager Ron Saunders, the Canaries began their most successful era, achieving promotion to the First Division for the first time in the 1971–72 season. Although they were relegated after two seasons, new manager John Bond, took them straight back up.

One of Bond's first acts was to appoint Ronnie Brooks to his coaching and scouting staff. Brooks was a man with considerably broader experience of life than most people involved with professional sport. His playing career with Norwich was ended almost as soon as it started, by a knee injury when he was still a teenager. He went on to work for the Electricity Board for 30 years and became a local councillor and a magistrate. Throughout this time he coached young players. Back with Norwich City, Brooks was keen to bring new talent to the club. He claimed to have found Justin through the network of sports teachers he knew through his work on the Education Committee. Other accounts, though, have Justin first spotted by another coach, John Sainty. Either way, appearing in trial matches the 13-year-old made a big impression. Tall, strong and determined, he simply rampaged through defences. He was way ahead of other boys of his age and Brooks was determined to sign him to the club as soon as possible. This meant signing him on 'schoolboy forms'. The club would provide regular coaching and in return would retain first option on signing Justin as an apprentice when he was 16.

Brooks knew he would have no difficulty persuading Justin but he also had to deal with Betty Jackson. She was not thrilled that Justin wanted to take this first step towards a career in professional sport but her reservations must have been somewhat allayed when she met Ronnie Brooks. He was clearly someone who would have Justin's welfare at heart. His goal was always to help the youngsters he coached become better people as well as better footballers. She gave her consent and in 1975, aged 14, Justin signed up. But Betty and Alf were never enthusiastic about Justin's sporting career. They did not watch him play and even after Justin was established in the Norwich first team, Betty was filmed for a TV programme saying rather despondently 'It would have been nice if he'd been a scientist or a doctor or something like that but that's the way it goes', before adding rather harshly: 'He knows this is a short lived thing and he will be a nobody again.' It may have been a remark which passed Justin by but it is possible to look at his self-promotion, determination to prolong his football career after serious injury and efforts to stay in the public eye long after he stopped making headlines through football as stemming from a stubborn refusal to ever be the nobody that Betty Jackson predicted.

The Biography

Ronnie Brooks described the young Justin as 'mischievous, boisterous and self-opinionated – a lad I had to keep under my thumb a little bit because of his natural ebullience', a remark which illustrated how differently Justin behaved away from the constraints of the classroom and the family home. Brooks realised that Justin needed a father figure and that's what he became. Over the next few years, he spent a great deal of time with Justin, providing the closeness, guidance and discipline that he sought. Although their contact was sporadic after Justin left Norwich City, Justin turned to Ronnie Brooks when he faced the biggest crisis of his life.

*   *   *

If anything was going to stop Fashanu succeeding in football, it was the prospect of a career in another sport. Boxing coach, Gordon Homes, had moved from London to the village of Walton, around eight miles from Shropham, and opened a gym. A friend persuaded the 12-year-old Fashanu to go along and Homes immediately spotted his potential. Justin's first competitive fight was in December 1975 when he was 14 years old. Before the fight he had to undergo a strict medical examination organised by the Amateur Boxing Association (ABA). Homes was concerned that Justin was getting out of breath easily and mentioned it to the doctor. He was able to diagnose a blood condition, associated with people from the Yoruba ethnic group of West Africa including Nigeria, which could be treated with medication. Lives turn on such moments. Without that intervention he may never have become a professional sportsman. Within weeks Justin won the East Anglia regional final of the ABA schools competition and made it to the national quarter-finals before having to retire with a cut eye.

Justin's big year came in 1977 in the National Schoolboy Championship. At 5ft 11in and 11 stone, he was in the heavyweight division. He appeared unstoppable. By the time he reached the quarter-finals, he had won his previous eight bouts, in all competitions, all in the first round. The quarter-final, against a highly acclaimed opponent, Paul Hedges, was a long contest by Justin's standards; he took two rounds to knock him out. In the semi-final, the usual pattern was restored; Justin won in the first round. The final was to be held at the Pontin's Holiday Camp in Blackpool, some 250 miles away, but local people eagerly bought tickets so they could go to support him. Gordon Homes told the papers there was no doubt in his mind that Justin would go right to the top as an amateur and make international status.

His opponent was the experienced Liam Coleman, who had already won the title twice. But that did not stop Justin steaming into him in the first round which he won on points. In the second round, Coleman steadied himself and came back strongly. All depended on the third and final round. Justin started well, cheered on loudly by his supporters, but Coleman rallied and came back at him. No one could predict what the judges would decide but they came down narrowly in favour of Coleman.

'We're all disappointed, obviously' said Gordon Homes 'but we have no complaints. Justin has taken it well and is keener than ever'. He was keen; to the point of saying he preferred boxing to football. Looking forward to leaving school in the summer, the 16-year-old told the press he hoped to go on a catering course while he continued his boxing career. He was enjoying the company he kept and they liked being around him. The wife of a local boxing coach affectionately remembers him as being 'gorgeous, cheeky, cocky and with plenty of spunk'. But Justin did not lose the politeness and good manners he was also known for. On trips he would be teased by other boys for being so well behaved.

His next major tournament was the ABA Championship for his age group. Again, he pummelled his way to a final against Liam Coleman, and again they fought out the full three rounds. The verdict was in the hands of the three judges and they awarded the title to Coleman. Gordon Homes is still convinced Fashanu won, 'A miscarriage of justice', he calls it. There was nothing to be done but prepare for the next fight and, seeking out suitable opponents for him to practice against. Homes took him on a trip to Bremen in West Germany where he came up against a 20-year-old. According to boxing regulations they should not have fought but Fashanu insisted on going ahead and beat him easily. His opponent's coach turned to Homes and said: 'That's another Muhammad Ali you've got there.'

Even more than football, boxing is a sport taken up almost exclusively by young men from tough working-class backgrounds. Despite the disruptions of his early childhood, Justin, as he said himself, was from a relatively privileged background for a footballer. What then was the attraction of boxing and why, according to Gordon Homes, was his greatest attribute his ruthlessness? What did this former chorister get out of whacking other boys hard? Perhaps there is a clue in the nightmares Edward Jackson remembers him having; sitting up in bed and lashing out with his fists. On one occasion, he even punched through his bedroom window. Although he largely kept it under control, Justin undoubtedly had a temper. Roger Haywood remembers him punching out a panel of a door after somebody had insulted his family. There has to be a reason for this rage that surfaced in Justin's dreams and the aggression with which he attacked his boxing opponents.

Apart from providing an opportunity to channel his anger, boxing may have held another attraction. It was the sport in which black men had enjoyed the most success.

The Biography

Among his heroes was Liverpool-born John Conteh, who became the Light Heavyweight World Champion in 1974. His father was from Sierra Leone and his mother, Irish. Muhammad Ali was the biggest star in any sport. Justin later said of Ali: 'He was a good idol because he was one of the first black guys who wasn't stereotyped in those days; you know the '60s type of drug dealer with the big hats and bell bottoms.'

It was Ronnie Brooks' job to persuade Justin to choose football over boxing. He argued with him: 'I said that if you lose a boxing match you can't move the following day but if you lose a football match you're back training for the next one.' But it seems to have been simple economics that won the day. Justin was keen to make his way in the world. Norwich could offer him a wage almost as soon as he left school and football was undoubtedly preferable to catering. With boxing, he would be dependent on prize money, which he could not even begin to earn until he was 17.

Leaving school in the summer of 1977, Justin spent six weeks working as a steel erector before signing for Norwich City as an apprentice. But he expected to carry on with boxing and Gordon Homes thought he could succeed in both sports. Homes was shocked when he phoned John Bond to ask if he could take Justin sparring in London and Bond would not hear of it. And, as Justin put it: 'Then, lo and behold, at 17 I'm in the first team. So I couldn't jack it in when things were going so well.' Justin never boxed competitively again but even after becoming a star with Norwich City he talked to friends such as Roger Haywood, about going back to it. Homes, who went on to work with David Starie, the Commonwealth Super Middle Weight Champion, believes Justin would have been a world champion.

Justin benefited from his brief boxing career in several respects. There was his relationship with Gordon Homes who, like Ronnie Brooks, was a father figure to him. Homes and his wife became friendly with the Jackson family and their home became a second home for Justin. Gordon Homes recalls: 'He would turn up at any time, tyres screeching on the road, bounce in and ask if there was anything in the fridge. He was like the big puppy who first turned up at the gym.' Then there was his strength and fitness. Boxing training is tougher than football training and this gave him an advantage against other players. And knowing how to use his fists turned out to be useful on more than one occasion.

*　*　*

The role of apprentice was a testing one for young footballers. Wages were low and they had to work hard, not just training but undertaking manual jobs around the club.

For youngsters who had dreamt of scoring goals at Wembley and the adoration of the crowd it was an introduction to a more mundane reality of being a professional sportsman. After each home match Justin had to go round the pitch replacing dislodged pieces of turf and pick up the litter from the stands. Another task was cleaning the boots of senior players and he was allocated to Tony Powell, 14 years older and coming to the end of his career as a hard tackling defender. Like Fashanu, Powell had been a boxer before he became a professional footballer.

The apprentices were used to being the best players on the pitch – football came easily to them. But once they were matched with others of equal talent, they had to show they were wiling and able to learn and improve. They had to demonstrate the mental toughness to come back after a bad game and play better next time. Most teenagers who have the talent to become professional footballers fail at this stage because few have the right attitude to succeed. None of these challenges were a problem for Justin. He enjoyed the atmosphere of a professional football club, was a dedicated trainer and completely determined to succeed. And if he stepped out of line there was always Ronnie Brooks to put him straight. Brooks, who also knew how to box, remembers once giving Justin a couple of sharp punches to the ribs. The next time he saw Betty Jackson, she said: 'So you're the man who keeps hitting my boy.' 'Sometimes they need it' replied Ronnie. She conceded: 'You're probably right.' John was also showing promise as a footballer and, like his brother, Justin, looked to Ronnie Brooks as a father figure. Brooks remembered fondly the times they spent together in the summer holidays. Along the Norfolk coast were a string of holiday camps where he ran football skills sessions and he recruited the Fashanu boys to help him out.

Playing at youth level, Justin was unstoppable. Every manager wanted a big, strong centre-forward to 'lead the line'. He had to take passes with defenders snapping at his ankles and lay the ball off to another player, win headers and generally scrap for the ball. He was expected to score goals but there was usually an equally sought after player – often smaller, quicker and more skilful – who would play off him and be more adept at getting the ball in the net. Justin did both jobs at once. During his first year as an apprentice, when he played for the youth and reserve teams, he scored 43 goals – a ridiculously high number, especially from someone who contributed so much to team play. With the odd exception, his goals were not especially spectacular or memorable. He was effective rather than flamboyant. No one was complaining.

Justin's step up from youth to reserve team football came in March 1978, his first season and a month after his 17th birthday. It was a big test. With his physique honed by boxing training, Justin could dominate defenders in his own age group. But could he do it against grown men with years of experience? In those days defenders aimed to clatter opposing forwards to the ground early in the game to establish their domination. At worst they would concede a free-kick for a challenge that today could get them sent off. Players trying to get picked for the first team were not going to tolerate being given the run around by a mouthy 17-year-old. Some would be particularly keen to subdue a mouthy 17-year-old who was black. Justin relished the confrontations. The harder they kicked him, the harder he kicked them back. He was demonstrating all the attributes that would bring him success: speed, strength, fitness, determination and self-belief allied to a keen football brain: knowing when and where to run, when and where to pass the ball. He scored twice on his debut for the reserves, at home to Reading, and three more in five other reserve matches that season. Justin had blossomed into an outgoing, confident teenager with all the attributes to succeed in professional sport.

Chapter 3

The Black Canary

Playing standards were high at the top level of English football in the late 1970s and early 1980s. The First Division produced European Cup winners six years in a row: Liverpool won it three times, Nottingham Forest twice and Aston Villa once. But off the pitch the game was in serious trouble. Crowds were dwindling, put off by the risk of getting caught up in violence between opposing supporters. The atmosphere in grounds was often passionate, boisterous and hostile with alcohol-fuelled fans singing, chanting and gesturing their hatred of the opposition. In many ways it was a great outlet for young men's pent up aggression. Crowds could be witty and good humoured with a touch of pantomime in their expressions of rivalry. But there were also violent clashes in stadiums and surrounding streets. In Norwich there was so much trouble that the police advised shoppers to stay away from the city centre on match days. At a home game against local rivals, Ipswich Town, there were 57 arrests and Ipswich manager, Bobby Robson, was hit by a missile. On their way home Ipswich fans rioted in the market town of Diss. As the authorities clamped down on the violence, football stadiums began to resemble prison camps. High steel-mesh fences were erected, and guarded by rows of police officers. Away supporters were herded onto special trains – usually too dilapidated to be used on regular services – and marched between station and stadium.

The Biography

The atmosphere at football matches reflected the strife and conflict of the wider society. It was a time of strikes, demonstrations, riots and IRA bombings. The 1978–79 'winter of discontent' was followed by the election of Margaret Thatcher's Conservative government, bringing mass unemployment in its wake. As ever, in times of economic hardship, racism was rife. It was stirred up by Thatcher claiming, in a 1979 speech, that she understood 'the fears of the British people of being swamped by coloured immigrants'. Meanwhile the National Front, intent on recruiting from disaffected working-class white youth, targeted football supporters, selling its magazine, *Bulldog*, outside grounds. In opposition were the Anti-Nazi League, organising huge demonstrations, and Rock Against Racism, setting up gigs of punk, reggae and two-tone bands with an anti-racist message.

As the time approached for Fashanu to make his debut for the first team, the status of black professional footballers was of great interest to racists, anti-racists and the media. Black men had played professional football in England for decades, overcoming prejudice and hostility to succeed. Although their careers may have been modest they caught the attention of aspiring black youngsters such as Justin. He name checked Clyde Best of West Ham in an interview for *Radio Times*: 'I used to think "He's black, I'm black; he's done well, I can do well".' In the late 1970s, more black footballers, often the sons of people from the Caribbean who arrived in the 1950s, began to break into the first teams of professional clubs. Their numbers were still not great, but in a society so sensitive to the presence of black people, they made an impact. This was especially so at the West Midlands club, West Bromwich Albion, where manager Ron Atkinson picked three black players for his team: striker Cyrille Regis, winger Laurie Cunningham and full-back Brendan Batson. Not one to miss a publicity opportunity, Atkinson called them The Three Degrees, arranging for them to be photographed with the black female vocal group of the same name.

Young men, who usually just wanted to succeed in their sport, found themselves in the media spotlight more for their skin colour than their footballing skills, embroiled in the debate about the position of black people in Britain. They became targets of abuse from opposition supporters and players, and sometimes even their own supporters, teammates and coaching staff. Whatever they felt inside, these players were expected, by their white bosses, to act as if it did not bother them, though they did not always succeed. Brendan Batson had just been appointed as West Bromwich's managing director when he was interviewed for *The Guardian* in 2002. Looking back on his football career, he recalled: 'The worst crap I experienced was the hurling of bananas and verbal abuse such as "nigger", "coon" and "blackies go back to the jungle".'

He was sent off three times in his career, twice when playing against Tony Coleman of Manchester City, who enraged him by making monkey noises. Off the pitch black footballers had to contend with hate mail. When Cyrille Regis was called up for the England squad for the first time someone sent him a bullet with a note saying: 'If you go to Wembley and put on the England shirt you'll get one of these through your knees.'

As Fashanu started his second season as an apprentice at Norwich, another black footballer was about to make history. It was November 1978 when Viv Anderson, the Nottingham Forest full-back, became the first black man to play for the full England team, in a game against Czechoslovakia. It was an achievement full of symbolism – a black man, donning the England shirt, standing shoulder to shoulder with his white teammates for the national anthem, representing his country, England. It provoked a media frenzy with the home of his Jamaican-born parents, on a housing estate in Nottingham, invaded by TV cameras. Anderson dealt with all the fuss like a typical sportsman. As his biographer, Andrew Longmore, put it: 'As he came out for his international debut, his thoughts were not of the thousands of black kids who might be inspired by him, but of making sure his winger didn't score a hat-trick.' (Although Anderson is generally acknowledged as the first black player for England, he may not be. Phil Vasili, author of *Colouring Over the White Line: The History of Black Footballers in Britain*, believes a player with unacknowledged black African heritage played for England before Anderson.)

*   *   *

While the Norwich City first team was enjoying its fourth successive season in the First Division, Justin was making rapid progress in the youth and reserve teams, scoring 20 goals by Christmas. Despite some reservations John Bond signed him up as a full professional, two months before his 18th birthday, the youngest Canaries' player to achieve this distinction. International recognition followed when he was picked for the England Youth squad. These landmarks were quickly followed by his first-team debut for Norwich on 13 January 1979.

The catalyst was a third-round FA Cup tie at Leicester, then a struggling Second Division side. It was a freezing cold day and as the more glamorous games were called off, the *Match of the Day* cameras honed in on Leicester's Filbert Street stadium where the pitch had been protected by a huge balloon. So the humiliating 3–0 defeat of John Bond's team was witnessed by millions on TV. Some may still recall the unusual sight of Leicester winger, Keith Weller, keeping warm in a pair of white tights as he skidded past several defenders on the icy surface before striking the ball past the Norwich goalkeeper. John Bond was furious with his team, accused some of his players of lack of effort, and put three on the transfer list. They included the veteran former England striker, Martin Chivers. The search for a replacement began immediately, with chairman, Arthur South, promising the necessary funds.

Having failed to sign a replacement for Chivers by the following weekend, Bond reluctantly turned to Fashanu. When he first watched him as a 15-year-old, Bond had not been impressed; he could not understand what John Sainty saw in him: 'His feet and brain didn't seem to work together at all while his control and passing were virtually non-existent. I couldn't see how he was going to develop as a footballer.' Admitting he had been wrong he conceded: 'What Justin did have was this ability, when he was anywhere near the goal, to put the 'frighteners' on people. He had this natural aggression. He was fearless. In the box he would put himself where angels fear to tread. And he scored lots of goals.' No one doubted Fashanu's physical strength and courage but managers, coaches, journalists and fellow players would disagree about his technical ability throughout his career. When his assistant, Ken Brown, suggested he give Fashanu his first-team debut, Bond's first response was that he must be mad to propose it but Brown persisted and eventually persuaded him.

The game was at home against West Bromwich Albion who would go top of the League if they won. Publically Bond talked Fashanu up despite his reservations: 'It's a hell of a match for him to come in to but he has confidence, ability, strength, and is a proven goalscorer'. His strike partner was another young star, 21-year-old Kevin Reeves. They were up against one of the best central-defensive partnerships in the League, John Wile and Alistair Robertson.

Justin's debut was always going to be noticed, as much for his presence as a black man in the Norwich team, as for his footballing ability. Rather than play it down he, as fan Graham Dunbar, put it: 'Showed his sense of the big occasion with a theatrical centre-circle handshake with Cyrille Regis and Laurie Cunningham seconds before kick-off.'

The result was a creditable 1–1 draw and according to *Eastern Daily Press* reporter, Malcolm Robertson, Fashanu proved himself a real handful to the Albion defence and went close to scoring a dream goal: 'The teenager rose above the Albion defender to send a rousing header only inches over the top.' Post-match, Justin demonstrated another attribute which impressed the Robertson who wrote: 'He is a member of that rare breed in British football – the character. Fashanu is not one of the game's more modest exponents, and possesses a cockiness and sense of fun that is all too rare these days.' In fact, Justin's comments demonstrated both the cockiness and the doubt which coexisted in his assessment of his own ability: 'I feel I did enough to justify being picked again. I wasn't nervous. I couldn't afford to be because it might have been my only chance.' Fashanu had been compared to Muhammad Ali for his boxing ability and Robertson referred to his 'Muhammad Ali-like tongue'. Ali used his wit to calculating effect to gain an advantage over opponents as well as to entertain. Fashanu did not have that talent or intent but always had plenty to say and seemed oblivious to managers' expectations that their players restrict themselves to talking in polite clichés. His willingness to tell reporters exactly what he thought would get him into trouble on more than one occasion.

Fashanu was given more opportunities in the first team that season and took them well. But he had to wait six games for his first goal. It came in a 2–2 draw away to Leeds. Remembering the match, Justin described how 'a cross came over and I flung myself at it to score with a diving header'. MP, Colin Burgon, a Leeds United fan, recalled the goal 20 years later in the House of Commons. He had been horrified at the amount of racial abuse aimed at Justin throughout the match which 'was enough to turn my stomach'. Referring to Justin's goal he said: 'It was probably the only time in my life that I have cheered when an opponent put the ball in the back of the Leeds net.'

Fashanu would have to endure racial abuse from the terraces throughout his career. Outwardly, he handled it coolly. While still at Norwich he told a friend: 'These people don't matter'. In the *Radio Times* interview he explained: 'If I thought they actually hated me it might bother me. But they're not actually getting at Justin Fashanu the person; they're getting at Justin Fashanu the image.' When black footballers became more accepted and present in greater numbers it was easier for them to admit to being hurt and offended by racist abuse. In the 1970s and 80s they were expected to handle it without emotion. They were given no support from football administrators or managers who were unable or unwilling to distinguish between the personal abuse regularly hurled at players and racist abuse with its history of imperialism and belief in racial superiority, and the threat of violence which accompanied it. It was the determination and persistence shown by Fashanu's generation which enabled black players to become established as an integral part of British football.

For Fashanu, there must have been particular complexities in his response to racist chanting from the terraces. He was brought up, from the age of four, by white people in a white community, with a fragile sense of what it meant to be black. But to

National Front supporting racists he was just another 'black bastard' to taunt and threaten. And the abuse was not confined to the terraces. Though at least when it came from opponents on the pitch it was easier to retaliate. 'I'd rear up on footballers if they said anything and footballers aren't the bravest people in the world so they used to think twice before they said anything to me', he told Ernest Cashmore for his book about black sportsmen. Justin was sent off for violent conduct many times. Judging from these comments it seems likely that on some occasions he was punished for responding to racist abuse.

The young Justin was certainly gaining a reputation for intimidating, rather than being intimidated by, tough defenders. Aston Villa's centre-half, Ken McNaught, was injured in an accidental clash with him and ended up in hospital. The last game of the season was at home to Nottingham Forest who were about to become European champions. Their central-defenders were Larry Lloyd and Kenny Burns. In the words of journalist and Forest supporter, Daniel Taylor, they formed the 'ugliest, meanest, most fearsome defensive partnership in the country'. More than any other defenders playing at the top level, they went out to hurt and intimidate forwards. Fashanu took them on single handed. Burns was the first to have a go at him. Fashanu left him on the ground, receiving treatment. Lloyd then appeared to butt Fashanu in the face, leaving him with a gashed lip. They kicked him throughout the match but they could not stop him. Meanwhile, strike partner, Kevin Reeves, was left free to show his skills and head a brilliant goal, gaining a creditable 1–1 draw for Norwich. As Malcolm Robertson wrote: 'Despite the appealing look and the innocent smile, Fashanu is a tough character.'

Justin began the season as an apprentice, wondering if he would make the grade as a footballer or go back to boxing. By the end, he had played 13 full games for the first team, come on as a substitute three times and scored five goals. He had played in front of crowds of over 30,000 at Manchester United's and Manchester City's grounds, big crowds in those days. And he had played with one of his heroes, Martin Peters. Peters was in the England team which won the World Cup in 1966 when Justin was five years old. Coming to the end of his career, Peters was still an influential figure in Norwich's midfield. Justin was in awe of his ability. Known as 'The Ghost', Peters had the knack of losing his defender and drifting into the penalty area unseen. He had done it against West Germany in the World Cup Final and was still doing it 13 years later. Peters was Norwich's top scorer that season.

* * *

As soon as the season was over Norwich embarked on a tour of New Zealand and Australia where Justin continued his good form. But he must still have wondered if he would be lining up for the first team in August. Young players, however talented, tend to be inconsistent. Managers like to bring them on slowly, rather than rely on them to perform week after week. But John Bond, with a tiny transfer budget, tried and failed to bring in a big, experienced forward and so had to persevere with Fashanu.

The opening game of the 1979–80 season was away to Everton and the Canaries could not have gone into this fixture with a lot of confidence. Norwich had a dreadful away record, they had not won away in the League for two years, and Everton had finished fifth the previous season. The result was a shock. Everton went into the game with two small central-defenders who could not cope with the height and power of Fashanu – by this time the 18-year-old had grown to 6ft and 12½ stone. He scored twice in a resounding 4–2 win. Norwich fans must have thought they were dreaming when the next game brought a 4–0 victory at home to Tottenham Hotspur, with another goal for Justin. This was followed by a home win, over Leeds United, and the Canaries were top of the First Division for the first time in the 77 years since the club was founded.

The next two games were lost and then came a home match against Nottingham Forest. Kenny Burns and Fashanu had already picked up three bookings each and both were warned by their managers to avoid a confrontation. Marked by Larry Lloyd, Justin came out on top again, scoring with a header and 'going past the Forest player almost at will in the second half', according to Malcolm Robertson. The Canaries won 3–1. Forest's goalkeeper, Peter Shilton, ended up with a black eye after holding Fashanu in the penalty area. Having seen off the European champions, Norwich went up to Anfield, home of League champions Liverpool, and drew 0–0. Their next game was another huge test, a League Cup match at home to Manchester United, second in the League the previous season. Norwich produced, possibly, their best performance under John Bond, winning 4–1. Fashanu and Reeves took Scottish international defenders Gordon McQueen and Martin Buchan apart, Justin scoring yet again, with a header. The following game brought a 2–1 defeat of Bolton Wanderers and another goal for Fashanu, Robertson writing: 'Justin Fashanu improves significantly with every match', and 'there is now a delicacy about his game which scarcely seems credible in a big man'.

With six goals in his first 10 games, Justin was making an impact way beyond anyone's expectations. His fabulous autumn got even better when he was called up to the England B squad to play against New Zealand, coming on in the second half. Then he was named as Young Player of the Month for September by a panel chaired by

England manager Ron Greenwood. Justin donated the prize money to a local children's charity and Dr Barnardo's.

In October a National Front conference was held at the Norfolk seaside resort of Great Yarmouth. A row about it had been brewing for months, ever since the Conservative Council gave its approval, with the Labour Party and trade unions planning to hold demonstrations. Eventually the conference and the protests were relatively low key but around this time Fashanu experienced a more personal and less peaceful encounter with the National Front. He found himself in the same pub as a contingent of NF supporters who became increasingly abusive and threatening to him. Fashanu's response was to punch one of them so hard it broke his jaw. The victim ended up in hospital having his face put back together. Remarkably no charges were pressed and the incident received no publicity. Perhaps the victim was advised that the sympathy of the Norfolk public would be almost entirely with Fashanu.

Fashanu was rarely militant in his statements about racism, choosing to focus on his potential as a role model, showing what young black men could achieve. But the National Front brought out his anger. In his *Radio Times* interview he told the reporter about NF members offering him their paper: 'I suppose they were trying to insult me.' He went on to say: 'They don't frighten me but I think they have under-estimated the power of the coloured people – and not just the blacks. If they did go too far overboard you could have a civil war. But I don't think they'll ever take off; there are not enough people interested in it.'

Meanwhile he continued to battle on the pitch. He revealed his struggles in an interview in the Norwich City programme, though typically for the time the word 'racism' was implied but not used: 'I'm a special target for the trouble makers who know my situation and sometimes it's hard to keep yourself in check when you know someone is winding you up.' He had retaliated against another player in the game against Tottenham and been fined through the club's internal disciplinary procedure. Fashanu told the interviewer that he still practiced his boxing occasionally, it being good for working the aggression out of his system and for 'the odd spots of depression', a rare admission of emotional lows that were usually well-hidden.

Justin was a popular figure in the dressing room, his exuberance endearing him to the other players. He used to enjoy showing off his strength by picking up two of his teammates at once. Interviewed for the book, *12 Canary Greats*, Kevin Reeves remembers 'a real sociable lad, a very funny lad as well with a good sense of humour and a cheeky way about him' but also that he did not always have an easy time. Choosing his words carefully Reeves recalls: 'Remember we're talking about a young lad who has come in and held his own in a fairly strong dressing room. And Norwich hadn't had too many coloured lads at the time. So the two of them – Justin and John – needed to be strong characters from day one.'

*   *   *

Fashanu's and Norwich's form dipped. His goals dried up and Norwich slipped towards mid-table. A home game against Southampton in November 1979 saw Norwich 1–0 down and Fashanu displaying a lack of confidence and conviction. Then he seemed to come to life, scoring with a lob over the goalkeeper in the 79th minute and setting up a late winner with 'a sizzling solo dribble' according to the *Daily Express*. Afterwards he explained his sudden burst of form to the reporter: 'I'd been trying to play like a recognised striker is expected to. You know, staying in the middle as a target man and knocking the ball on as soon as it reached me. That made it easy for Southampton. But then it dawned on me that I didn't want to be stereotyped and in any case I can't play that way. I'm me and nobody else and so I started doing my own thing at last.' It sounded as much like a personal manifesto as an explanation for his improvement during the match. And it cannot be over-emphasised that young players are not supposed to talk like that. If they say anything at all it is usually about how much they have to learn and how much they appreciate the efforts of their teammates and managers to help them.

In truth Fashanu may have caught the Southampton defence by surprise on this occasion. His best assets were his power, courage and ability to put the ball in the net. Sizzling dribbles never did become a regular feature of his game. His challenge was to make maximum use of his physical attributes while keeping within acceptable limits. This he failed to do when he was sent off for allegedly kicking Aston Villa's Allan Evans although he claimed to be completely innocent. The Norwich crowd responded angrily to the referee's decision. A smoke bomb was let off and dozens of coins were hurled at Jimmy Rimmer, the Villa goalkeeper. After the game he displayed marks on either side of his neck where he had been hit. Play was suspended and only resumed after both managers appealed for calm. A month later, in January 1980, there was more crowd trouble when Norwich visited Yeovil in Somerset for an FA Cup match. Local youths attacked the police, delaying the start of the game and twice causing it to stop.

All this violence was causing people to stay away from football grounds and clubs were struggling to cope with diminishing revenue. Norwich was no exception and, a year after Fashanu made his debut, Bond was driven to say that he might have to sell him. Fashanu told the press: 'I am happy at Carrow Road [the Canaries' stadium] but I'm an ambitious player and if the right offer was made I'd have to consider moving on.' They were the first words in a saga that would drag on for 17 months. Crystal Palace, managed by Terry Venables, was the first club to show interest. But any manager watching Fashanu would have been unimpressed. His slump in form had continued and he had scored only twice in four months.

The fixture before his 19th birthday was at home to Liverpool, the League champions, drawing a big crowd of over 25,000. The game was given added significance because it was to be played in front of the *Match of the Day* cameras. As the supporters gathered and began their chants and songs, and the two sets of players warmed up on the pitch they had no idea they were about to witness and take part in a match which would be stay in their memories the rest of their lives.

In a thrilling game of end-to-end action it took only 70 seconds for Martin Peters to head Norwich into the lead, but David Fairclough equalised for Liverpool then put them ahead. Kevin Reeves shot home from close range and the half-time break came with the teams level at 2–2. On 75 minutes David Fairclough completed his hat-trick to put Liverpool ahead once more. But soon the Canaries equalised.

Kevin Bond passed the ball from the middle of the pitch out to John Ryan on the right. Ryan played it up to Fashanu who received it on the edge of the penalty area, with his back to goal and the defender, Alan Kennedy, close to him. As Ryan sprinted forward, calling for a return pass, Fashanu flicked the ball up with the his right foot, turned inside and volleyed it with his left beyond the reach of England goalkeeper, Ray Clemence, as he dived to his right. Turning calmly away, Fashanu pointed to the sky, as if to say 'I'm number one', and began walking towards the centre circle before being mobbed by his teammates as the crowd roared their approval. Liverpool snatched a 5–3 win with goals from Dalglish and Case in the last two minutes but, on this rare occasion, the spectacle was more important than the result.

That evening the football watching nation enjoyed highlights of the match on TV with Fashanu's goal making a great impact. What made it so memorable was the element of surprise. No one on the pitch or in the stands saw it coming. It suggested that Justin was more than a good all-round footballer who was exceptionally tough; he also possessed the special attributes of imagination and nerve. It was an audacious goal. *Match of the Day* viewers voted it Goal of the Season and it still crops up in discussions about the best goals of all time.

Fashanu showed maturity beyond his years in putting the goal and people's reactions in perspective. He reflected on it in a book, *Our Way – Norwich City,* published at the end of the season: 'It's funny how you can work yourself to a standstill week in and week out plying your craft as honestly as you know how without making any great impact on the fans or on the media. It is fair to say that some of the best things you do go totally unnoticed because they are the workaday aspects of the game. This has never been brought home to me more forcefully than when I scored that celebrated goal against Liverpool this year at Carrow Road. It is the big talking point of people you meet on the street or at the pub and it dominates any appraisal of my form last season. Goals like that are one-off things. The opportunity rises out of the blue and if you make all the right decisions and luck is on your side then the miracle of perfection takes place.' He added: 'I had just scored what may be the greatest goal of my career.'

Chapter 4

Money, Fame, Cars and Girls

Justin was being filmed for a TV documentary, one of a series called *The Pace-Setters*. He was asked what he wanted for himself and how he saw his life developing over the next 10 years. He flashed a huge smile at the camera and said: 'I'd like to get richer and more famous.' He added: 'Being a celebrity at my age, you can have one or two of the rewards: a nice car and of course there are one or two girls coming my way.' Girls loved Justin. People attending a memorial service for him were asked to write down their memories. Recalling their teenage years, two women wrote together: 'We will always remember Justin's smile and how if Justin was on the dance floor every girl wanted to dance with him. [We] were lucky enough to do that a lot.' Another wrote: 'Many happy memories at Cromwell's nightclub dancing to The Commodores. Think of you every time I smell Paco Rabanne – never smelt as good on anyone else.'

In *The Pace-Setters* Justin spoke of the minor hassles of celebrity before concluding: 'I like it most of the time because it shows that you're wanted, it shows that people love you and it's something that you'll miss when you're not in the limelight.' Most young footballers would have talked about winning medals, playing for their country, scoring goals. But as sports writer, Mick Dennis, noticed about Justin: 'He was desperate for fame as a young person, desperate more than anyone I've come across. He really, really wanted to be famous.'

Fashanu loved celebrity and the trappings which went with it but was never aloof. He was always ready to mix with the fans or lend some glamour to a charity event. A typical fan's memory comes from the journalist Matthew Clark. He was at school when Justin was playing for Norwich and his school football team were raising money to finance a trip to the USA. They asked the Norwich players for some help and Justin came along for a photo shoot at a sports shop where they were being fitted out with new kit. Clark remembers: 'He was lovely. He was incredibly friendly and never acted the star.' He also remembers Justin's car, an orange MGB GT. Justin loved his flash motors though he was not a great driver. On one occasion he took part in a charity event at Norfolk's Snetterton racing track and crashed his car. Fortunately he was not injured when, travelling at only 30mph, he misjudged a corner and went into a skid. The usually mild-mannered Ken Brown – by then the manager – was furious and barred him from driving there again.

Once Justin had to miss a game through injury and endeared himself to the fans by joining them on the terraces in the most raucous part of the ground, the Barclay End. When he was on the pitch they would chant: 'Keep on scoring Fash-an-u.' Although black footballers took a lot of stick, football also provided a rare forum where young black British men were idolised and celebrated.

Fashanu became friends with a public relations man, Roger Haywood and asked him for advice especially about handling the media. Haywood became his business manager and gave him an intensive course in how to speak fluently in interviews and avoid the usual clichés. Fashanu was a willing and capable student, so much so that he got his own sports programme on Radio Norfolk which he would record during the week for broadcast on a Saturday. His ambition was to become a commentator when he retired from football. He was given his own column in *Match Weekly* and Haywood negotiated a four page fashion shoot for *The Sun*. Justin had the physique, looks and personality to carry off wearing the most outrageous outfits. They recorded some music with Justin on lead vocals. Unusually for such a young player, Fashanu was ever aware that his career in football could be cut short. He had seen colleagues at Norwich have to retire early through injury but perhaps, also, he was conscious of being out there on his own with no family to fall back on. His formal links with the Jacksons ended on his 18th birthday although he did not move out immediately and was always welcome at the family home.

The Biography

Money and fame came early and he was not always able to handle the responsibilities which went with it. This was illustrated by his accumulation of parking tickets. He seemed to believe that, because he was becoming a famous footballer, he could park his car anywhere. He would leave it on a double yellow line and refuse to move it. As Ronnie Brooks put it: 'He became a bit more difficult to control and look after. He'd come in with a huge bundle of parking tickets and say "What am I going to do with these? I tell them I'm Justin Fashanu".' Brooks would tell him: 'They don't care who you are, if you've transgressed against the law, you must pay the penalty.'

The acclaim and attention was damaging Justin's relationship with John, the brother he had been so close to. John spoke about this period in *Fallen Hero* a TV documentary made after Justin died and seemed still to seethe with resentment about living in his older brother's shadow. He felt abandoned, waiting on the sidelines as Justin talked to teammates and journalists after matches. He too was hoping to be a professional footballer but did not quite have Justin's ability. Norwich took him on as a schoolboy but let him go. John felt that having the Fashanu name was a hindrance rather than a help as he was constantly compared unfavourably with his brother. But he worked hard, was signed by Cambridge United and eventually won a contract as an apprentice back with the Canaries.

One particular incident summed up the difference in their status. When Justin saw John signing autographs after a youth game he strode up to him, took the pen away and snapped it. 'Earn the right to sign your name', he said. 'These children only want your name because of the success I've had. You earn your own name, earn the right to have them idolise you.' John told this story twice in TV documentaries. In *Fallen Hero* he gave it as an example of Justin's unbearable arrogance. In *Going Back* John revisited Flint House, the Jackson's family home and reminisced about his childhood. This time he suggested Justin was rightfully coming down on him, telling him he had to make a success of himself. Either way, this period saw the beginning of the breaking of the brotherly bond which had held them so close.

*   *   *

That goal against Liverpool is the moment in football Justin Fashanu is best remembered for but it did nothing for his immediate prospects. He continued to struggle for form and three games later was dropped from the team. It was Kevin Reeves who made the big money exit, moving, in March 1980, to Manchester City for

£1 million. When Reeves played his last match for Norwich, Fashanu was turning out for the reserves. Mel Machin, the reserve team manager, offered some words of encouragement: 'The rest from the pressure of being in the first team is doing him a world of good. He is only 19 and has lots of time. I think he will eventually be one of the best strikers in the country.' But Bond gave a more mixed appraisal: 'For one so young Justin has done a marvellous job for us this season. Lately, however, he hasn't been doing justice to his ability and that's why I've left him out. He has to learn about dedication and hard work and it's my job as manager to teach him from an early stage.' A few months later Bond expanded on those remarks: 'There is only one thing that will stop him from being really special. He must put the same effort into every game and not live on what he did in the previous match.'

In most respects Justin was aware of his limitations as a player and eager to improve. Justin felt that he was not jumping high enough to win headers and Roger Haywood, who used to train with members of the Norwich squad at a local gym, suggested that Chris Roberts, who ran the gym, could help him. Roberts devised a programme of exercises to increase the suppleness and strength of his jumping muscles. Using the programme Justin was able to add five to six inches to the height of his leaps. And he was putting in extra stamina training, showing his insecurities when he told a reporter: 'The big worry I have is that I'm going to let the lads down by not having a bit left towards the end of the game…I go back to London to see one of my brothers and I know that not every black kid in England has had my chances. It makes me determined to really work.'

After missing a few matches Fashanu was restored to the first team. The break had worked and he was back to his best form, scoring a clutch of goals and winning his first cap for the England Under-21s, coming on as a substitute and scoring in a 2–1 defeat to East Germany. But as the season drew to a close Fashanu and Bond had a row. The incident which set them off was Fashanu headbutting Bristol City's defender, David Rodgers, leaving him with blood pouring from a fractured cheek. It was missed by the referee but seen by Norwich staff. In the dressing room Bond showed his fury. As Fashanu sat with his head down, taking off his boots, he yelled: 'Look at me when I'm talking to you.' Fashanu responded by telling him to shut up. Bond told him if that was the sort of thing he was going to do in a Norwich shirt, he was finished. They were so angry with each other that assistant manager, Ken Brown, and coach, John Sainty, had to pull them apart.

The row could have blown over but Fashanu prolonged it by threatening to call in the players' union and publicly criticising Bond: 'I realise I was out of order in butting

Rodgers', he said, 'but the manager has over-reacted by blowing his top. Rodgers had been having a go at me throughout the match. And in my position you have to give as good as you get. In that situation, someone is bound to get hurt sooner or later. I'll be seeing the boss as soon as possible and if we can't sort things out I will be asking for a transfer.' Bond was equally unrepentant, saying he would fine Justin heavily and report him to the Board of Directors, adding: 'If that's the way Justin wants to carry on his football career then he won't do it under my management.' Bond and Fashanu resolved their differences but this was by no means the last time Fashanu would fall out with a manager and demonstrate a strong impulse to make sure the fans knew his side of the story.

The 1979–80 season had been one of highs and lows for Fashanu but he ended as Norwich's leading scorer with 13 goals in the three major competitions. The team completed its fifth successive season in the First Division, finishing in mid-table.

When the season was over, Norwich embarked on a tour of China and midfielder Peter Mendham has fond memories of Justin from that trip. They were good friends, having come up through the junior teams together, and among the group of players who hung out at the CEYMS (Church of England Young Men's Society) club after training, playing snooker or challenging local table tennis stars, Richard and Martin Stevenson, to a game. On trips they roomed together. Like others who knew Justin well at the time Peter had no idea Justin was gay but when interviewed for this book he was keen to say that had he known it would not have made the slightest difference to their friendship. He remembers him as 'a terrific man and a real gentleman'.

The Canaries were only the second professional team to visit China and made quite an impact. Peter remembers he and Justin going into Beijing's Tiananmen Square. They joined some children who were kicking a ball about and attracted a lot of attention, Justin with his black skin and Peter with his white skin and red hair. Soon they were surrounded by several thousand curious spectators as they showed off their ball skills. Another incident is typical of the anecdotes former professionals like to have a laugh about when they meet up for reunions. John Bond was always impeccably turned out and was greatly annoyed when his case went missing and he had to put together an emergency wardrobe. Meanwhile, a case stood in the corner of Peter and Justin's room, each assuming it belonged to the other. It was only when they were leaving and neither claimed it that they realised it was John Bond's missing case – and they were going to have to tell him.

Having impressed on Norwich's tour of Australia the previous spring, Fashanu was signed up to play five games for Adelaide City during June. He made an impact on and off the pitch, the newspaper, *Soccer Action*, reporting: 'He thrilled boys at Australian Soccer Camps with his demonstrations of skill and with his enlightening talks.' He even made a film for the Education Department. Adelaide, and former Australian national coach, Ralé Rašić could not praise him enough, saying: 'Few top class professionals are able to come from the top down to our level, without trying to make it obvious that they are different to us. Not so with Justin. He was merely one of the boys.' Justin scored three goals, helping Adelaide to four wins out of five, and one may have been the closest he ever got to emulating his goal against Liverpool, lobbing the goalkeeper from over 30 yards – 'an unbelievable goal' according to *Soccer Action*. This was Justin's first taste of living and playing abroad, promoting football where it was a minority sport. It suited him.

* * *

For the 1980–81 season Fashanu's new strike partner, replacing Kevin Reeves, was Joe Royle. He had won England caps but although only 31 his best days seemed to be behind him; he cost just £60,000. Like Fashanu he was a big, tough player and their similarity could have worked against them but in practice their partnership was a success. With Royle taking on some of the responsibility for battling with defenders Fashanu was freed up to score goals.

The season could not have got off to a better start. In front of their own supporters Norwich walloped Stoke City 5–1 with Fashanu scoring three in the first half. His first was a shot from 18 yards; he took the ball round the Stoke goalkeeper to score his second and headed in his third from a cross. He was unplayable that day. After the game Bond described him as 'a bit special', before adding, 'trouble is, he wants more money every time he scores'. The previous day Fashanu had signed a new, improved three-year contract which, according to *The Times*, ended speculation about his future.

By this time Fashanu and Bond had got over their row about the headbutting incident and spoke well of each other. Bond said that it was a privilege to have him in the side. Of his manager Fashanu said: 'There was a time last season when I wanted to leave but that is all over now. Because the manager and I have had our ups and downs, the bond – and I apologise for the pun – between us is much stronger. I love that man and now whether or not he plays me is immaterial.' Both referred to his disciplinary record, Bond saying of Fashanu's sending off against Aston Villa: 'If he had continued along that path he would have destroyed himself.' As ever, Fashanu was eloquent in his defence: 'Being coloured in a white community and having a Dr Barnardo's background makes you become more dependent on yourself at an early age. You make your own decisions. You become your own man rather than rely on others. When I started in League football I was just a little young and some people played on it. I was under a lot of provocation from some of the older players at other clubs who should have known better than to try winding me up. But that, we all know, is a tactic of the game. I'm not a naturally aggressive sort of fellow. I'm very placid as a rule. But when I'm aroused things start to happen. Discipline is important to me but people can get much more out of me by sitting down and talking things out.'

Following the win against Stoke, Norwich lost the next four games and went on to have a poor season but Fashanu continued to play remarkably well. In October he was picked again for the England Under-21s and also named as back-up for the senior squad by manager Ron Greenwood, with several of his usual strikers being injured. He was the leading scorer in the First Division with 10 goals but Norwich were third from bottom. After seven successful years, John Bond had had enough of keeping the team afloat with so little money to spend on players and accepted an offer from Manchester City. His assistant, Ken Brown, was appointed to replace him. Sensing that Fashanu might be unsettled by Bond's departure, Leeds made an offer, thought to be £750,000, which was turned down by the club with Fashanu obviously tempted: 'I feel a move might be good for me.' Chairman, Arthur South, declared that they would only let him go for a British record fee of £2 million. It was a figure designed to put off potential buyers. With the economy in recession and football hit by falling attendances, a bid of half that figure was unlikely.

Norwich were keen to hang on to Fashanu for the rest of the season – he represented their best chance of avoiding relegation – and in December offered him another contract which would have made him one of the best paid players in the country. Fashanu rejected it, clearly indicating his wish to leave. The list of clubs reported to be interested in signing him grew to include Nottingham Forest and Manchester City. John Bond was eager to pair him up with Kevin Reeves again. In January 1981 Manchester City inflicted a humiliating defeat on Norwich in the FA Cup, a 6–0 home win. With his son, Kevin, playing for Norwich Bond derived no pleasure from seeing his former team perform so ineptly. 'Every time a goal went in I looked at poor Kevin's face. I wish we had stopped at three', he said after the game.

As his future remained uncertain Fashanu was becoming increasingly frustrated by his colleagues and his feelings boiled over the day after his 20th birthday. The ITV highlights programme, *On the Ball*, captured the Canaries' seventh successive defeat, away to Birmingham. They held out until 15 minutes from time but then collapsed, conceding four goals. As usual, Fashanu was getting most of the attention, being watched by Brian Clough and Peter Taylor from Nottingham Forest, and Terry Neil and Don Howe from Arsenal. 'Fashanu loped belligerently around the field' reported *The Times* and he was certainly belligerent when interviewed immediately after the match, delivering an epic rant to the TV cameras: 'We've got to fight, we've got to battle and it's going to be bloody hard – if you'll excuse my French – to get out of the relegation zone, and I think it's about time the players in the team – I hope the manager doesn't mind me saying this – have got to look at themselves, myself included. We're here in the First Division and love everything that goes with it. We've got nice suits and nice cars but in the Second Division it's going to be a blasted hard struggle. I can't understand why we can't be determined, ruthless and let's get ourselves out there. Because all we've got to do is just be a little bit nastier. You see, players at this club are too nice.' Whether this was a rallying cry or an attack on his teammates is debatable but it certainly shows a young man running out of patience but never lost for words.

Justin was struggling for form himself at the time and with good reason. He was suffering from a rare illness which was not diagnosed for several more weeks. The club did not disclose what it was but, according to Justin, his stomach swelled up, he could not eat or drink much and lost almost a stone in weight. He was completely shattered after games. He was about to be admitted to hospital for rest and extensive tests but a specialist diagnosed the problem and prescribed medication to clear it up. It was typical of Fashanu's determination and the club's desperation that he only missed one game during this period.

In March he was approached by a big PR company, Public Eye Enterprises Ltd, and agreed to sign up with them. He was not entitled to do so, having a contract with Roger Haywood, but it was rather typical of Justin that this did not occur to him. Haywood was not only put out but concerned about Justin. He had never made money out of working with him and saw him as a friend. He felt that this still young and somewhat vulnerable star needed people around him who cared about his wellbeing. Haywood feared that a bigger company would exploit him as a cash-making commodity. He could have taken legal action but decided to preserve their friendship while losing Justin as a client. Roger Haywood did not know this was the second time he had reneged on a contract in his short career. Justin already had a legally binding contract with his boxing coach, Gordon Homes, to represent him in business matters when Haywood signed him up. Like Haywood, Homes indulged Fashanu and let it go. As John said of his brother, looking back on his life: 'He came from lovely Norwich where the people were sweet, so nice, and they'd protect him.'

Justin was not the most reliable person. Roger Haywood explained: 'I would arrange, for example, a media interview and phone him up and say "Justin, where are you, what's going on?" and he'd say "Something more important came up". I'd say "Hang on a minute, you made an appointment, you do it" and he'd be embarrassed and apologetic, and come over and fix it.' He added: 'I wouldn't say he was selfish but I don't think he had a sense of responsibility.'

With Justin's illness affecting his performances and his evident desire to leave Norwich, some of the supporters turned against him and started barracking him after he missed a couple of chances in a home game against Middlesbrough where, once again, he was being watched by Peter Taylor from Nottingham Forest. The match proved a turning point for Fashanu as he overcame his tentative start to put in his best effort for some time and help his team secure a rare win. He always seemed to play well against Nottingham Forest and did so again in an away fixture at the end of March. He put Norwich ahead with an excellent near-post volley before they subsided to another defeat but must have impressed yet again the Forest management.

A few days later he played in a testimonial match for Ces Podd which says much about the position of black footballers at the time. Podd was one of the small number of black players turning out for English professional clubs when Fashanu's generation were growing up, and endured a great deal of abuse. He played over 500 times for Bradford City at right-back and was popular with the supporters there, choosing to stay when bigger clubs, including Manchester United, showed an interest in him. 'I got on well with the Bradford fans. They were my security,' he explained. The testimonial game featured a Black All-Stars team with Fashanu turning out alongside players such as Brendon Batson, Cyrille Regis, Luther Blissett, Remi Moses and Garth Crooks. Podd was not a high profile player and it was an act of solidarity for these stars to take part.

With six games to go Norwich gave themselves a chance to avoid relegation with an impressive run of four successive wins. Fashanu would have enjoyed the goal that defeated local rivals, Ipswich Town, ending their chances of finishing top. He was invariably on the receiving end of racist abuse from Ipswich supporters, taunting him with monkey chants and shouts of 'where're the bananas?' A 1–0 defeat to Manchester United left the Canaries with a slender chance of staying up. A draw in their last match of the season would be enough if the teams immediately above them all lost. They were at home against already relegated Leicester City. But it was not to be. Nerves got the better of them and they were 2–0 down after 22 minutes. In a dramatic game they drew level with goals from McGuire and Fashanu only for a third Leicester goal to confirm relegation.

Fashanu's goal was his 19th League goal of the season – making him the third highest scorer in the First Division, a remarkable achievement for one so young and playing for a team which created so few chances. In all competitions he scored 22 goals for Norwich. Notable also was his feat in avoiding being sent off or suspended, suggesting a maturing talent.

Norwich had held on to their prize asset until the end of the season but it was inevitable he would leave before the start of the next. Meanwhile Fashanu's summer break was once again filled with football. First the Norwich squad flew straight out to the USA where they played three matches in three days, against Florida International University, Atlanta Chiefs and Fort Lauderdale, Fashanu getting sent off in one match. Then he was picked again for the England Under-21 squad, playing in Budapest against Hungary and scoring the winner. His globe trotting continued as he signed up once more for the newly named Adelaide City Juventus. This time Justin played eight games, scoring three goals and put in a typically whole-hearted series of performances. One resulted in yet another controversial sending off. After several confrontations between Fashanu and opposing players, one went down claiming he had been headbutted and Fashanu was shown the red card. He claimed the referee had been conned: 'If I had really headbutted him I'd have broken his nose.'

When Fashanu returned to Norwich in early August there had been no firm offers from other clubs. He began pre-season training with his old team and turned out in a friendly against Peterborough. The report of this match in the *Eastern Daily Post* could not have made it clearer that after two and a half years as a prominent player for Norwich Fashanu was still subjected to racial prejudice in its many forms: 'Justin Fashanu was in his element in what might have been his last match in NCFC colours. A bandaged head left him Zulu-like in appearance and his determined charges caused great consternation amongst the Peterborough defenders. Peterborough too demonstrated primitive instincts of their own. McGuire confidently stroked in a 45th minute penalty to make the scores 2–2 after Fashanu had been upended in the box.'

Just two weeks before the 1981–82 season kicked off Nottingham Forest made an offer of £1 million which was accepted by Norwich. Fashanu travelled to Nottingham with Ken Brown to negotiate a personal terms with Brian Clough. By this time Manchester City had made a late bid. Brown remembers turning away as Clough ushered Fashanu into his office only to find that almost immediately Fashanu was back beside him. Clough had offered to make him one of the best paid players in the League and he took just seconds to accept. The achievements of black players were still sufficiently newsworthy that Fashanu was heralded as the first £1 million black footballer.

*   *   *

Justin had recently got engaged to his girlfriend, Julie Arthurton, and she moved to Nottingham with him. His life was following the trajectory expected of a talented sports star. But all this was about to change dramatically in three ways. Within months he would be failing as a footballer, become a born-again Christian and start leading the life of a gay man. Could any of this have been predicted?

Justin's achievements as a young footballer were impressive. Few make such a solid impression at such a young age. His spectacular goal against Liverpool was a one-off but his goalscoring and all round performances in Norwich's relegation season provided more convincing evidence of his ability. Thirty years later only one footballer of his age had surpassed his feat of scoring 19 League goals in a season in the First Division (or Premier League). That was Robbie Fowler who was playing for Liverpool, a team which created far more chances for forwards than Norwich. But Fashanu had his limitations. Roger Haywood noticed them and talked to him about them. He was not great at controlling the ball or tricking opponents to take the ball past them. Norwich could play to his strengths, laying the ball off and collecting the return pass, shooting and heading powerfully, and generally rampaging around. But in a team playing at a higher level with more skilful players these limitations could become exposed. Haywood regarded him as more of a £250,000 player who could have stayed at Norwich for 10 years and had a great career there.

Interviewed for *12 Canary Greats*, Fashanu's strike partner, Kevin Reeves (who left before Justin's last and best season), was highly complimentary but, when recalling the famous goal against Liverpool rather damned him with faint praise: 'He wasn't particularly strong with his left foot but that was what he was capable of. He could go from looking gangly to produce a bit of quality like that.' Greg Downs, Norwich's left-back that day, was even more circumspect about the goal, claiming that Fashanu miscontrolled it with his right foot and when he hit it with his left it could have gone anywhere.

Success in football is about more than skill, and confidence is key for a striker. Ronnie Brooks felt that Justin was not as confident as he appeared and Brian Clough was the wrong sort of manager for him. Speaking in the documentary, *Fallen Hero*, he said: 'Had I have known he was going to Nottingham Forest, I would have advised him quite strongly not to have gone there because Brian Clough was a very abrasive sort of person who would not wait to put down a player if he felt he wasn't doing something he wanted doing.' There was bound to be a personality clash between Clough and Fashanu. Clough expected his players to keep quiet and obey his commands. Fashanu was never going to do that. Questions were raised about how carefully Nottingham Forest staff had monitored his performances before splashing out £1 million. More to the point, if Clough had read any of his interviews he would have seen that Fashanu was an opinionated, outspoken, stubborn man much like himself. He would almost certainly have decided there was only room for one such character in his club and looked elsewhere.

Until Justin came out as gay in 1990, people who knew him well, when he was playing for Norwich City, such as Ronnie Brooks, Peter Mendham, and Roger Haywood and his late wife, Sandra – who was also very fond of Justin and treated him like her younger brother – had no idea he was gay. Neither, it seems, did members of the Fashanu and Jackson families. While at Norwich he dated young women and was engaged. Possibly less surprised by his coming out was Marilyn Powell, wife of Tony Powell, the player whose boots Justin cleaned when he was an apprentice. He left Norwich just before Fashanu and moved with his family to California. A couple of years later, according to accounts she has given in interviews, Marilyn discovered he was gay when she returned unexpectedly to their home and found him having sex with a young man.

A few days after Justin came out she spoke to the *News of the World*, an article appearing under the headline, 'Bitter wife's first clue to macho Tony's gay secret – Night My Hubby Kissed Football Star Fashanu'. In it she recounted how she knew of Justin's difficult childhood and felt sorry for him. She said: 'When Tony started spending lots of time with him, I was sure he felt the same way.' Justin told her that he idolised Tony. She described how: 'I often caught Tony staring at Justin in a strange way, but I always put it out of my mind.' She then related an incident when Justin turned up in tears because a friend or relative was sick: 'Tony jumped up, threw his arms round Justin's neck and kissed him. They were just like two girls comforting each other. I told myself I was being silly. Who suspects the father of her children is a practicing homosexual.' In an interview in 2002, she had some kind words for Justin: 'When my marriage ended and I found out the truth about my husband, Justin Fashanu was the only person who kept in touch. He was a sweet boy. He came to see me and told me, "I'm so sorry". Justin admitted to her that he had known Tony was gay.

When talking about discovering his sexual preferences, Fashanu never referred to Tony Powell. He mentioned having felt different at school and having gay friends from the age of 15 who he turned to for support and advice in 1982. He also wrote an article for a book, *Stonewall 25: The Making of the Lesbian and Gay Community in Britain*, in which he revealed: 'I had just been given a £1 million transfer to Nottingham Forest and there was a big party. I had a few drinks and ended up in bed with my best friend. It wasn't planned. From then on, I started to experiment more and more.'

Although Justin relished fame and money there was also a more reflective side to him. He had not entirely jettisoned the Christianity he was brought up with. He kept a Bible in his flat and would object to people blaspheming by for example using 'Jesus Christ!' as an exclamation. But he was also exploring other belief systems or at least ways of achieving inner peace, trying out yoga and meditation. He featured in a book, *Fitness with Fashanu*, in which he demonstrated exercises developed by Gordon Haddock, a partner in the Norwich Natural Therapy Centre – not the sort of place associated with the world of the 1980s professional footballer – a world of clubs and pubs. Justin inhabited that world too although he seldom drank more than a pint of beer or glass of wine.

His interview with *Radio Times* to publicise the documentary about him, *The Pace-Setters*, was published at the end of his last season with the Canaries. Justin told the interviewer that he was Piscean, a bit of a day dreamer and enjoyed reading science fiction and Tolkien. 'It's narrow just to be a footballer' he said: 'When my time comes to die – which I hope won't be for a while yet – I want to be able to say "All right you can come and take me now because I've had a go at everything I've wanted to".'

Chapter 5

Everything Changes

Nottingham Forest was a club enjoying unprecedented success with the legendary partnership of manager Brian Clough and his assistant, Peter Taylor. They had first met in the 1950s when playing for Middlesbrough, Clough's home-town team in the north-east of England. Clough was a brilliant forward, scoring 204 goals in 222 games before moving to Sunderland where he scored 63 in 74. But his career finished in frustration. He played only twice for England, feeling he should have had many more caps, and it was ended by a knee injury which occurred when he was 27, forcing him to retire at the age of 29. Taylor, a goalkeeper, was born in Nottingham and enjoyed most success as a player with Coventry and Middlesbrough.

Their managerial partnership began at Hartlepools (now Hartlepool) United, 14 miles from Middlesbrough. Soon they moved to Derby County, a Second Division club in the East Midlands of similar stature to Norwich City. They achieved promotion in 1969 and won the First Division title in 1972, reaching the semi-finals of the European Cup the following season. Shortly after, Clough resigned, leading to a tumultuous couple of years which included a campaign to get him reinstated, a brief time managing Brighton with Taylor, and a disastrous spell at Leeds United. This period was captured in David Peace's novel, *The Damned United*, and the film of the same name.

The Biography

In 1975 Clough was recruited by Nottingham Forest, 15 miles from Derby and, like Derby, when he had become their manager, in the Second Division. He persuaded Taylor to join him and they achieved promotion in the 1976–77 season. The next season Forest won the First Division title and the following two seasons, the European Cup, while finishing second and fifth in the First Division. Their achievements at Derby were impressive but this was spectacular, elevating Brian Clough to the status of one of the greatest ever managers in English club football.

The values Clough brought to managing a football club stemmed from his family background and, in particular, his mother. While his dad was working long hours managing a sweet factory, she presided over a family of eight children, running the home with order, warmth and authority. He expected his players to be well turned out, to respect referees and obey his instructions. In return, he engendered a family spirit of togetherness that enabled them to achieve far more as a team than could be expected from the sum of their individual talents.

He was at his best with players who had previously achieved little in their careers, and knew they owed their success to him. Winger, John Robertson, was going nowhere in the reserves when Clough arrived at Forest. Under his guidance Robertson became a key member of the team and one of the best Nottingham Forest players of all time. Another player to benefit from Clough's management was the midfielder John McGovern. He followed Clough from Hartlepools to Derby, Leeds and Forest, and was team captain during Forest's greatest period of success. Yet he was never selected to play at senior level for Scotland. In contrast, Clough's attempt to manage a team of established stars at Leeds United was a disaster. He took over a team which had just won the First Division under manager, Don Revie, and alienated players, such as Johnny Giles and Norman Hunter, with his criticisms.

Brian Clough is not just remembered for his achievements as player and manager. He was a man who craved attention and earned it through his arrogance, wit, eccentricity and outspoken views. He was a natural on TV, making memorable appearances, with other opinionated characters such as Derek Dougan and Malcolm Allison, on a panel commenting on the 1974 World Cup, and was a popular guest on chat shows such as *Parkinson*. He became, not only one of the most successful managers, but one of the biggest and most loved personalities of English football. But he possessed a withering tongue and a tendency to brag and bully. He was not a man to get on the wrong side of.

The calming influence of Peter Taylor was crucial in keeping Clough's impetuous and volatile nature in check or repairing the damage when he did not succeed. But that was just one of several critical contributions he made to their partnership. Another was as a judge of players to bring to the club. Less easy to pin down in a job description was his role as best mate. Football management can be a lonely and stressful job. Taylor was the man with whom Clough could wind down, have a laugh, chuck ideas around and trust completely. In most respects it suited Taylor to stay in the background. He was an anxious man who could not cope easily with the limelight.

Clough and Taylor needed each other and were generally willing to acknowledge it and appreciate the other's contribution. But they could also resent their mutual dependence and Taylor felt he did not get enough credit. In the autumn of 1980 a book, *With Clough by Taylor*, was published. It was Peter Taylor's account of their partnership and his role in its success. He had not told Clough he was writing it and Clough was not pleased. He felt Taylor was trading on his name and should have given him some of the profits. Taylor pointed out that Clough had never shared the proceeds of his newspaper columns. This petty row over a few pounds marked the beginning of the deterioration of their relationship.

It was not helped by the unsatisfactory 1980–81 season in which Forest slipped to seventh place and failed to qualify for European competition. Looking back, Clough accepted that they moved on too many of their ageing squad too quickly and their replacements were generally inferior. He was particularly dissatisfied with their expensively assembled trio of strikers, Trevor Francis, Ian Wallace and Peter Ward.

Trevor Francis was one of the biggest stars in English football and became the first player to be transferred between English clubs for £1 million when he joined Forest from Birmingham City. Clough admired his skill but was not convinced his best position was striker, often playing him out wide. Ian Wallace arrived from Coventry, also for £1 million and Peter Ward from Brighton for half that amount.

Clough wanted a strong, brave centre-forward. In his column in the *Daily Express* he wrote: 'Wearing the No 9 shirt in football has gone out of fashion but Justin Fashanu might soon put it back. Even kids have stopped talking about wanting to be centre-forwards. And why? Because everyone realises it is the most difficult job on a football field to fill that role successfully.'

Roger Hayward felt that for Justin, Clough's desire to sign him was the validation of his talent he craved. His insecurities about his true ability were assuaged by a top manager's judgement that he could make the difference to a team looking to reclaim its position as the best in Europe. Fashanu said of Clough: 'He impresses me greatly because he is a winner and makes those around him winners.' Peter Taylor made it clear that Forest had wanted him for some time and that he was signed to be the premier striker at the club, the other striker's position going to whoever slotted in best alongside him.

For Justin, this was not just about a move to another club. He was leaving the area where he had found stability after the upheavals of his early life. He was moving away from the parental figures in his life: Betty and Alf Jackson, Gordon Homes and Ronnie Brooks; from his brother, John, and good friends. He had grown up with Norwich City and was a fans' favourite.

Nottingham was a more ethnically diverse city than Norwich with an established black population. As a black man, Justin would stand out a little less in the team as well as in the city. Nottingham-born right-back, captain and England international, Viv Anderson, was also black and there were black players coming through the reserves, such as Chris Fairclough and Calvin Plummer. Fairclough, who went on to win a First Division title with Leeds United, remembers his excitement at Forest signing Fashanu, feeling it showed what black footballers could achieve. To some extent Fashanu was carrying the hopes of Britain's black community as well as those of Forest's supporters.

* * *

Until they could find somewhere more permanent to live, Justin and Julie moved into the penthouse suite of one of Nottingham's top hotels, the Albany. But Justin had to leave immediately to join his new teammates on a pre-season tour of Spain. He did not get off to the best of starts, first arriving at the airport without his passport and then being sent off in his second game. Forest were playing Real Zaragoza in a four-way tournament and in a stormy match he picked up two bookings, the second for dissent. It would not have gone down well with Brian Clough who strongly believed in players respecting referees even when they made mistakes. An alert reporter for *The Times* noted Fashanu had earned 'a place in the history books' having been sent off three times in the summer break while playing for three different clubs on three different continents; the previous occasions having been for Norwich in the USA and Adelaide in Australia.

Fashanu's competitive debut for Forest came in a home win against Southampton. Wallace lined up alongside him with Francis playing out wide. Clough and Taylor demonstrated their growing disunity by making contradictory statements about Francis. Taylor said that Francis might leave; Clough insisted he wanted Francis to stay. But then, after one more game, he was sold to Manchester City. Fashanu had hoped to play alongside Francis and publically expressed his disappointment: 'From what I have seen at the start of the season I think he's the best player in the First Division.' Once more he would have incurred Clough's displeasure. Clough though chose to praise his early performances, saying that they had strengthened his faith in Fashanu's ability. Fashanu also drew praise from Ian Wallace who scored a hat-trick in the third match which was lost 4–3 away to Birmingham City: 'Every time Justin went for the ball he took two men with him. Because they were marking Justin very carefully, it gave me more room and greater opportunity.'

Despite Fashanu's reasonable start, Clough soon developed a strong personal dislike of him and distain for his abilities as a footballer. And this may well have begun with an incident involving the Stoke defender, Denis Smith, who was marking Fashanu. Smith gives his version in his autobiography: 'When you've got that kind of price tag I was the kind of player who would test you out. So straight from the kick-off I was all over him, both in terms of giving him a real buffeting in aerial challenges and in tackles on the deck – smack. I also got into him mentally, nicking the ball off him, not letting him settle, reducing his confidence, probing his weakness.' He goes on to describe how Fashanu, unable to cope, went over to Clough and asked to be taken off. Clough refused and, according to Smith, Fashanu burst into tears as he walked back towards him. Smith concluded that he was 'mentally weak'. Clough claimed, in his autobiography, to have realised after a few weeks that Fashanu was 'a playboy rather than a footballer' and 'he tried to portray the macho image but he wasn't macho, he was flamboyant'.

This behaviour was utterly untypical of Fashanu who usually relished battles with defenders and gave as good as he got. It appears to have been a one-off. But it was becoming apparent that he was not the player Forest hoped to have signed. Frank Clark, who had played for Forest and was on the coaching staff, talked about Fashanu's strengths, limitations and the problems he faced when he first arrived at Forest, in an interview for the website www.tacklemedia.co.uk in 2010: 'I'd played against him when he was at Norwich and he knocked Burnsy and Larry Lloyd all over the place, and you've got to be very tough to do that. That's why Forest bought him, Taylor especially remembered the chasing he gave Larry and Kenny. So he was tough but not a great footballer. He needed to be at a club where he was regularly working with the ball you know…Forest weren't like that…very often [laughs]. Plus Brian was very autocratic and Justin was a bit of a maverick.'

Brian Clough had an unorthodox attitude to training and fitness. Once the season began, training sessions tended to be short and light-hearted. He believed the players should save their energy for matches. There was little work on technical skills. Like many of his methods – getting a player out of bed to drink champagne on the night before a Cup Final comes to mind – they look as if they should not work, but no one can argue with his success.

Someone else who noticed Fashanu's limitations was Steve Hodge, who went on to play for England, but then was a youngster hoping to break into the first team. In his autobiography he recalls how, soon after joining Forest, Fashanu asked him and a few other apprentices to stay behind after training for some extra shooting practice: 'These simple shooting drills turned into a nightmare for him, and us apprentices displayed far better technique than the £1 million player. His shots continually flew high and wide or were miscued.' This was a young man who had scored 22 goals for a struggling side the pervious season. He did not do that by being a dreadful finisher. A striker's technique needs to be backed by confidence. The signs were that Fashanu's confidence was rapidly being drained.

Forest's matches were being covered in the *Nottingham Evening Post* by a young journalist, Duncan Hamilton, who later wrote an award-winning memoir of the times he spent with Brian Clough. Several games into the season he wrote of Fashanu 'straining for effectiveness'. But Fashanu put in some decent performances. In October Forest were back at Birmingham for a League Cup match and Hamilton, while noting that Fashanu had yet to score a goal, credited him with laying on all three in a 3–2 win. It was 10 games into the season before he did score, away to Middlesbrough, but Hamilton continued to give him some credit, commenting on his partnership with Wallace that 'the pair look to be operating more successfully together than the Wallace – Francis partnership last season'. Fashanu perhaps had his best match for Forest in a 0–0 away draw with Manchester City. Hamilton wrote: 'City, it appeared, viewed Fashanu as a moving target. Virtually every effort at either controlling or running with the ball ended with a defender dumping him on the sodden turf. Nevertheless, this was the Fashanu that Forest paid £1 million for. He proved to be far more mobile and threatening than at almost any other stage this season.'

Into November, the goals started coming at last – four in successive games. First Fashanu scored the only goal to win a League Cup tie away to Blackburn. Then he finally scored in front of the home supporters at the City Ground, even if it was for the England Under-21 team against Hungary. His first home goal for the club came just three days later in a defeat to Arsenal, followed by another, in a victory away to Sunderland.

One man taking a keen interest in Fashanu's form was Terry Carpenter, the managing director of Auto Cars garage which was involved in various sponsorships with Forest. When Justin's representative approached him to see if he would provide Fashanu with a sponsored car Carpenter, was happy to oblige. He had seen the TV documentary about Fashanu, *The Pace-Setters*, and reckoned he was the hottest thing in football. He agreed to supply a top of the range Toyota with Justin's name emblazoned along the side. Auto Cars would benefit from the association and also from Justin's agreement to add his presence to their occasional open evenings.

Soon Justin became a regular visitor to the garage because he kept damaging the car. He was turning up every couple of weeks. Carpenter put it down to carelessness: 'Justin was very aware of the public. He wanted to be really popular with everyone he met. He would like to be recognised and lapped it up. He'd probably turn round and wave to somebody and run into the car in front.' At least Auto Cars benefited from his outgoing nature. At the open evenings, he would introduce the event and go round talking to people and shaking hands, charming everyone he met. He was brilliant at it and appeared to love doing it. With Justin's goal tally beginning to look more respectable, Terry Carpenter came up with a charity fundraising scheme. His idea was for local companies to sponsor Justin's goals. Every time he scored, a firm would pay for a sticker, illustrated with a football, to be placed on the side of Justin's car. This way he hoped to raise £7,000 to buy a minibus for the local branch of The National Society for the Prevention of Cruelty to Children. No one could have imagined there would be no more goals.

Meanwhile, Justin and his brothers, John and Phillip, had been searching for their father, Patrick, and found him running a law firm in Lagos. They were eager to visit him and Justin told the local paper he would be meeting with Brian Clough to ask his permission. It was not a wise move. Clough was from an era where he played for Middlesbrough on the day he got married and was unlikely to indulge Justin's wish for time off in the middle of the season. The trip was postponed.

Clough and Fashanu were finding plenty to disagree about. Another point of conflict was the attitude towards parking tickets that Fashanu brought with him from Norwich. Clough was informed by a policeman that he had accumulated something like 30 unpaid fines. Clough wrote that the policeman said: 'I'm sorry Brian, but we're going to have to do him.' Clough claims to have responded: 'Don't tolerate it a minute longer; put him in jail.' Justin paid up. Two points emerge from this story. First, although Justin was treated badly by Clough, he did not always help himself. Secondly, such was Clough's status and his air of authority that, from time to time, he acted and was treated more like the Sheriff of Nottingham than the manager of a football club. This was to become apparent in a more public incident involving Clough, Fashanu and the police.

Meanwhile, Justin had been picking up yellow cards and faced a three-match ban. His last game before it started was an away win at Swansea in mid-December.

Fashanu's time at Forest in invariably remembered as an unmitigated disaster and his £1 million transfer considered one of the biggest wastes of money in football history. So it is worth noting that, up to this point, he had played every minute of Forest's season, not even being substituted, let alone dropped. But this was as good as it got for Fashanu and Forest.

Christmas and New Year are traditionally a busy time for footballers, with extra matches squeezed into the holiday period, but the suspended Fashanu was going to miss out. Facing a break, he told the *Nottingham Evening Post* he would use the period to work on his fitness. Justin had thrived on hard work in training, using his physical edge to out run and out muscle his opponents. Clough's casual training methods were not working for him. In fact, nothing about this manager's relationship with his player was working.

Neither of them had a good festive season. On 29 December Clough was rushed into the coronary section of Derby's Royal Infirmary suffering from chest pains. He did not get a firm diagnosis but was strongly advised to take a break. The next day, Justin made the front page of the *Evening Post* when he drove his car into a bus, the car coming off worst, being badly scraped and dented down both sides but Justin escaping injury. Once more it was back at Terry Carpenter's garage.

Peter Taylor was not doing too well either. Always a worrier, he felt bad about players he had recommended performing poorly for the club and he was not helped by Brian Clough holding him entirely responsible. Clough told Duncan Hamilton: 'Whenever anyone mentions Justin Fashanu to me, I say one thing. I didn't buy him. It had nowt to do with me. The person who did buy him didn't do his job properly. We signed an idiot.' Maurice Edwards, a scout who worked for Clough and Taylor for years, blames Taylor for 'not doing his homework on this particular signing', saying he had been too influenced by seeing Fashanu's wonder goal against Liverpool on TV. But Clough and Taylor had both seen him perform exceptionally well against their own team on several occasions and newspaper reports from the time show that they watched him in other matches.

Perhaps if they had seen the cover art for the record Fashanu had made with Roger Haywood they would have realised he was someone they could not cope with. Justin was featured on both sides wearing an orange leather suit dotted with studs and matched with slip-on yellow shoes. The record was released on the independent East Midlands label, Rondelet Records, best known for its roster of punk bands such as Riot

Squad, The Fits, and Threats. The A side, *Do It 'Cos You Like It*, was a funky dance track and the lyrics could well have been written for someone thinking about exploring their sexuality: 'Sometimes when you see something it's no good thinking twice / there's no point being cautious you shouldn't hesitate / just go out and get it if you've got what it takes.'

* * *

With severe winter weather causing games to be postponed, it took six weeks for Justin to serve his suspension. Forest did not do well in his absence, being knocked out of two Cup competitions. Losing away to Spurs in the League Cup was acceptable; a 3–1 defeat at home to Second Division Wrexham in the FA Cup an embarrassment. Justin was back for a home game against neighbours Notts County.

It was a big match for the fans. Notts County may well be the world's oldest senior football club and the Forest v Notts fixture the oldest local derby. Under manager, Jimmy Sirrel, Notts had climbed up through the four divisions and were enjoying their first season in the First Division since 1926. Local pride was at stake and Forest were expected to win. Instead they lost 0–2. Justin did not come out of it well, taking heavy criticism from the crowd. After another poor performance in the next match he felt obliged to apologise: 'I can understand the supporters are becoming impatient. They have every right to be. I was bought to score goals and I've not done it.' Sounding uncharacteristically plaintive, he added: 'I can't seem to do much right at all.'

The fans were disappointed with their team which, in 11th place, were not even matching the previous season's form. Fashanu seemed to epitomise Clough and Taylor's failure to replace their European Cup winning squad with players of similar quality. With Clough away in Spain recuperating from the illness that had put him in hospital, one of the few stars left had had enough. John Robertson, who had been unsettled for some time, put in a transfer request.

On Clough's return he did his best to offer Fashanu some sympathy, saying he knew what it was like for a striker to have a lean spell. But, never one to play down his own achievements, he could not resist adding that his lean spell had been considerably shorter than Justin's. He could never resist an opportunity to remind people of his abilities as a striker. Centre-half, Willie Young, told *The Sun*: 'He was always boasting. I remember when he signed Justin Fashanu and Ian Wallace for £1 million each and neither was scoring. Cloughie kept telling them what an amazing amount of goals he had scored. I had to butt in and say, "Yeah, but all your goals were in the effing Second

Division". It was true but I didn't last long after I reminded him. There was no place for an opinionated loudmouth like me with Cloughie at Forest.'

Clough revealed that is was not only Justin's goal drought that was bothering him: 'What I have to say is private. It concerns him, me and this club.' He had been getting phone calls from people telling him about Justin's presence at a gay club, or as Clough put it in his autobiography: 'He was a regular visitor at a club notorious for the gathering of homosexuals.' Clough evidently assumed that this meant he was gay, though Justin might not have been sure himself at this point. Clough wrote: 'That in itself didn't bother me too much – it was just that his shiftiness, combined with an articulate image that impressed the impressionable, made it difficult for me to accept Fashanu as genuine and one of us.' He then claimed to have 'put him to the test' with the following exchange:

Clough: 'Where do you go if you want a loaf of bread?'

Fashanu: 'A baker's, I suppose.'

Clough: 'Where do you go if you want a leg of lamb?'

Fashanu: 'A butcher's.'

Clough: 'So why do you keep going to that bloody poofs' club in town?'

According to Clough, Justin shrugged and 'knew what I meant'. Clough seemed to think he cleverly trapped Fashanu into admitting he was gay, and this anecdote is repeated in articles and books about him. But even if the conversation did occur, it revealed nothing and, when asked about it years later, Justin replied, as if embarrassed for Clough: 'I'm afraid he never said it.'

It was true Justin had started visiting a gay club, Part II. He spoke about it to *The Sun*, when he came out in 1990 and to *Gay Times* the following year. He described his fiancée, Julie, as a wonderful girl who would make someone a beautiful wife but said he had realised he had sexual feelings about men. He recalled seeing in the lounge of the hotel where he was living: 'Four guys with a lot of style and charisma who were clearly enjoying themselves. They stood out from the more traditional guys with girls and interested me more than anyone else.' One of them was Ross Smith, who managed the club and invited Justin to it. At first he went with Julie but then started going on his own. He recalled: 'The atmosphere was electrifying and sensually stimulating and I had a whale of a time. It was the atmosphere of people enjoying freedom. I found that gays were attractive, fun people who really knew how to party. I could relax with them. And I found myself attracted to them…If I was stuck in a room full of women with just one man there – he would be the one to catch my eye.' Contradicting the account he gave of sleeping with a man at the party to celebrate his transfer to Nottingham Forest, Justin told *The Sun* that the first time was with a man he met at the club early in 1982.

Clough's attitude gave Justin good reason to be secretive about whether he was gay and, during this period of experimentation, he was probably unsure himself. His attraction to men threatened his relationship with Julie and threatened to make his life as a professional footballer very difficult indeed. It would have taken time for him to come to terms with it. Of course, as an employee of Nottingham Forest he had no obligation to talk to his manager about his sexuality. His manager should instead have been focused on making the most of Fashanu's talents as a footballer and helping this young player improve. Brian Clough told a story about how Justin introduced him to a beautiful young woman, saying she was his girlfriend and they were engaged. He wrote: 'I realised it was a con, a charade. It was Fashanu's way of trying to convince me he wasn't gay. That's how big a fraud I believed him to be.' Whatever Justin believed about himself and his future on that day, the young woman was undoubtedly his fiancée, Julie.

*   *   *

February 1982 was another dreadful month for Forest who lost three, drew two and won only one of their fixtures. Clough announced that he still had confidence in Fashanu: 'I know I can get him scoring goals again.' Five days later, he put him on the transfer list, along with strike partner, Ian Wallace and captain, John McGovern, then flew off to Cyprus for a family holiday. Dropped from the team, Justin tried to sound upbeat: 'The great thing about the Clough – Taylor partnership is that they are not frightened of changing things if they think they've got it wrong.' But he also defended himself, pointing out that he was still only 20 years old, seven or eight years younger than most strikers playing in the First Division: 'I have plenty of time in which to prove my critics wrong.'

There was little chance of him moving to another club. Football was in financial meltdown, with falling crowds and income. Clubs were unwilling to pay high transfer fees and wages. Several years later, Justin talked about this period of his life. He said he had realised that fame, flash clothes and expensive cars were not making him happy. He was feeling empty and lonely: 'I thought, even if I get richer and better known, I can't see it changing the way I feel.'

Following his collision with the bus, Auto Cars had repaired the Toyota but Justin could not be bothered to collect it. He owned his own jeep and with all his parking tickets a second car had become a bit of a nuisance. But after a couple of months Terry Carpenter persuaded him to pick it up. He remembers when Justin arrived in his office: 'He looked a bit dejected – I think he'd had a bad time with Brian Clough – and I looked him straight in the eyes and said: "Justin, I think your life is a little bit of a mess, at the moment, isn't it." He looked at me as if I'd dared to say anything about the way his life was going and I said: "I think I know someone who can help you." And he said: "Who's that Tel? Who can help me?" I said: "I believe that Jesus Christ can help you", and he got very alive and said "Tell me more".

Justin later told an interviewer about their conversation: 'At first I was sceptical. Everyone seemed to want me for something, and so few seemed really genuine. But without trying, this bloke showed me he was concerned for me and my own best interests. He wanted to help me for no other reason than I needed help. There was a sense of peace and conviction about him that I wanted very much.'

Terry Carpenter's own moment of revelation had occurred many years earlier. He grew up in London, above the grocery shop where his dad worked. He was used to his parents' constant rowing and was delighted and curious when it suddenly stopped. When he asked why, they told him they had been to a rally led by the American evangelical preacher, Billy Graham, and become Christians. Impressed, nine-year-old Terry asked if he could go to the next one, to be held in Harringay speedway stadium. At this event he too invited Jesus into his life and became a born-again Christian.

As he found himself speaking to Justin, Terry believed it was God who was giving him the words. Justin wanted to know more, and more. After a couple of hours, they went back to Terry's house for some lunch and carried on. Terry asked if he could say a prayer for Justin. Then Justin said one himself: 'I got down on my knees and asked for God to come into my life. And he did.' Terry Carpenter introduced him to the evangelical Christian Centre, where he was helped to feel welcome by the Senior Minister, David Shearman, a sports enthusiast.

In a few tumultuous months, Justin found himself setting the priorities that would stay with him the rest of his life. They were regaining his reputation as a top class professional footballer, pursuing his gay lifestyle and being a good Christian. They were not easy to reconcile with each other. Trying to do so was to be his biggest challenge of all.

Chapter 6

Glad to be Gay?

Being gay in 1982 was tough. Although homosexual acts between men had been decriminalised in England and Wales in 1967, gay men did not enjoy equality with heterosexuals. For example gay sex was only legal for men over 21 years old, an age Justin Fashanu reached in February of that year. It was still illegal for male couples to behave in public like heterosexual couples, kissing or holding hands, which gave the police an excuse for harassing them. Then there were the plain clothes 'pretty police', entrapping gay men into breaking the law. Gay men lived in fear of violent attacks – queer bashing. There were no laws to protect gay men (or lesbians) from discrimination, including harassment in the workplace. Being known to be gay risked attracting ridicule and retribution. In this atmosphere of hostility few public figures were out, even in the supposedly liberal world of show business.

No professional footballer was or ever had been out as gay but there was nothing extraordinary about it. Football mirrored the rest of society. There were, though, reasons why life might be even more difficult for a gay footballer than for people in other jobs. Footballers had more physically intimate relationships with their work colleagues than in just about any other occupation. They showered and changed together. In the 1980s they were still sharing communal baths. They were always bumping into each other and grabbing each other in training – mucking about generally. And there were the goal celebrations – the most hugging, kissing even, you were likely to see between men in public; expressions of unbridled joy, affection and admiration.

The possibility of being sexually attractive or attracted to another man scared many straight men. Straight footballers were no different. They tended to handle the physical and emotional closeness by making the strict assumption that their teammates were straight. There was no reason to think straight footballers were more hostile towards, or scared of, gay men than other straight men. But their capacity for relaxed acceptance of gay men as work colleagues was going to be tested more. This did not mean professional football could not accept the presence of gay men, but it did require a more significant shift in attitude from those who were uncomfortable or felt hostile towards them than in most work situations.

Brian Clough tended to take the sort of horseplay footballers indulged in to extremes. On occasion, in another context, he could have been accused of sexual assault. Someone rumoured or known to be gay acting the same way would probably have horrified people who were prepared to tolerate Clough. The front cover of Maurice Edward's memoir of working with Clough and Taylor shows them with the European Cup. Wearing suits and ties, they had been posing for some formal photographs. But in this one Clough has his hand firmly on Taylor's testicles while Taylor responds with a comical expression which could be from a *Carry On* film. Edwards has called his book: *Brian and Peter: A Right Pair*.

Diego Maradona was probably less amused when Clough pulled the same stunt on him. The incident is described in Steve Hodge's autobiography. The Nottingham Forest and Barcelona teams were lined up ready to walk out into Barcelona's Camp Nou stadium for a friendly match. The Argentinian, Maradona, was on his way to becoming one of the greatest footballers of all time. Brian Clough walked up to him, said 'You might be able to play a bit but I can still grab you by the balls', and proceeded to do just that. Hodge also recalls an occasion when the Forest squad were staying in a hotel in Scotland where a wedding reception was being held. As the newly married couple took to the floor for their first dance, Clough – to use Hodges words – '…appeared from nowhere, grabbed the groom's kilt, and did an impromptu checking of the poor man's wedding tackle'.

In the laddish, boozy world of British professional football it was difficult to say where banter became abuse and horseplay edged into assault. But wherever the line was drawn, Brian Clough was one man who repeatedly went over it with his repertoire of insults, humiliations and occasional violence, sometimes fuelled by alcohol. Some men who played for him remember Clough fondly as entertaining, unpredictable and outrageous. He could be warm and witty and sometimes showed a touching vulnerability. But in their reminiscences this moody man often sounds more like a boastful bully.

A professional football club was not the easiest place to keep secrets. Footballers got to know each other well. They spent a lot of time together, waiting around, travelling and staying in hotels where even well-paid stars roomed together. They socialised and, if they were single, went to nightclubs together hoping to pick up women. It was not easy to turn down an offer to go out, brush off an enquiry about what you did last night or explain why you did not have a girlfriend.

When retired footballers are asked if they miss the game, a common response is 'not so much the football, it's the dressing room banter'. For those of us whose dreams of football glory never came to fruition, missing hanging around with a bunch of blokes joking about each others' haircuts, clothes, idiosyncrasies and ethnic origins more than the thrill of actually being paid to play football in front of admiring crowds may be mystifying. Perhaps it is their way of saying they miss the closeness. War analogies are cheapened by over use in football. It is commonplace to compliment a teammate by saying that he is the sort of man you would want in the trenches with you. But it does demonstrate the sense of commitment and solidarity that footballers feel for each other, reliant as they are, on each player to make his contribution for the good of the team.

Joking around is one way that closeness is built and expressed, and tension eased before a match. For some, it's an opportunity to demonstrate their wit and raise a laugh. Those who tend to be on the receiving end are obliged to come up with a humorous retort or at least appear not to take offence. But there is a thin line between teasing intended to include and taunting intended to exclude. A gay footballer, especially one unsure of his status in the dressing room as Justin was at Forest, would have good reason to fear being taunted. But Justin was good at handling his teammates with a light touch. The magazine, *Attitude*, reported Viv Anderson remembering John Robertson asking Justin 'Are you queer?' and Justin replying with a big smile, 'Give us a kiss and I'll tell you'.

But Justin was always a bit of an outsider at Forest and Steve Hodge explains why: 'I always found Justin Fashanu to be an articulate and friendly character but his ways were very different to your average First Division footballer in the 1980s. All the first team players at Forest had a blue towel with a number stitched on but Justin preferred to bring in his own towels for use after training. It was little things like that that made him stand out from the crowd, never a good thing in a football dressing room.'

The Biography

Justin was employing a personal trainer and assistant, Osman, a man with a martial arts background. He used to bring Osman into the changing room to give him a massage before training. As Hodge puts it: 'The other players saw it as "a bit precious".' Then there was Justin's habit of going off on his own rather than socialising with teammates on trips. These displays of non-conformity no doubt reinforced Brian Clough's view that Justin Fashanu was not 'one of us'.

Apart from the dressing room culture, there was another aspect of being a professional footballer, especially in the 1980s, which distinguished it from other forms of employment and even other sports. It was the presence of fans of opposing teams who felt they had every right to abuse players without restraint; indeed felt it was their duty to support their own team by riling, distracting and intimidating the opposition. Fashanu had been targeted for racial abuse but at least knew the experience was one he shared with the increasing numbers of black players coming into the game. If he came out, or was outed, as gay he would be on his own.

For Justin, coming to terms with his homosexuality was complicated by his newly found religious beliefs. The relationship between Christianity and homosexuality is a contested one, with different churches and religious leaders expressing a range of beliefs. In the evangelical form of Christianity he had embraced, the Bible was seen as the word of God, to be taken literally and followed to the letter. All sex outside of marriage was regarded as sinful. Being an out and proud gay man was incompatible with being a member of his church. He told *The Sun* that he and Julie had stopped sleeping together and drifted apart, but he continued to have sex with men.

For any public figure, coming out to friends and, especially, family can be more of a challenge than dealing with the reactions of people they do not know. As Justin admitted to *The Sun*, he had deceived Julie at first and was faced with having to deal with the future of their relationship. But he also had to wonder about the possible reaction from his two families, the Jacksons and Fashanus. How would John respond? What about his father, who he was still planning to meet?

'Coming out' is a not entirely satisfactory term covering a whole range of subtle choices. But, given that rumours about his sexuality were beginning to circulate beyond the Nottingham Forest dressing room, he was likely to be faced with a stark choice. He would have to publicly deny or confirm. The British tabloid or 'red-top' newspapers liked nothing better than a sex scandal involving a public figure that they could splash over the front page, with a lurid headline and promises of more revelations inside.

JUSTIN FASHANU

*   *   *

In the early 1980s gay people were campaigning for equality, protesting against mistreatment and proclaiming a positive identity. The unofficial anthem of gay politics was the Tom Robinson Band's *Glad to be Gay*; not the affirmation of gay pride its title suggests but an angry, sarcastic attack on homophobia in all its forms. Alongside the politics was the partying. Gay people were becoming a little more confident about enjoying themselves in public. Gay clubs were never exclusively gay but did provide space for gays to meet on their own terms. The unofficial anthem of gay partying was Gloria Gaynor's *I Will Survive*. Part II was one of the best gay clubs in the Midlands; Heaven, in London, set the standard. Radio presenter, Paul Gambaccini, described it as the first industrial-sized nightclub for gay men.

It was at Heaven that Justin met Peter Tatchell, who remembers the occasion well: 'I was dancing with some friends. He was on the edge of the dance floor, drinking a glass of beer. I noticed he was staring at me over the top of his pint, as he sipped it. So when I clicked that he was quite persistent with his looks I went over, introduced myself and asked him for a dance. He said "no", but we ended up chatting and drinking together. He seemed very friendly, personable, attractive, quite interesting. We chatted about gay clubs and music, a bit about current affairs and about our family backgrounds. We exchanged numbers and said goodbye at about 2am. Then he phoned me the next night and we began a series of mostly long, late night phone conversations, occasional meetings and attendances at various public events he was doing.'

Both were dealing with challenges about how open to be about being gay. Peter Tatchell had never hidden it but was having to reconsider his position. He had been selected by the London constituency of Bermondsey, a working-class area on the south bank of the River Thames, to stand as Labour candidate in the next general election, replacing the sitting MP, Bob Mellish. Nationally the Labour Party was in disarray having lost the 1979 election to Margaret Thatcher's Conservative Party. Its leader was Michael Foot, a man with a radical past who was desperately trying to stop right-wing Labour MPs defecting to the recently formed Social Democrat Party. Tatchell was an outspoken, unapologetic socialist – much as Michael Foot had been – but Foot was under pressure to demonstrate he was purging the Labour Party of its more left-wing elements. Foot and the National Executive Committee of the party refused to endorse Tatchell as the Labour candidate while his constituency party refused to deselect him. This dispute rapidly became the subject of headlines in the national press, portrayed as a battle for the soul of the Labour Party. With most newspaper proprietors eager to keep the Labour Party out of power, their papers launched into personal attacks on both Foot and Tatchell.

Realising that homophobic attacks could overshadow his campaign, Tatchell reluctantly took the position of refusing to answer questions about his own sexuality while stating that he was a supporter of gay rights. This did not stop him being attacked anyway, even by senior figures within the Labour Party. Neil Kinnock, who eventually took over from Michael Foot as leader, said: 'I'm not in favour of witch hunts but I do not mistake witches for bloody fairies.' In the press Tatchell was lambasted equally for being Australian, left wing and gay, as he describes in his book, *The Battle for Bermondsey.*

Newspapers were intent on unearthing a scandal that would undermine Tatchell and went to extraordinary lengths to do so. There were people photographing everyone who visited his flat, others persistently knocking on his door from early morning to after midnight. People followed him, sifted through his rubbish, called on neighbours pretending to be Council Officers and trawled through gay bars offering money for stories. Tatchell had to leave his job working in a day centre because it was virtually besieged by journalists. His family in Australia was harassed – once a journalist secured admission to their home by saying Peter had been involved in a serious accident. Press coverage stirred up hatred, causing him to receive death threats, survive several attempts to run him down in a car, and have bottles and bricks thrown at him.

Politics was often the subject of Fashanu and Tatchell's late night phone calls. Tatchell was determined to convince the Conservative-voting Fashanu that, as a gay, black man he should be supporting the Labour Party. He would go through the parties' policies on the health service, employment, immigration and so on, and on each one Fashanu would agree he preferred the Labour Party policy. At the end of the conversation he would tell Tatchell he had convinced him to support the Labour Party. Then by the next conversation he would have gone back to the Conservatives and they would start again. Peter Tatchell felt that Justin's aspirations for wealth and personal success ended up overruling his political analysis.

Other times they would talk about being gay and how Justin could reconcile it with his Christianity, or about coming out. Tatchell thought it would be a bad move for Justin to come out while his football career was in the doldrums. Generally Justin agreed but then took risks which suggested he might find it a relief if he was outed by the press. On one occasion he invited Tatchell to join him and members of his birth family at an event celebrating the achievements of black people. To Tatchell's alarm he found himself sitting with them at a table on the stage in full view of the audience and media. A photo, linking them would be a dream for the editor of one of the more homophobic newspapers and he was surprised and relieved when none appeared.

Peter Tatchell was made welcome by the Fashanu family, who must have known about the public speculation that he (Peter) was gay. Pearl even told Justin she thought Peter was a nice person and he should get to know him better. He was invited round to the family home and Justin's brother, Phillip once met him for lunch to talk politics.

* * *

Meanwhile, Fashanu had a football career to rescue. Forest were in a mess. Clough and Taylor took it in turns to absent themselves for family holidays, fuelling rumours that they had fallen out with each other. Clough announced that Justin would not get back in the team, saying the crowd would not accept him anyway, and then contradicted himself by giving him a chance as a substitute. It was a home fixture against Manchester City and he came on with 25 minutes to go, helping to secure a draw. Peter Taylor's compliment must have been music to his ears: 'As soon as he came on a lot of possibilities opened up for us.' After a break with the England Under-21s where he played well, Clough started him in a fixture away to Leeds. Marking him in the Leeds defence was Kenny Burns who he had battled with when Burns was at Forest and Fashanu with Norwich. Duncan Hamilton reported: 'Fashanu relished the physical challenge of a hard personal duel with Kenny Burns and produced a performance that could easily have been capped with a goal.' He was even more enthusiastic when reporting on the next game, an away win against West Ham United, saying of the Wallace – Fashanu partnership: 'Their display, the sustained level of which was far above anything else they have produced over the last seven months, won over a few of the sceptics.'

Justin's performance was a feat of focus and courage given what he was dealing with at the time. The *Sunday People* had constructed a story about the possibility of him being gay and before the match approached him for a quote. It was decision time. He could say it was true and risk ruining his career in football, possible rejection from family and friends, and condemnation from fellow Christians. He could deny it and be forced to maintain a life of secrecy and lies, knowing that he could be exposed at any time by a newspaper coming up with more solid evidence than the *Sunday People*.

The Biography

It was an unenviable choice and he made the same decision as just about every gay man in public life at the time – he denied it.

The story appeared on the front page of the *Sunday People* the day after the match with the headline: 'Soccer SuperStar Justin Fashanu Answers All the Gossips – The Truth About My Love Life'. The paper's lawyers had no doubt cautioned it to avoid any claims that could not be proved and nearly all the story was devoted to quotes from Justin 'kicking back against the malicious gossips who have been saying he's homosexual'. Justin accepted that rumours were circulating: 'The stories have got so bad even my best mate in London, Garth Crooks of Spurs, told me last week that people were saying I was bent.' And he went on to deny them in no uncertain terms. He cited his relationship with Julie and claimed 'men do not figure in my personal life', suggesting that the rumours started because he mixed with unconventional people not usually associated with football players. This was, he explained, because he was not a drinker and so did not spend much time with other players. He told the reporter that some of the people he mixed with 'may be gay' and he did go to gay clubs, and complained that there were people following his every move, which he found sickening. Then he went on the attack: 'I will sue if any of this gossip is said openly.'

Fashanu might have considered that he got off lightly. No specific evidence of his homosexuality was offered. Thanks to the solidarity of the gay men he was spending time with there was no 'kiss and tell' account. If the story had been carefully presented to make it still appear to the reader that Fashanu was gay, it did not succeed. Had it done, opposing fans would have latched on to it and started mocking chants. They did not. No doubt Fashanu was also protected by the inability of most fans to conceive that a professional footballer could be gay, especially one as physically tough as he was. So his decision to sue the *Sunday People* was surprising, even perverse. It could have back-fired on him horribly.

This was demonstrated by a similar situation developing in the USA. A month before the *Sunday People* article, the magazine, *Sports Illustrated*, made some serious accusations about the highly successful coach of South Carolina University women's basketball team, Pam Parsons. They included one that she was having a sexual relationship with a young woman in the team. Parsons was not out as a lesbian, partly because of her Mormon background. To protect her reputation she decided to sue the publishers. But during the trial she and the young woman, Tina Buck, were shown to have lied when they denied having frequented a lesbian night club, Puss N Boots, together. Both were sentenced to four months in prison for perjury. Justin was potentially heading in the same direction.

Just as Fashanu's football fortunes were taking a slight upturn he experienced a series of setbacks. They started with a gashed leg requiring five stitches, which troubled him for the rest of the season. Then he picked up a 10th booking of the season after an off-the-ball challenge on his old adversary, Aston Villa centre-half Allan Evans. He was suspended for two games, and fined two weeks' wages by the club. In his autobiography, Clough did not let the facts spoil his argument. He claimed Fashanu was sent off 'again and again'. In fact, he was sent off twice during his Forest career, both in pre-season friendlies in Spain. He was wrong and his comment was unfair but Fashanu was not helping himself by picking up two suspensions in one season.

Before his return to football action Justin was shaken by the death of his foster father, Alf Jackson. He was a decent man who helped provide the stability and support for Justin and John to recover somewhat from their earlier traumatic experiences. Losing him was another destabilising event in a year of upheaval.

As the end of a disappointing season for Nottingham Forest approached, rumours that not all was well in the Clough – Taylor partnership turned out to be true. Taylor announced his immediate retirement, citing 'mental and physical strain'. Maurice Edwards told journalist, John Gibson, that the signing of Justin Fashanu had 'tortured Peter Taylor and turned him into a chain-smoking, nervous wreck while Cloughie raged at Fash's sexuality'. After his own retirement Clough told Duncan Hamilton that the trust between them had been shattered by the publication of Taylor's book and the signing of Fashanu had finished the partnership off. Justin was inadvertently responsible for the break-up of one of the most renowned managerial teams in English football.

By this time the relationship between Clough and Fashanu had broken down completely, not helped by Clough seeing Fashanu's newly found religious beliefs as yet another sign of his instability. Viv Anderson describes Clough as having been 'merciless in his criticism'. Hamilton remembers that Fashanu became so terrified of Clough he broke into a sweat just talking about him. 'It's the way he looks at me', he told Hamilton: 'You just know you're going to get a right bollocking. He doesn't like me. Never will.' Clough complained: 'He used to burst into tears if I said hallo to him.'

Having served his suspension, Fashanu was recalled for the last home game of the 1981–82 season, against Tottenham Hotspur. Forest were desperate for a win. They had not won any of their previous 10 home games – it was their away form that kept them clear of a struggle against relegation. And Justin was desperate for a goal having failed to score for five months. Forest won but there was no goal for Justin, who was left with one last chance to redeem himself, at Ipswich.

Instead he endured his biggest row with Clough so far. His gashed leg was still giving him trouble and, perhaps because they were barely communicating, it was only just before kick-off that Fashanu told Clough he was not fit to play. According to Hamilton, the furious Clough hit him with a flailing arm. Writing for the *News of the World* in 1996 Clough boasted: 'When I was in my prime at Nottingham Forest, I was a law unto myself. I whacked more than a few of my players. I hit them – and I don't mean verbally or financially. Justin Fashanu got it from me more than once – just for being who and what he was.' Referring specifically to their row before the Ipswich game he also claimed to have said to Fashanu: 'There are three possibilities. You can leave voluntarily; I can call the police and have you removed or you can politely ask me to sit down for a minute and reconsider.' Fashanu stayed but Clough closed the door of the team coach on him, telling him he could walk back before relenting and allowing him on.

* * *

Ideally Justin would have enjoyed a typical footballer's close season; first a complete break – perhaps a relaxing holiday somewhere hot – a time to put the disappointments of the last season behind him and recharge his batteries. Then he would have come back, in July, for a rigorous programme of pre-season fitness training followed by some carefully selected friendly games, designed to prepare the team physically and tactically for the first competitive match of the new season, at the end of August.

It was nothing like that. In the 15 week close season, he played football in Morocco, Nigeria, the Far East, and mainland Europe. He met his father for the first time for 18 years, won a libel case and was embroiled in an international row about apartheid in South Africa. He also found time to move, with Julie, from their hotel into a newly built house in an exclusive gated community, The Park.

At least he scored a few goals. There was a testimonial game for the former Derby County player, Mick Fletcher. Forest beat a Burton Albion XI 7–0, with Justin scoring three. Then they flew off to Morocco for a game against Kuwait. The Kuwait team were preparing for the World Cup, having qualified for the Finals for the first time. Justin scored in a 1–1 draw.

In June he was off to Africa again. This time the purpose was personal. With brothers Phillip and John, he was going to visit his father, Patrick. He set off full of optimism, sending a postcard to Gordon Homes saying that he hoped to learn a lot. He had also arranged to play some football on this two week trip, guaranteeing his visit would attract media attention. He was captured on TV cameras sounding a little defensive about his father: 'I never said he abandoned us, I just said he'd returned to Nigeria.' After moving back to Nigeria, Patrick had married a white Scottish woman and they had four children together who his three sons from England were meeting for the first time. The visit did not go well and Justin never saw his father again.

While he was in Nigeria Justin's libel case against the *Sunday People* was proceeding in the High Court in London. His counsel, James Price, must have done an amazing job because the *Sunday People* conceded the case, Justin accepting an undisclosed 'large sum' in damages which was later reported to be several thousand pounds. Price made a statement: 'Mr Fashanu's sense of outrage at the publication remains but he has decided nothing further is to be gained by pursuing this action.' Desmond Browne, counsel for the publishers of the *Sunday People*, said that they wished to make clear that the gossip reported was malicious and without foundation and they did not seek to imply otherwise.

It appeared to be an extraordinary victory. A newspaper had done no more than report rumours that Justin was gay, which they had given him ample space to deny. Justin was gay. Nevertheless, he had won damages on the basis that the article could have given the impression that there was some truth in the rumours which, of course, there was. Given Justin's desire, need even, to keep his homosexuality secret, this was, on the surface, an incredibly useful verdict; not only for its own sake but because it would scare off other newspapers from making similar claims in the future. It gave him a sort of immunity but at a price. He had lied, which could not have been easy to live with. If he was ever to be exposed as gay, the implications would be worse than before because he would be shown to have misled the court. Should he ever decide he wanted to come out, he would also have to face the legal implications from this case. On a personal level, the need for secrecy would make it virtually impossible for him to develop a loving, committed and secure relationship with a man. Perhaps it was not a victory at all.

On the day his libel case was concluded, Justin returned from Nigeria and walked straight into another controversy. He had been named, provisionally, as a member of a sanctions-busting squad of players to tour South Africa. Under the Gleneagles Agreement of 1978 Commonwealth countries were committed to stop all sporting links with South Africa because of its apartheid policies. This policy had a tremendous impact on the sports mad South Africans and contributed to the climate that brought about the ending of apartheid. But South African businessmen, politicians and sports organisations were determined to break these sporting sanctions. They did this by taking advantage of the greed and political naivety of sports stars who were invited on unofficial tours.

Taking a key role in organising the tour was Jimmy Hill. In a long and distinguished career in football he had often been a pioneer. Among his achievements were leading the Professional Footballers' Association to a ground-breaking victory against the frankly feudal relationship professional footballers had with the clubs which employed them. And he was also responsible for introducing the analysis of matches shown on TV that we now take for granted. At this time, he was chairman of Coventry City and presenter of the BBC's *Match of the Day*. He could claim some justification for his role with the planned tour. Football in South Africa was significantly more integrated than other sports. But the Gleneagles Agreement still applied and, as a former union organiser, he might have appreciated the value of solidarity.

The tour organisers planned to use a mix of players who were out of contract and ones drawn from the squads of Nottingham Forest and Southampton. To be able to justify the tour politically, they were keen to include at least one black player in the party and were suggesting Fashanu would be involved, without having actually spoken to him. Despite the possibility of players being suspended from domestic football for taking part in the tour, Forest chairman Geoffrey Macpherson and manager, Brian Clough, said they would stand by anyone who joined it. So Justin was left to make his own decision. He issued a press statement, turning down the invitation and saying: 'I'm afraid some of the players on this tour are just going for the money, not to help black or coloured players. I have nothing against those going but I think the tour will only aggravate the political situation over there.' So this fan of Margaret Thatcher and the Conservative Party had taken a stand against apartheid, unlike his Labour Party supporting manager.

The tour went ahead before collapsing because of political rows. It emerged that the black clubs taking part had been coerced into doing so by a mixture of threats and financial inducements. But following discussions with black consciousness organisations they refused to turn out. The tour broke up with only three of the six scheduled matches having been played.

Justin's next trip was to the Far East, at the end of July. It was supposed to raise some cash for the club and begin the team's preparation for the new season. Fixtures against, Java, Selangor and the national team of Malaysia were arranged. Three of Forest's star players, Peter Shilton, Viv Anderson and John Robertson had been playing in the World Cup Finals over the summer and so were missing the trip while they recuperated. But when the hosts found out they would not be playing, Java and Selangor cancelled their matches. This long and exhausting journey was made for one game of football against Malaysia.

All was quiet on the transfer front. There was some talk of a loan move to Manchester City but nothing materialised. Pre-season preparation continued in Germany and Spain where, for the second year in succession, Justin was sent off. This time it was against Athletico Bilbao, after just 10 minutes for an 'off-the-ball incident'. It was while he was in Spain that an incident occurred which perhaps demonstrated the tensions Justin had lived with all his life and which had been building to a crescendo during this most difficult year. He had suffered from violent nightmares in his teens but none had caused the drama of this one. In the middle of the night his room-mate, Viv Anderson, was startled awake by a loud banging sound. Looking round, he discovered Justin had smashed through the door with his fists. Also, woken by the sound, coaching staff, Ron Fenton and Colin Lawrence, rushed to the scene to find the door in splinters with a huge hole through the middle. Viv Anderson was cowering under the sheets while, still in shock, Justin was silently bathing his damaged hands in the wash basin.

Chapter 7

Snakes and Ladders

The artist, Colin Yates, specialises in portraits of black footballers. His portrayal of Justin Fashanu shows him merged with a snakes and ladders board game. It is an apt image. Justin's life was seldom steady for long and, during the next couple of years, his football career went through some steep highs and lows. By the end of the 1981–82 season he had slid down a snake and nearly off the board but two months into 1982–83 he was climbing the ladder to success. In nine League games he had scored three goals, he had found his form with the England Under-21s and even drawn praise from his manager. But the manager was not Brian Clough and the club was not Nottingham Forest. Nor had he made a dream move to another club. Instead, his two month loan to Southampton had just ended and Justin's troubles with Brian Clough were about to burst spectacularly into the open.

Southampton was a similar club to Nottingham Forest. It had a modest history but was enjoying a successful spell in the First Division under a charismatic manager. The manager was Lawrie McMenemy and Saints – Southampton's nickname – had finished seventh the previous season, five places ahead of Forest. Saints' ambition was demonstrated by the signing of Forest's goalkeeper, Peter Shilton. But plans for the forthcoming season were disrupted when former European Player of the Year, Kevin Keegan, suddenly left for Newcastle United.

McMenemy's short-term solution was to bring in Fashanu on a month long loan. Brian Clough was no doubt delighted to see the back of him for a while. He had no intention of playing Fashanu and was about to bring his European Cup winning striker, Garry Birtles, back from Manchester United. Although still determined to succeed at Forest, Justin must have realised his best chance lay in proving himself elsewhere. He told the *Southern Evening Echo*: 'No one can replace Keegan. The man is a football institution. I'm just Justin Fashanu, footballer, hoping my career is going to take an upward turn with Southampton. All I'm concerned with is that I start scoring goals again. After a disastrous year at Forest, I think everyone agrees a change will be as good as a rest for me.'

And it certainly was. Unlike Clough, McMenemy was willing and able to help Justin sort himself out and regain his form. His first goal came in the third game of the season, giving Saints a 1–0 home win over the new European Cup holders, Aston Villa. Fashanu's performances were not spectacular but he did well enough for McMenemy to extend his loan for a second month.

His best game in this period came with the England Under-21 team, in the first leg of the European Championship Final against West Germany. The match was not a major event, being played at Sheffield United's ground in front of just 6,354 spectators. But it was a significant occasion for Justin who was brought on as a substitute in the 38th minute. 'Justin Fashanu, a £1 million embarrassment in the First Division, has amazingly become a star on the international stage,' wrote Joe Melling in the *Daily Express*: 'From the moment he came on the West Germans were on the run. Fashanu was lithe and lethal. He crashed in the second goal and provided the pass for the third.'

After the match Justin spoke modestly but optimistically: 'I have certainly known the highs and lows of professional football. It is nobody's fault what has happened to me in these last few months and I have no intention of shouting from the roof tops now. I am a young man who has learned a lot recently. All I can say is that I am enjoying playing again and it's a long time since I showed such excitement at scoring a goal. I think I am at the start of a new lease of life.'

McMenemy said he could not afford to buy Fashanu but was keen to keep him on loan for a third month. It looked an easy decision for Justin and the two clubs but he turned down the opportunity, saying he wanted to 'come back to Forest and give it a go'. Perhaps he felt he needed to sort out his future permanently but there may have been another reason. In Nottingham Justin had accomplished the difficult task of keeping his gay life separate from football and religion. A move away could unsettle this delicate balance, leading to potentially dire consequences. He may have been thinking along these lines when he phoned Duncan Hamilton in the middle of the night pleading: 'Couldn't your paper get me a move to Notts County? I like Nottingham but I don't want to stay at Forest. Not with him.' The feeling was mutual. Brain Clough told the press: 'I would have thought the prospect of playing for Southampton's first team would have appealed to Fashanu but he has back-heeled it. I don't know what the lad wants…After all we are talking about Southampton and not a northern Fourth Division club.'

A move to Notts County was not beyond the bounds of possibility. For the 1982–83 season they had appointed a promising young coach, Howard Wilkinson, to work with the first team, Jimmy Sirrel taking a step back to the position of general manager. Wilkinson was a coach with the England Under-21s and so was in a good position to make his own assessment of Fashanu as a person and a footballer. If they wanted him the problem would be money. For Notts to afford him, Forest would have to agree to a massive loss on the transfer fee, and Fashanu a greatly reduced salary.

Justin left Southampton with an endorsement from McMenemy: 'Justin Fashanu remains a great source of untapped potential. When the lad came here in August, he was a right mess both on and off the field. You wouldn't believe it now. Outwardly, lots more confident; on the field he has regained much of his old sharpness. I do feel we have helped him as much as he has helped us. I enjoyed his stay here. He's a willing worker, an interesting character and he has certainly helped us through a lean spell.' McMenemy claimed Clough as a friend but he was also a rival. It is hard to ignore the implied criticism in this comment.

*   *   *

Justin returned to Nottingham at the end of October and the next few weeks were to prove pure farce as he and Brian Clough publicly battled over his future. It began with Clough naming him in the third team only to change his mind at the last minute and put him on the substitutes' bench for a League match against Luton. It was the nearest he would get to first-team action. Then Peter Taylor re-entered the story. Bored with retirement he took up an offer to manage Derby County, the club with which he and Clough had enjoyed great success. Derby were back in the Second Division, cash-strapped and short of players. Clough offered to help out his old mate with some loans and Taylor made a bid to take Fashanu. Evidently, even if he shared Clough's reservations about Fashanu's ability at the top level, he had not developed the same personal dislike of him or felt so disturbed at the prospect of him being gay. But once again, Justin opted to stay in Nottingham.

Shortly after, he was handed a letter by the club secretary, suspending him on full pay for 14 days and banning him from the ground and training facilities. According to the club chairman, Geoffrey Macpherson, it was because Justin had not turned up for a League Cup tie and for other instances of general indiscipline. Justin, who had not been in the squad for that match anyway, claimed to have missed it because he had been negotiating the possible loan move to Derby. Justin had, apparently, torn up the letter without reading it and believed he was suspended because of refusing to go to Derby. Having sought advice from the Professional Footballers' Association, he defied the ban and turned up at the training ground. Finding the first-team squad were away, he insisted on training with some youngsters. Through the PFA he appealed against the suspension to the Football League.

While Justin was still suspended, Norwich City manager, Ken Brown, tried to take him on loan. Norwich were back in the First Division and it might have been tempting to return to the club where he had enjoyed so much success. But Norwich wanted Forest to continue to pay some of Justin's wages. This time it was Brian Clough who ruled out the move saying he would only allow it if Norwich were prepared to buy him at the end of the loan period.

When Fashanu turned up at the training ground again Clough ordered him to leave. Fashanu refused. This was to be Clough's Sheriff of Nottingham moment. He called the police and asked for two officers to be sent down to take him away, which they did. He was reported to have left quietly, 'visibly distressed'. Although no one else appears to have seen it, Clough later claimed to have kicked Fashanu on the calf when he refused to leave. Fashanu told the press: 'I felt humiliated. But it was my own fault for being there. The boss said I have got to learn lessons but I don't know what they are unless he tells me.' Ever hopeful, he added: 'All I want to do is play football – preferably for Nottingham Forest even if it means being in the youth team or the schoolboys. I just want to win back my first team place.' Clough commented: 'This young man must learn to follow orders. The sooner he does so the better for all concerned.'

Fashanu was receiving strong backing from the PFA, which encouraged him to continue to defy the ban. 'Justin has been found guilty without trial', claimed the PFA secretary, Gordon Taylor. Fashanu turned up the next day, only to find the training ground deserted – the first-team squad were meeting later to travel to Sunderland for a match. He returned once more as the squad was assembling. Later that day he was given a boost by the Football League which ruled that he should not be denied training facilities until any alleged misconduct was proved.

The Biography

The Football League Commission appeal was held in London with Fashanu represented by Gordon Taylor and Forest by their assistant secretary, Paul White. It was a victory for Fashanu as the Commission ruled that Forest had not come up with sufficient evidence. The panel ordered that he be allowed to return to training immediately and expressed their hope that Clough and Fashanu could get together to resolve 'their obvious difficulties'. Some hope. Fashanu was delighted with the ruling: 'It establishes that I was right.' There were no grudges on his side, he said: 'I want to sit down and talk about it with Mr Clough.' Clough declared: 'Fashanu has no future at this club.'

The next club hoping to take Fashanu on loan was Manchester City, still managed by John Bond. His assistant, John Benson, who had also been on the coaching staff at Norwich claimed they could get him playing as he did in his Norwich days inside a month. Fashanu turned down their first approach saying that he had decided to stay at Forest to battle it out for a first-team place. Presumably Clough finally persuaded him this was never going to happen because a week later he agreed to the move. All seemed set until Clough suddenly called the whole thing off. He had agreed a transfer fee with another club and was not going to turn down the opportunity to get rid of Fashanu for good.

That club was Notts County and the transfer fee reported to be just £150,000, negotiated over four meetings between Brian Clough and Jimmy Sirrel. Defending the financial loss he made on the deal, Clough resorted to one of the most disparaging remarks ever made by a manager about one of his own players: 'The fee is substantial for a commodity that has little appeal to others and is not wanted here.' Justin's wish to stay in Nottingham was granted but only if he was prepared to take a massive salary cut.

Supporters of both clubs were fully aware of the negotiations when they gathered at Notts County's Meadow Lane stadium for a League fixture. Justin was watching from the stands and would have heard the chants coming from the opposing sets of fans. With Forest's singing 'We've got rid of you Fashanu' to the melody from a British Airways advertisement, the Notts' fans responded with 'We don't want you Fashanu' and 'Christie is better than Fashanu'; Trevor Christie being the forward most likely to lose his place to Justin. He may, at least, have enjoyed the result, Notts beating their illustrious neighbours 3–2.

Justin's basic wage was around £50,000 a year, making him one of the best paid players in the country. It was double what Notts could offer and chairman, Jack Dunnett, was not hopeful of persuading him to make the switch. But the opportunity to get away from Brian Clough while staying in Nottingham was too good to turn down. After several meetings and many phone calls a deal was done. That day Fashanu and Clough must have finally found that they had something in common – relief that they would never have to deal with each other again. But Clough could not resist a parting shot, telling Howard Wilkinson that Fashanu would get him the sack.

* * *

The second edition of Brian Clough's autobiography was published after Justin's death. In a chapter entitled, 'I Should Have Tried to Understand', he wrote: 'When you hear of a lad taking his life in such squalid circumstances like that, a lad you once worked with and were responsible for, you have to look back and wonder if you could have done things differently. I know now that I should have dealt with Fashanu differently, certainly with a little more compassion and understanding.'

He admitted that his wife, Barbara had criticised him at the time, telling him that Justin's sexuality was his business and he was entitled to be who and what he was. Then he tried to make out that his problem was not with Justin's sexuality but his secrecy, writing: 'Unless people come to terms with what they are they must suffer very, very long periods of loneliness and frustration.' Contradicting himself, he concluded: 'On reflection, I don't believe I was wrong to confront him about his sexuality but I should have done it more privately. I did it in front of the other players and in front of almost anyone I talked to. I was extremely unkind to him.'

Apologising for anything did not come easily to Clough and this was a genuine attempt. But even with the help of a journalist to craft his words, this most articulate of men comes across as someone who is flailing around, way out of his depth. He simply did not have the capacity to relate respectfully and constructively to a person he could not easily understand and control, and used his power and authority as manager to attack and humiliate him. So disturbed was Clough by his experiences with Fashanu that at least once he asked a high profile player he was about to sign for the club whether he was gay.

In contrast, Fashanu was always considered in his comments about Clough, while he was at Forest and afterwards. Speaking eight years after leaving, he even told *The Sun*: 'My biggest regret in life is that Brian Clough and I didn't have a friendship.' In 1992 Justin was asked about his time at Forest on a TV programme, *Open to Question*, and allowed himself some criticism. He suggested that Clough had bought a young player with potential but had failed to nurture that potential and bring it out.

It was potential that Howard Wilkinson picked up on in his column in the local paper: 'In Justin Fashanu we have a player that had a reputation of being a good player but is now, in our eyes, back to being a potentially good player. That is why we were able to compete, because his reputation now is not as high as it was during his days at Norwich City.'

*　*　*

Notts – known as the Magpies because of the team's black and white stripped shirts – were enjoying their second consecutive season in the First Division, a fine achievement for a club which had languished in the lower divisions for so long and whose home attendances were frequently below 10,000.

Jimmy Sirrel had gathered together a bunch of interesting characters in a squad which was remarkably cosmopolitan for the time. They included defender and captain, Pedro Richards. He was the son of a Spanish mother and African Caribbean father who had met in London, but was brought up by his grandparents in the Basque Country until the age of 11. Then he joined his mother and her new partner in Nottingham, living on The Meadows council estate, close to the Magpies' ground. Temperamentally he was the opposite of Justin, shunning celebrity – he was said to be uncomfortable even signing autographs – and continuing to live on The Meadows estate through his nearly 500 game career with Notts.

Five years older than Fashanu, he came into the game when there were even fewer black players in British professional football. In 1985 he commented on racism to the *Nottingham Football Post*, advising younger black players, 'Don't worry – it's not as bad as it used to be'. When he signed for Notts County, he recalled: 'All the aggravation was directed at a tiny band of black pro footballers. Today virtually every club has at least one black player. It has cooled considerably over the last five or six years even though it is still bad.'

The winger, John Chiedozie, was born in Nigeria, his parents separating when he was a baby. He was also brought up by grandparents, and constantly uprooted by the events of the Biafran war. Aged 12 he joined his father who had moved to England to work in the Ford motor plant at Dagenham. In 1981 Chiedozie was picked to play for the country of his birth, making his debut for Nigeria in a World Cup qualifying match against Tunisia in front of a crowd of 100,000 – quite a change from playing for Notts.

Alongside him in attack was Rachid Harkouk, born in London to an Algerian father and a mother from Yorkshire. His international debut, for Algeria, was even grander than Chiedozie's with 130,000 turning up to watch a friendly with West Germany. He is best remembered not only for having a spectacular shot but also for acquiring a criminal record when playing for his previous team, Crystal Palace. He was caught trying to sell forged bank notes which came into his possession after Palace had played a friendly match against a prison team. With the St Kitts-born Tristan Benjamin and Aki Lahtinen from Finland playing in defence, and Serbian goalkeeper, Raddy Avramovic, Justin was joining a club which was ahead of its time in the diverse backgrounds of its playing staff.

Fashanu made a quiet debut on 18 December 1982 in a 1–2 home defeat to West Ham United which left the Magpies in 15th place. His first goal came in the next match, helping to secure a 2–2 draw away to West Bromwich Albion. There were two in a 3–2 victory away to Leicester City in the FA Cup and a stunner to give Notts a 1–0 win over Arsenal, a bullet header which one fan remembered 25 years later as the best goal he had ever seen at Meadow Lane. Fashanu was winning over the majority of Notts' fans, helped by the positive influence of Howard Wilkinson. He was a complete contrast to Clough, relying less on the power of his personality and more on a scientific approach to fitness and preparation. Justin, who was eager to train hard and learn, took to this approach immediately. And Notts' more direct style of play suited his talents. Wilkinson clearly liked him as a person and believed in him as a footballer. Soon the fans were using the British Airways tune to sing: 'We'll take good care of you, Fashanu, Fashanu.'

Justin celebrated his 22nd birthday – 19 February 1983 – with the goal that brought a 1–0 win at Manchester City. Interviewed in 2008 for the BBC East Midlands TV programme, *Inside Out*, Wilkinson remembered him from that time: 'He played well, he played happily, he looked happy, he seemed to be living happily…He always seemed a fighter. He didn't shirk a challenge on the pitch physically. He didn't shirk a challenge in training in terms of putting himself through the barriers it is necessary to put yourself through.' He described Justin as 'mentally strong'.

* * *

As usual with Justin, nothing stayed constant for long. A month after his birthday he was ruled out for the remaining weeks of the season with shin splits – his first serious injury. It must have been frustrating to find himself sidelined but he could look back on the season with some satisfaction. Twelve goals in 27 matches for Southampton and Notts County suggested his football career was back on track. At his age he could still expect to improve and, provided he steered clear of Brian Clough, fulfill his ambitions.

Justin's sexuality and the fears that went with it were presenting him with some conflicts and dilemmas. There was his relationship with Julie which clearly did not have a future. Not only was he destined to lose the relationship but also the cover she provided, giving credence to his appearance of being straight. Meanwhile his friend

The Biography

Peter Tatchell's experiences were a reminder of the hostility that could be directed at anyone in the public eye who was thought to be gay.

In November 1982 Bob Mellish, had resigned as MP, forcing a byelection when the Labour Party was still in disarray. Tatchell was finally endorsed as the official Labour Party candidate just weeks before the election which was to be held in February 1983. Among the long list of other candidates was Bob Mellish's political colleague, John O'Grady, who stood as Real Bermondsey Labour; this former council leader seeking to stir up prejudice against the official candidate of his own party. The Liberals and Social Democrats had formed a pact and chose Simon Hughes as the Liberal/SDP Alliance candidate. The Conservative candidate did not stand a chance in Bermondsey.

Despite the disunited state of the Labour Party and the controversy surrounding Peter Tatchell, he was still expected to win quite easily. Bermondsey was one of the safest Labour seats in the country, Mellish enjoying a 12,000 majority in 1979. But the campaign became something of a fiasco, as it eventually become apparent that senior figures in the Labour Party were sabotaging it. Meanwhile, Simon Hughes began to attract tactical voters as opinion polls indicated he stood the best chance of beating Tatchell. Tatchell later wrote: 'In the last few days of the byelection campaign, the atmosphere of hatred and irrationality reached fever pitch. It was an almost fascist-like mass-hysteria, more reminiscent of Germany in the 1930s or McCathyite America than British politics as we know it. Pilloried as a communist, foreigner, draft-dodger, traitor, homosexual and nigger-lover, I had to run a daily gauntlet of threats and obscene abuse, as did many of our Labour canvassers. Such was the climate of fear and violence that people displaying 'Vote Tatchell Labour' posters had their windows smashed and many others were threatened that if they didn't take them down they would get a brick through their window in the middle of the night.'

The Alliance was not above exploiting the situation. One day, its male canvassers wore badges saying 'I've been kissed by Peter Tatchell' or 'I've not been kissed by Peter Tatchell'. Bizarrely, this stunt was thought up by members of the Liberal Gay Action Group, claiming it was a protest against Tatchell going back in the closet. An Alliance leaflet pointedly described the contest as a 'straight' choice between it and Labour. The unimaginable became reality, Simon Hughes not only winning the election but doing so with a majority of nearly 10,000. It was a disastrous day for the Labour Party and for gay rights. Hughes waited until he was safely elected before condemning the campaign of personal abuse directed at Tatchell.

There was to be a twist to this tale 23 years later. In 2006 Simon Hughes stood as a candidate for leadership of the Liberal Democrats, the party formed in 1988 from a merger of the Liberal and Social Democrat Parties. For years he had denied rumours about his sexuality but *The Sun* obtained records showing he had phoned a gay chat line. Under pressure he was forced to admit to the paper: 'I have had both homosexual and heterosexual relationships.'

Given the vicious attacks on Peter Tatchell and the simmering violence, hatred and lawlessness that pervaded the football stadiums of England, Fashanu must have wondered what forces would be unleashed if his sexuality became public knowledge.

On top of rampant homophobia, gay men were facing another threat – Aids. In Britain and elsewhere it was among gay men that its devastating effects first became apparent. Ignorance bred fear, with health workers wearing protective clothing like space suits when treating Aids victims. In some quarters fear of Aids, combined with homophobia, grew into paranoia, illustrated by the occasion when engineers refused to remotely repair the telephone line of a gay helpline for fear of catching the disease. Aids provided a new opportunity for gay bashing. An example was the comment from James Anderton, the Chief Constable of Manchester and a Christian with a particular take on morality. He referred to gay men as 'swirling around in a cesspit of their own making'. The threat of Aids may have been exaggerated by ignorance and paranoia but was still real enough. Aids cast a shadow over the gay community. Gay men were dying and it was a desperate time.

Meanwhile, Justin's religious practice was taking up more of his time and attention. This driven young man, who craved money, acclaim and celebrity through stardom on the football pitch, had found something which meant more to him. He was beginning to spread his wings away from the Nottingham Christian Centre. Once he arrived there accompanied by tennis star, Sue Barker, and her partner, pop singer, Cliff Richard, another man having to deal with rumours about being gay. Justin met them through Christians in Sport, an organisation eager for him to speak publicly about his faith. He also came under the influence of an inspirational preacher called J.John, meeting with him once a week for mentoring. The particular form of Christianity Justin embraced was lively, straightforward and joyful; quite different from the more sedate and circumspect Church of England Protestantism he had grown up with in Shropham. Such was the contrast that Betty Jackson, herself a practicing Christian, complained to Gordon Homes, his old boxing coach: 'I don't know what to do with him; he just goes on and on.'

With Julie departing, Justin was joined by a housemate, Les Cleevely. He was a 17-year-old goalkeeper who Justin had met at Southampton. He recalls Justin saying: 'If you ever need help, let me know.' As Cleevely comments: 'A lot of people make that kind of offer but when I did contact Justin he really put himself out.' Cleevely was looking for a better contract than what he was offered by Southampton and Justin offered, not only to try to get him fixed up with Notts County, but for him to share his home. Over the summer they concentrated on getting fit together, going for long runs, often with Howard Wilkinson. Osman was also living with them and would take them through stretching exercises four times a day and encourage them to eat well. Les Cleevely has gone on to be a successful goalkeeping coach with Chelsea and other clubs and believes Justin was way ahead of his time with his attitude to health and fitness. Justin invited him to the Christian Centre and, although it was not for him, Les liked the people he met there and says that neither they nor Justin tried to 'push their beliefs down my throat'. At home, Justin would sometimes go to his room for private time to pray and read the Bible.

With the 1983–84 season approaching, Howard Wilkinson left Notts to take up an offer to manage Sheffield Wednesday. Such was the bond they had made in these few months that, unusually for people in the peripatetic business of professional football, Fashanu and Wilkinson remained friends, Justin describing him as 'a real person with a brilliant mind'.

* * *

The new team manager was a surprising choice, Larry Lloyd. He was the Nottingham Forest centre-half Fashanu had impressed against when at Norwich. A member of the European Cup winning team, he was one of the players Clough chose to move on perhaps too early. He had become player-manager of Fourth Division Wigan and took them to promotion in his first season. But the following season he was sacked after a run of eight defeats. Lloyd had hardly demonstrated the talent or gained the experience to manage a First Division team and his associations with Forest did not endear him to the fans.

With Lloyd's arrival, Les Cleevely lost his chance with Notts and moved on to Crystal Palace. He felt the fitness he had built up over the summer helped him to earn his contract. Les and Justin remained friends, sharing their enjoyment of tennis by going to the Wimbledon tournament together. Justin being Justin, he obtained access-all-area tickets for them through his friendship with the African American player, Camille Benjamin.

Pre-season saw a trip to Spain, Justin's third in succession and the first in which he was not sent off. He scored goals in both games and Lloyd declared him to be fit and looking sharp. Before the 1983–84 season began Lloyd was able to bring in his fellow European Cup winner, Martin O'Neill, who had moved from Forest to Norwich, enjoying two spells there with a stint at Manchester City in between.

Once again the Magpies' ambitions did not extend much above hoping to avoid relegation for another year but their start briefly promised much more. The first game was a 4–0 win at Leicester, followed by a home win over Birmingham. But then the decline set in. The next game, also at home was lost 2–0 to Ipswich, Justin scoring an own-goal and describing his performance as his worst ever. After three more defeats Lloyd dropped him from the team. There was no clear cut explanation for Justin's loss of form. He may not have fully recovered from his injury. Perhaps he would have been performing better if Wilkinson was still in charge. He never enjoyed the same rapport with Lloyd. The growing influence of religion in his life may have taken the edge off his dedication to football.

After two more defeats Justin was recalled for a League Cup tie at Fourth Division Aldershot, scoring in a 4–2 win. And so he secured a place in the team to face Forest at the City Ground. This was always a highly anticipated fixture and even more so on this occasion with Lloyd and O'Neill returning as heroes and Fashanu the villain. He of course was desperate to do well, needing to show his own manager and fans that he deserved a place in the team as well as wanting Clough and the Forest fans to see they had underestimated him. Determined though he was to play, there was a dilemma for Justin. The game was on a Sunday and to take part was to go against his Christian beliefs which required it to be a day of rest and worship. On this occasion football won out over religion but this conflict added a further layer of tension to Fashanu's mind.

With Forest supporters singing 'We're sick and tired of you, Fashanu' 45 minutes before the match kicked off Fashanu knew he was in for a torrid time. Once the game began a rejuvenated Forest team quickly demonstrated their superiority, going one up after eight minutes. Then Fashanu made his first impact, bursting into the penalty box where he was brought down by Colin Todd, Trevor Christie converting the penalty-kick to bring the scores level. But by half-time Forest's class had defeated Notts' industry and they were 3–1 up.

Fashanu was being constantly kicked by Forest's defenders with little protection from the referee and shortly into the second half it all got too much for him. He retaliated to what he perceived to be another foul, causing the linesman to flag against him. He turned to the linesman and said 'you must be joking'. Later Fashanu described his response: 'The linesman looked at me as if I'd got no right to be there.' He was not more specific but clearly deeply offended. Whatever abuse then came from Justin's mouth was enough for him to suffer the humiliation of being sent off, making the referee, according to the *Evening Post*, 'the most popular ever to set foot on the City Ground'. Notts fell to their seventh successive defeat in League matches.

The Biography

Justin had a weekly 'Fash on Football' column in the *Nottingham Evening Press* and wrote about his poor start to the season. In that pompous way celebrities sometimes talk about themselves he said: 'At least one man is confident that rumours about Justin Fashanu being a spent force are totally unfounded. That same man is certain that Fashanu will draw the crowds again. That man? Me.' He found a more thoughtful tone when talking more generally about the Magpies' struggles: 'Disappointment is something we all have to live with but my feeling is that is the time when you grow as a person, handling these disappointments and coming through them individually to indicate your depth of character.'

Into November, Notts and Fashanu found some form, winning away at Southampton, astounding their supporters with consecutive home wins, 5–2 against Aston Villa and 6–1 against Sunderland, and briefly climbing out the relegation zone. Two heavy defeats were followed, on 27 December, by a fine performance which saw them draw 3–3 away to Manchester United, thanks to two late goals from Fashanu, the last being his sixth of the season.

In his final column before Christmas he had been characteristically open about his religious beliefs: 'I hope this Christmas will be one full of peace, joy, happiness and an awareness of Christ. Because we are finding more and more people are being separated from Christ and his teachings.'

The next game was a New Year's Eve fixture away to Ipswich. It was Justin's first visit there since his disastrous bust up with Clough at the end of the 1981–82 season and was to prove even more calamitous. Six minutes before half-time a challenge from defender Russell Osman caught him on the side of the right knee. He was helped off the pitch limping badly and bleeding. A week later Justin reported, through his column, that he had needed four stitches, was suffering from severe bruising, his knee had swollen up to the size of a football and he was running a temperature. His knee had twice been drained of fluid. He had been given pain-killing and sleep-inducing drugs, powerful enough that he could remember little of what had happened. Despite this suffering Justin, being the character he was, was photographed sitting up in bed with a big smile; a nurse on one side and on the other a girl who had just had an operation and whose autograph book he was signing.

After another week Justin left hospital having been told by the consultant that he had an inflamed knee lining. He hoped to get back to training but it was not to be. Soon after, his leg was in a full length plaster and his season over. He was powerless to help his team avoid relegation. Worse still – although he did not know it at the time – this injury would ruin Justin's chances of ever again being a top class professional footballer.

Chapter 8

A Man Apart

Justin's injury healed sufficiently for him to join a trip to Kenya at the end of May. It was an exciting event for the players, organised to raise money for the Kenyan Olympic Fund, and featuring matches against three local sides. A highlight was the luxury train ride taking them from the capital, Nairobi, to the coastal resort of Mombasa.

It was also about relaxing and having fun after a grueling season and just the sort of occasion when footballers could be expected to chase after women, bantering and boasting about their sexual exploits. Concerned about the players picking up sexually transmitted diseases, the club doctor took 50 shots of penicillin for the party of 15. On the return flight Larry Lloyd asked if he had used any of them. The doctor told him there were only three left.

Justin would have been uncertain if any of his teammates knew he was gay. There were rumours but no one was sure what to make of them. They knew he was a regular at Part II but it had the best sound system and lights in Nottingham, which could be a good enough reason to go there. Justin was different from most footballers of that era. With his adventurous dress sense, big personality and exuberant Christianity, teammates were not sure what to make of him although he was popular enough. One described him as 'a man apart'. It never occurred to Les Cleevely that Justin might be gay, even though they talked about women and occasionally went to nightclubs together.

The Biography

After Julie left Justin dated other women. Whether his motives were purely to appear to be heterosexual is not clear but it certainly helped. One teammate remembers taking Justin to a party where many of the people there were gay men. Justin ended up taking a young woman he met there for a meal, much to the annoyance of his teammate who had been interested in her himself. Justin was a good looking, outgoing, charming man who was undoubtedly attractive to women as well as men.

Despite the *Sunday People* story of rumours about Fashanu being gay, opposition fans had not latched on to them. Some Notts County fans recall there was chanting by their own supporters of 'Fashanu is a homosexual' at the match with Forest just before his transfer. But others have no such recollection; chants can be started but fizzle out if not taken up by enough people. There does not appear to have been any other homophobic chanting at Fashanu until he came out. An informal survey of Notts supporters suggests that most had no idea Fashanu was gay although some heard rumours and others knew but did not feel obliged to spread it around.

Back to Kenya and, having arrived at Mombasa, the players spent an evening at the Bora Bora nightclub. There Justin danced with a young woman, possibly not realising she expected to be paid for sex. At the end of the evening he thanked her for the dance and said he was going back to the hotel. The young woman was furious and stormed over to a group of players asking 'What's the matter with him?' to which Pedro Richards responded 'He doesn't go with girls, he goes with boys'. She went back to Fashanu and pointed towards Richards as she spoke to him. Fashanu left.

The next day, in training, Fashanu let Richards nutmeg him (push the ball through his legs, run past and collect it). As Richards passed him, Fashanu swung a punch so hard Richards collapsed on the ground. He tried to get up only for Rachid Harkouk to shout 'I'd stay down if I were you or he'll kill you'. Larry Lloyd asked Justin what he had done it for. He replied 'Ask Pedro'. The training session was abandoned and the incident not mentioned again.

*   *   *

One man who would have been impressed with Justin's punching power was Ronnie Kray. He and twin brother, Reggie, the notorious criminals from London's East End, were both imprisoned for life in 1969 for crimes which included murder. Ronnie was diagnosed with paranoid schizophrenia and incarcerated in Broadmoor Special Hospital. Intent on spreading the word of God, Justin wrote to him and arranged, through the hospital, to visit. A bonus for Justin was the newspaper headlines his visits attracted – headlines he could no longer command through his performances as a footballer.

He and Ronnie Kray had more in common than their East End origins. Both could have been professional boxers and Ronnie was bisexual. He also had some Christian faith although more low key than Justin's. He wrote of Justin: 'He spent much of the time telling me how he'd become a born-again Christian. I think he was hoping to convert me, but I told him, "I don't need to be reborn to have good thoughts and to look after other people". Maybe it wasn't what he wanted to hear, but it hasn't stopped us being friends.'

Reggie Kray was in Parkhurst Prison on the Isle of Wight and, in the summer of 1984, Justin tried to visit him. He told *The Sun* he was not allowed to see Reggie but spent time with his cellmate instead and described what happened when he left: 'The atmosphere was full of oppression and hate. I came out of it in a buzz, drove down the road and the car crash seemed to happen in slow motion. My car was a write off. I ended up in the passenger seat. If I hadn't done that I'd have lost both my legs.' He may have been exaggerating. It was the fourth day of his coming out story; he was running out of material and resorting to making some things up. But the crash was real enough. The *Isle of Wight County Press* reported that he had come out of a side road and driven straight into another car. Justin was fined £60 for driving without due care and attention.

Justin was as unreservedly open about his religious beliefs as he was secretive about his gay lifestyle and he endured being mocked about it by Brian Clough and Larry Lloyd among others. In his autobiography Lloyd describes an incident which occurred when he was out having a meal and drink with the former Forest player, John Robertson: 'Sitting there, minding our own business, we were interrupted by Fash who, it would appear, had something profound to tell us. "Larry," he began. (He didn't address me as Boss, which put my back up straight away.) "Remember, it took the Israelites 2,000 years to come out of the wilderness".' Lloyd, who was in danger of losing his job, claims to have replied: 'Fash, I ain't got 2,000 fucking minutes to save my job. Now fuck off.'

In his attitude to Fashanu, Lloyd places himself firmly in the Clough camp. He writes: 'I can't say he wasn't pleasant, and at times, likeable, but he was a liar and a wind-up.' He was convinced Fashanu was suffering from dreadful levels of paranoia and delusion, saying 'Poor old Fash. I guessed he wasn't terribly well', but doesn't attempt to justify the comment. The contrast in Clough and Lloyd's attitudes towards

The Biography

Fashanu and those of McMenemy and Wilkinson is remarkable; and the contrast in Fashanu's form when playing under these managers, equally so.

Fashanu's attempts to share his religious beliefs with other people in football were not always rebuffed. Graham Daniels was a young professional at Cambridge United and 'new to faith'. He decided to invite his teammates round for a meal and to listen to Justin talk about Christianity. It could have been a daunting assignment but Daniels remembers it going well because Justin was so at home in the situation. Daniels recalls him joking with the manager, John Ryan, who had been in the Norwich team when Justin scored his famous goal against Liverpool. Ryan reminded him he had been running up the wing screaming for the ball when Justin turned the other way and unleashed his shot. Daniels describes Fashanu as 'a consummate communicator' and for Justin it was a rare occasion when he was able to bring together two of the disparate elements of his life – football and religion.

But there was a problem about Justin being so public about his Christianity. It put even more pressure on him to keep his gay life under wraps. To be exposed as somebody who was spreading God's word but going against it would have been devastating for him. Of course he still had to live with knowing, in his own terms, that he could not hide from God. There were these two strong forces in his life, Christianity and homosexuality, and he could not reconcile them.

Justin was interviewed about his Christianity for a book aimed at teenagers, *Nick's Christmas Mix*. It was produced by Nick Beggs, the bass player with pop group Kajagoogoo, and a Christian. The book also included interviews with singers David Grant and Donna Summer. Justin talked about how the difficulties in his career had forced him to re-evaluate his relationship with God: 'I reckoned that since God was my father and protector, he would be a kind of insurance policy against problems and hardship. But I've come to realise that I will still face problems. God gives me the strength to cope with the trials. He doesn't take them away. Just recently, I've been laid on my back with a severe knee injury. It happened just after I'd scored two goals in a match at Manchester United. There I was thinking my goalscoring form had come back and suddenly I was out for five months. That was a severe blow. But God has used the lay-off, giving me the space to spend more time reading the Bible, talking to God and listening to what he has to say. My faith had been strengthened, not weakened.'

Justin was interviewed for the book by Malcolm Doney, himself a Christian, but with a different relationship to his religion from Justin's. They got on well and met on several more occasions. He describes Fashanu as naïve, with a trusting, simple attitude to life, treating the world as less complicated than it is and with a child-like belief in

God which Doney feels was about wanting a father figure – a familiar theme in Justin's life. He illustrates the difference in their attitude towards God with an example of when Justin wanted to contact him after a gap of several years. He found an old phone number and was amazed it worked, attributing his success in locating Doney to God's will. Doney's more mundane explanation was that he was still in the same job and had not changed his number.

Some time after they first met Fashanu asked Doney to collaborate on an autobiography and they met with a publisher. Fashanu asked for a ridiculous amount of money as an advance which Doney felt was based not so much on greed but on fantasy. Justin had failed to grasp that he was no longer the star of his Norwich days. His assessment of Fashanu was echoed by the words of Trevor Frecknall, a Nottingham journalist, who wrote that he 'behaves like an innocent at large, oblivious of how cynical or scathing his world of football can become especially when it intermingles with our world of journalism' adding that Fashanu talked a better game of football than he played.

∗   ∗   ∗

Relegated with Norwich, Fashanu commanded a £1 million transfer fee. Three years later, in the same situation, there was no talk of him leaving Notts County. There were no offers. Injury and erratic form had seen to that. The 23-year-old was contemplating his first season in the Second Division.

First he had to get fit. He took up cycling and when the squad met up for pre-season training he reported that he could bend his knee fully and put pressure on it riding up hill. In preparation for the 1984–85 season, Notts embarked on a round of friendly matches one of which brought him up against his brother, John. Having made just a handful of first-team appearances for Norwich, he had been transferred to Third Division Lincoln City in 1983 for a modest fee of £15,000. But it was John who shone in this match, scoring twice in a 4–0 win. He and Justin were quite close at this time. Lincoln was only 40 miles away from Nottingham and John visited regularly with his Spanish girlfriend, Maria Sol Acuña.

Justin had another housemate. Neil Slawson, who had been born in Britain and raised in the USA, and had a temporary contract with Derby County. Dissatisfied with his opportunities there he turned up at Notts for an informal trial. Justin offered him a place to stay which he was grateful to take up even though he returned to Derby County. Slawson soon realised that Justin had appointed himself as his mentor: 'Little by little he began to school me in the skills of life that I couldn't experience from always having lived at home with my parents. He also began to impart his knowledge of what it would take to make it in the game of football, from diet and exercise, to formal training techniques, to lifestyle, habits and public contacts.' Neil Slawson remembers an occasion when he was out with a girl in Derby on a Friday evening and missed the last train back having misread the timetable. He ended up spending the night before a match day on the station and this did not go down well with Justin: 'He was waiting to give me a tongue lashing. As soon as I walked in he questioned my dedication to the profession and threatened to pull his support from me. His brother, John, was over that day, sitting on the couch, shaking his head, also in disgust at my actions.'

Justin was not always so disapproving: 'He was always genuinely caring about your views on life matters, both in sport and about the world, always listening intently with that look of interest across his brow, nodding his head in urging you to "go on".' Neil felt confident enough to ask Justin about the rumours he was gay. Justin dismissed them, saying they had been made up by the newspapers after he visited Part II with Julie.

In the build-up to the new season there was alarming news of Justin's injury causing problems again. Lloyd blamed the hard summer pitches they were playing on. Fashanu later described how throughout the season there was swelling in his knee and when he played he was always in pain. During the summer Notts had to sell some of their better players and, in his autobiography, Larry Lloyd complains that he was left with a squad which was unprofessional, many being heavy drinkers and some using drugs. At least that was one accusation he could not make about Fashanu.

The season started dreadfully with four straight defeats, the second of which was a 1–2 loss away to Brighton. Justin, who scored Notts' goal, provoked hostility from the home crowd for his aggressive style of play which left defender, Jeff Clarke, injured. In his newspaper column Pedro Richards – who knew only too well how aggressive Fashanu could be – rather nobly came to his defence writing: 'I noticed that a lot of people were making a lot of fuss about very little last week – Justin Fashanu's alleged one man war on the Brighton team.' And continued: 'Big Fash's return to getting in where it hurts the most could not have come at a better time. He seems to be back to something like his Norwich City days, knocking the opposition around and generally making a nuisance of himself. With all his physical attributes, Fash has got to be that kind of player.' He could also have said 'with his limitations' because lacking from his Norwich days were the pace and sharpness to cut through defences.

JUSTIN FASHANU

Fashanu next hit the headlines in October when he was sent off in a home fixture against Cardiff played on a Sunday. Notts were losing by two goals when he was dismissed early in the second half for arguing with the referee after he thought he had been unfairly penalised. A fan ran on the pitch to remonstrate with the referee. This was the Magpies' eighth defeat in 10 league matches, leaving them bottom of the Second Division. Two weeks later Larry Lloyd was sacked and replaced by Richie Barker, a former Notts player who had managed Stoke City. For his first match he dropped Fashanu to the substitutes' bench. Fashanu demanded a transfer and Barker refused, saying he was still assessing the squad. Barker reinstated him for the next match, away to Norwich in the League Cup. A Nottingham journalist noted that although he was being booed by some of the Notts fans he was clearly still adored by the Norwich supporters.

Notts County continued to limp through the season with Fashanu in and out of the team as Barker tried and failed to put together a winning combination. In January Fashanu's wish was granted; he was put on the transfer list. But there was no rush of clubs eager to buy him. His career had reached a new low. This was far worse than being dropped by Brian Clough three years earlier. Then he was struggling in a team which was expected to compete for major trophies. Approaching his 24th birthday he could not get into a team at the bottom of the Second Division. Disillusioned he told Barker he no longer wanted to play for Notts but, with injuries to other forwards, Barker persuaded him to turn out, arguing that if he wanted to attract another club he needed to put in some performances.

Prior to the return fixture against Cardiff, also to be played on a Sunday, Barker announced he was thinking of playing Fashanu in midfield and told the press Justin had said he would play anywhere and do anything to help the club. But then came the event which finally pushed him into prioritising his religion over football. In contrast to Justin's career, his brother John's was on the up. He had been transferred from Lincoln to Millwall who were doing well in the Third Division, on course to swap places with the Magpies. They were also making good progress in the FA Cup and Justin travelled to Luton to see John play in a midweek quarter-final. Justin's career had been played out against a background of simmering violence on the terraces but what he saw that night took it to another level.

The Luton police were expecting 5,000 Millwall fans but 10,000 turned up, more than Millwall's average home gate. Word had got round to fans of other London clubs that there would be a punch up, attracting anyone who fancied it. Before the match they left a trail of broken shop windows. Then about 2,000 fans who did not have tickets smashed their way through the turnstiles. Within five minutes of the game starting they spilled out from the overcrowded terraces onto the pitch where it took hundreds of police and several Alsatians 25 minutes to restore order so that the game could restart. Luton won 1–0 and after the match people from the Millwall end ripped out seats and invaded the pitch, hurling the seats and any other potential weapons they could find at the police who were forced to retreat and regroup before they could quell the riot. Outside the ground the mob wrecked cars, smashed windows and attacked local residents.

Justin went home and prayed. The next day he announced he would not play in the match against Cardiff. He told the press the riot had shown where disobeying the laws of God was leading: 'I prayed long and hard about pulling out. It's not a case of not being bothered. Football cannot just divorce itself from the problems of society. I realise that if I continually disobey God I will take the consequences.' He explained he had previously been unhappy playing on Sundays and this may be why he had been sent off in the previous two Sunday fixtures. Instead of participating in the crucial relegation match he would be addressing young Christians in Gloucester. Richie Barker was diplomatic, saying it was a blow for the club but he respected Justin's point of view. He did not really have a choice. Some of the supporters were less charitable, barracking him in the next match until he scored in a rare win, against Wolves.

Although there were occasions when some of the home crowd were hostile towards Fashanu many fans remember him fondly, for his performances in his first year but also for occasions when they met him. They recall him standing with them on the terraces when he was injured and unable to play, as he had done at Norwich. Then there was the time when two supporters wanted to go to an away game in Birmingham but would not be able to get back because there was not a late train. One of them bumped into Justin when out jogging and asked if he could give them a lift, Justin being suspended from playing at the time. Justin not only agreed but invited them round to his house before they set off, showing them round and giving them tea.

One fan, Michael West, describes Fashanu as 'one of the nicest, most down-to-earth people you could ever wish to meet'. He gives as an example a time when his amateur team were having an informal practice match on a public recreation ground: 'A car pulled up and suddenly this huge black guy came strolling toward me followed by four white teenage lads, all kitted out for football and asked if they could join in with us. As a Notts fan my eyes nearly popped out of my head when I saw it was Justin Fashanu who was asking me if he could have a game with us.' One person did not recognise him and asked his name. West remembers: 'Despite being a high profile footballer in the national media over the past few years, and with his classic goal for Norwich against Liverpool being shown in the opening credits of *Match of the Day* every week, Fash did not show a flicker of annoyance at not being recognised and simply replied "Justin". He recalls that they joined in for half an hour or so; Justin making no attempt to show off and being quick to hand out praise. Fashanu was full of contradictions and it was typical of him that although he was one of the best paid of the Notts' players, lived in the poshest house and drove the flashiest car, he could also be the most approachable and unassuming.

After the win against Wolves, the Magpies lost five League fixtures in a row and Barker was sacked, leaving them second from bottom of the League with three teams to be relegated. Jimmy Sirrel was back in charge for the remaining five fixtures. Under his management they went on a great little run winning three and drawing one of the next four games with Fashanu scoring in all four, doubling his total for the season. The last of these was a home fixture against Manchester City who had been relegated from the First Division with Notts but would regain their place if they won. Ten thousand of their supporters swelled the crowd to nearly 18,000 – by far the Magpies' biggest of the season. Notts started superbly, scoring three goals in 13 first half minutes. But at half-time, in scenes reminiscent of those at Luton a few weeks earlier, City fans invaded the pitch, seemingly intent on getting the game abandoned. The police called in reinforcements and, with mounted police charging fans on horseback, order was restored after half an hour. Notts hung on to win 3–2 but the following week they lost 0–1 at Fulham, bringing relegation for the second consecutive season.

While that match was being played, 56 people died as fire spread rapidly through an old wooden stand at Bradford City's ground. A few weeks later, at the European Cup Final being played in the Heysel Stadium in Belgium, Liverpool fans attacked supporters of the Italian club, Juventus. As they tried to escape a wall collapsed on them killing 39 with 600 injured. Four years later, in 1989, attempts to control fans with higher and stronger fences backfired when 96 Liverpool supporters were crushed to death at an FA Cup semi-final at Sheffield Wednesday's Hillsborough ground.

These disasters, following on from the Luton riot and many other incidents of serious disorder, ushered in the era of all-seater stadiums, heavy-duty stewarding, and regulations and legislation to curb the behaviour of fans. Watching live professional football became safer but more expensive. Racist chanting was virtually eliminated and going to a match was a little more attractive to people from minority ethnic groups. Clubs encouraged a family atmosphere, welcoming to women and children.

The Biography

But many young working-class men found themselves priced out of watching live football. And the boisterous camaraderie of terrace culture which provided a welcome weekly dose of release from the restraints and politeness of everyday life had been subdued.

* * *

There was no way Notts could afford to keep Fashanu or that he would be willing to play in the Third Division. His flurry of goals at the end of the season attracted interest from managers who believed they could get him playing again at something like his best. Clubs linked with him in the press included, as usual, Manchester City and Norwich City; the Manchester club having been promoted back to the First Division and Norwich relegated to the Second. Chelsea, Birmingham and Oxford, all in the First Division, were said to be interested. He went close to joining Second Division Oldham Athletic, managed by his old strike partner, Joe Royle, who recollects the negotiations in his autobiography. He invited Justin to his home and after a long chat Royle thought he had convinced him to join, only for Justin to say he needed to think it over. The next day Royle phoned at an agreed time and when Justin did not answer continued trying until he picked the phone up. When Royle asked where he had been Justin replied 'with a strange air of detachment' that he had been talking to the Lord. 'So are you going to join?' enquired Royle. 'I'm not', Justin answered: 'The Lord and I don't think it is the right thing for me at the moment.'

Also interested in Justin was the manager of another Second Division team, Chris Cattlin of Brighton & Hove Albion. Feeling he might be a difficult player to manage, Cattlin decided to invite Justin to stay at his house for four days so they could get to know each other. They obviously hit it off and the transfer was agreed. Cattlin explained: 'Justin had a reputation of being a bit of a problem player with his other clubs but that is all in the past. In my dealings with him I've found him to be a smashing person and the sort of player our supporters will take to.' He told the *Evening Argus* that Justin was 'a dedicated player who has been asleep for a couple of years', adding 'I'm sure, with us, he will bring his talents to fruition'. For his part, Justin told *The Times*: 'I only took this step after a good deal of thought and prayer. I am convinced Chris Cattlin can get the very best out of me.' He described the move as the most important of his career. He must have felt it was his last chance to regain the form he had shown at Norwich and in his first few months at Notts County.

He signed in June 1985 for a fee of £115,000 and was given a generous three year contract, reported to be around £45,000 a year. He had passed his medical but there was an exclusion clause on his troublesome right knee. It would only be covered by insurance after he played 12 consecutive League games.

Before he left Nottingham there was to be one last appearance in a packed football stadium. Billy Graham, the evangelist who had made such an impact on Terry Carpenter's life, was holding a week-long mission at Sheffield United's Bramall Lane ground. Justin was invited to testify from the stage and it would be a massive occasion for him, with the event being televised in Nigeria, the home of his father. But, in the way which used to frustrate his business manager, Roger Haywood, he nearly missed it. Terry Carpenter happened to see Justin, who told him he was not going because both his cars were out of commission. 'It's rather important', Terry reminded Justin and drove him there himself.

Arriving in Brighton Justin was as eager to talk about his Christianity as he was to conceal his gay identity. He explained that he had spent the summer visiting Romania with a Christian group, that he observed the Sabbath and was a strict teetotaller. He told the *Argus* that he spent Sundays travelling round the country preaching the gospel: 'My life is dedicated to God.'

The city of Brighton and Hove was then two adjoining towns on the south coast. Brighton was known to be gay friendly, without having earned its more recent status as the gay capital of the UK. It had long been a popular destination for day trippers from London, with a reputation for intrigue and character, and was the setting of numerous books and films including *Brighton Rock* and *Quadrophenia*. Justin suggested that Albion supporters liked players with style and personality because they reflected the image of the town. The club found him a flat in Brighton's Regency Square, a prestigious and once grand address although one visitor remembers his flat being 'horrible and damp'. The Square could claim a link with a famous gay man from the past. Oscar Wilde and his lover, Lord Alfred Douglas, once crashed their horse and carriage into the garden railings. Echoing the title of one of his plays, Wilde declared it 'an accident of no importance'.

Brighton & Hove Albion had recently enjoyed the best spell in its history. In 1979 the club had been promoted to the First Division for the first time under manager, Alan Mullery. In 1983 it reached the FA Cup Final, drawing with Manchester United before losing the replay. The same year it was relegated and Chris Cattlin's job was to try to take it back up.

In the build-up to the 1985–86 season Albion played a series of matches against other English League teams in which Fashanu was outstanding. No doubt he relished starring in a 5–2 defeat of Nottingham Forest in which he had a hand in four of the goals. Justin's history suggested that he performed far better if he enjoyed a good relationship with his manager which clearly he did with Chris Cattlin. But Cattlin was getting a little carried away with his praise. After the Forest game he declared: 'It's high time they made room for him in the England squad. They were scared to death of him out there.' Responding, Justin named his three personal goals: to become a better Christian, fulfil his duties and obligations to Albion, and win a place in the England squad. He was settling in well, having become the PFA representative and saying how friendly he found the club.

There was some lingering ill-will from supporters over various incidents when he had played against them including the injury to Jeff Clarke the previous season. When still at Norwich, he had broken the nose of Brighton's defender, Andy Rollings, who was then sent off after swinging a punch at him. Dismissing the broken nose as arising from an accidental clash of heads, Justin claimed: 'I think I have become more subtle in my game. I would really hurt people in the past but that is all behind me, now.' But, as one Brighton supporter put it: 'He was the kind of player you couldn't stand because you thought he was dirty, then he comes to play for you and you think he's brilliant.'

Everything appeared to be going well but there was some cause for concern. After a pre-season match against Oxford United, Justin's knee had swollen. But he was fit to start the competitive season, making a quiet debut. The third match was at home to Bradford and with Albion 2–1 up Fashanu got into a dispute with the referee who was booking him for a foul, and refused to give his name. The referee sent him off but he took nearly two minutes to leave the field. At least the supporters got behind him. One remembers them singing his name, the loudest they had sounded for years.

As usual he was making a good impression with his friendliness and approachability. He started coaching the supporters' club team and is remembered as 'a fantastic bloke', 'infectiously enthusiastic', 'generous with his time' and 'a genuine lovely person'. After training he would buy everyone a round of drinks, sticking to blackcurrant and lemonade himself.

Fashanu's right knee became swollen again and it was decided he should have an operation. With that and the suspension for being sent off, he missed most of September and October. When he did return he clearly was not fit and had to sit out more matches. In his first game back he picked up his third booking of the season, and he spoke about his disciplinary record. He felt he was singled out by some referees but did not think it was to do with racism, saying that he stood out because of his size as well as his skin colour and had a reputation for being a physical player. He felt his brother received similar treatment and that some referees were obsessed with stamping down on them both. He claimed: 'I'm not a vicious player. You can ask other players and the majority will say I'm an all-or-nothing player, not a dirty player.' Sounding regretful he added: 'The day seems to have gone when a centre-half gave you a whack and you gave him one back.' He admitted that his emotions ran high when he was on the pitch, especially when he felt he was being unfairly singled out.

Finally he put together a run of 11 consecutive matches from late November to the end of January. He made a good impression on local reporter, John Vinicombe, who summed up his contribution to the team: 'Fashanu may not have scored many goals but he is a handful for any defence, awkward, uncompromising and difficult to shake off the ball – a striker whose diversionary runs and knockdowns have helped make Dean Saunders and Terry Connor such a deadly pair.' He may not have been attracting the attention of the England manager but was doing a decent job for his team. Brighton were performing reasonably well; going into an FA Cup tie with Hull City they were fifth in the League.

* * *

Moving from Nottingham, Justin had to find new ways and places to live his lives as a Christian man and a gay man while keeping them completely separate. Through Christians in Sport he was introduced to John Samways, a curate at All Saints Church in Patcham. John Samways remembers him coming to the church several times, at least once accompanied by his brother, John. He describes Justin as 'a delightful man'. He had no idea Justin was gay. He once visited Justin when he was struggling with his injuries and shared Psalm 125 with him: 'As the mountains surround Jerusalem, so the Lord surrounds his people.'

Soon after moving to Regency Square Justin met a gay neighbour, Terry Wing who, like him, had spent time in care. Terry became a good friend but not a sexual partner. Justin spent many an afternoon hanging out in Terry's flat and told him it was the place where he could relax. He felt he could be himself with gay men; but not always completely himself. He felt obliged to tell Terry that his Christianity was a way of covering up his homosexuality and succeeded in convincing him even though Terry himself was a Christian. Terry introduced him to Brighton Theatre Group, an amateur company staging musicals. They were preparing a production of Oklahoma. Justin enjoyed having a group of people he could spend time with away from football and became a sort of unofficial patron of the company. Terry Wing remembers Justin as 'a lovely guy, very handsome and well-presented; bubbly, soft and kind'.

Justin (left) and John with
family pet, Bubbles, in the
back garden of Flint
House.

Credit: Jackson family

Justin (left) and John.
School photo.
Credit: Jackson family

With Carol and Wendy Edwards, also from Shropham, 1970. Credit: Jackson family

Sue Jackson's wedding to William Anderson (centre). With bride's family including Betty (next to bride in blue outfit); Edward (third from right); Alf (right); Justin (front left) and John (front right), 1975. Credit: Sue Anderson

Some fun with Kevin Reeves while they pose with the match balls for the 1979–80 season.

Credit: Mirrorpix

Celebrating the Football League Commission panel ruling that Nottingham Forest were wrong to suspend him, November 1982.

Credit: PA

In his best season as a footballer Justin still keeps his boxing gloves close at hand, December 1980.

Signing for Notts County, flanked by Howard Wilkinson (left) and Jimmy Sirrel (right). December 1982.

Scoring for Notts County against Arsenal, January 1983.

In action for Torquay United.

Fashanu's Airdrie teammates congratulate him on scoring against Aberdeen, April 1993.

Credit: PA

A TV camera records Fashanu's impromptu press conference, Edinburgh, February 1994.

Credit: Action Plus Sports Images

With Nicholas, Edward, Jemima, Simeon and Rachel Jackson, Atlanta, October 1997.

Maria Sol Acuña, Exeter DJ Alan Quick, and Amal Fashanu at a football v homophobia event organised by the Justin Campaign, Norwich 19 February 2010.

The Biography

Being discreet about his sexuality, Justin generally stayed away from gay clubs in Brighton but managed one visit to a club at the Royal Beacon Hotel. It was a charity event and his cover was provided by him being invited as an honoured guest. His fellow honoured guest was Cynthia Payne, a brothel madam who had entertained the British public, at her trial, with tales of elderly men paying in luncheon vouchers to dress up in lingerie and be spanked. She had become something of a gay icon.

An acquaintance remembers Justin having sexual relationships with two men when he was in Brighton and what he observed highlighted the difficulties of being a wealthy celebrity with a secret gay life. In both instances he felt there was an element of paying for sex. He believed one of the men would not have been in a sexual relationship with him if it had not been for regular presents and being flattered by the attention of a famous person.

*   *   *

After an FA Cup match at Hull Fashanu's right knee swelled up yet again, causing him to miss more games. He was given an injection to calm down the swelling and was back for another FA Cup match, at Peterborough. It was played on a snow covered pitch, four days before his 25th birthday and he was taken off after an hour. It turned out to be the end of his season. His Brighton career was over after just 20 games and two goals. It would be nearly four years before he played another competitive match in England.

Chapter 9

Atlantic Crossings

After leaving the pitch at Peterborough Justin endured a miserable time as the seriousness of his knee injury became apparent. A month's rest failed to help and the club announced he was going to see one of the world's leading specialists. The *Evening Argus* headline 'Fash Future in Doubt' was followed by 'Fash Fears are Eased'. An arthroscopy (a technique to look at the knee with no major incision) revealed there was no ligament problem or arthritis. He would have a minor operation and be fit in three weeks. When the three weeks were up the club announced Justin needed more rest and would miss the remainder of the season. But with the season over, at the end of May, he was on crutches. A decision was made to send him to a rehabilitation centre to work on rebuilding the muscle round his knee. The centre was RAF Headley Court, a former stately home near Epsom in Surrey.

Justin had started the 1985–86 season with Brighton hoping to spend the summer in Mexico with the England World Cup squad. When that dream faded he decided to take a holiday watching the tournament. But soon after starting rehab it became apparent even this was beyond him and he would have to stay at Headley Court for a couple of months.

With Brighton's form dipping alarmingly towards the end of the season, Chris Cattlin was sacked and replaced by the returning Alan Mullery. As Justin emerged from the rehab centre still on crutches, Mullery was faced with a situation which was becoming a financial disaster for the club. Justin had not managed those 12 consecutive League matches which would have taken out the insurance exclusion on his knee. (His run of 11 matches included nine in the League.) The club was paying for his medical treatment and with the transfer fee and lucrative three year contract, Fashanu had cost a lot of money, with more to come and little prospect of him playing again in the forthcoming season.

The club issued a statement which began: 'After a full discussion with our medical staff, we have come to the reluctant decision that it would be in Justin's best interest if he didn't play competitive football as we could not see him being fit enough to return to football in the foreseeable future.' It was explained that he was still suffering from swelling and muscle wastage. His options were a course of injections, which would not be expected to provide a complete cure, or having his knee cap removed, which would only have a 50 per cent chance of success. The statement continued: 'We cannot wait another year to see if he is fit.' The club was offering to pay Fashanu six months of wages. Mullery told the *Evening Argus*: 'I feel terrible for the boy.' *The Times* quoted him saying: 'Justin isn't happy but I'm convinced we're doing the right thing.'

Fashanu had arrived at Brighton hoping the move would revive his career. Instead it appeared to have ended it. But there was a glimmer of hope. The club's statement had not completely ruled out the possibility of him ever playing again. He decided to pay for another operation himself. Terry Wing remembers Justin, staying in a London hotel at this time, obviously lonely, but always putting on a bright face, something Terry associated with having been in care. Once again the operation saw no improvement.

*　*　*

Justin was not ready to give up and found a surgeon, Dr Jim Tibone, in Los Angeles. His old housemate, Neil Slawson had returned to the USA and was training as a police officer, living with his family in Upland, on the edge of LA. Justin moved in with them. This time the operation worked. Dr Tibone told him: 'You had quite an infection in there but whatever it was has worked its way out now. The only problem is that you're got a hell of rehabilitation in front of you.' Justin stayed on in LA, attending the Kerlan-Jobe Orthopaedic Clinic for rehab up to four times a day. These gruelling sessions were enlivened by the presence of well-known sportsmen and women, including the tennis player, Tracy Austin.

In LA, Justin was more of a friend than a mentor to Neil Slawson but there was one occasion when he put on his mentoring hat: 'Justin once got annoyed with me because upon introducing me to Tracy Austin, I greeted her with, "Nice to meet you Trace". While driving away, Justin barked at me and schooled me that until you've arrived on the professional scene and made a name for yourself, it's not proper to abbreviate a superstar's name unless you know them personally.'

But Neil's memories of this time are mainly about having fun. He remembers, moments after being rather formally greeted by his parents, Justin went up the stairs to the bedroom they had allocated him only to turn round and slide down the stairs head first with his hands out in front of him, laughing all the way down: 'Justin was always so upbeat and playful; it was hard to tell he ever spent an unhappy day in his entire life.' And he valued the mentoring, believing it helped him enjoy a successful career with the police. When he graduated from the police academy he was proud to invite Justin to join his family at the ceremony: 'He had the biggest smile that day, because he had witnessed all of his hard work put into action, not in football but in police work.'

In April Justin was back in England for the 1987 PFA annual dinner and awards ceremony. It was held at the Grosvenor House Hotel in London's Park Lane and he attended with his brothers, John and Phillip. There he was forcefully reminded that the question of his sexual orientation could arouse strong feelings. He told *The Sun* what happened: 'I knew Simon Stainrod of QPR had been saying things behind my back. I heard that he was calling me a poof, or a fag or whatever, the usual stuff. At this dinner John stood up in front of everyone and yelled across to Stainrod: "Now tell us in the open what you have been saying about Justin behind his back". The guy was taken back, lost for words. He certainly wasn't prepared to start calling me names there and then.'

John gave a different version to Matt Allen, author of a book about Wimbledon Football Club, *The Crazy Gang*. He told him: 'I was so mad that he could insult Justin and my family that I took it really personally.' John said he followed Stainrod to the toilets and was about to attack him when Justin arrived on the scene: 'He flashed me a look as if to say, "Don't be stupid, John. Don't even think about it".' Either way, there was clearly a confrontation and Justin witnessed how offended John was by the accusation that he, Justin, was gay. Telling John it was true must have seemed more difficult than ever.

Back in LA, Justin was ready to step up his rehab by arranging to play for Autobahn, a part-time team in the San Fernando Valley's Budweiser International League. He played 20 matches that summer and although limited by his tender knee, he told the

The Biography

Los Angeles Times, he was hooked again. He became a good friend of Autobahn's goalkeeper Bob Ammann, even more so when Ammann picked up an injury and joined him for rehab at the Kerlan-Jobe Clinic. Ammann's ambition was to play in Europe and, impressed by his talent, Fashanu resolved to help him. With Fashanu hoping to revive his own career in England, both had the incentive to put in extra training together. Talking to the *Los Angeles Times*, Ammann described Fashanu as his coach and training partner, adding 'but more importantly he's my friend. That's the best part of it'.

Dr Tibone was certainly right about the amount of rehab Justin needed as he worked through the winter of 1987–88 but by the spring of 1988 he was ready to play football at a higher level. He signed for Los Angeles Heat as a player and assistant coach, bringing Bob Ammann with him. At the time there was no national outdoor league in the USA. The Heat were a semi-professional team playing in the Western Soccer Alliance; six teams along the Pacific Coast, from Seattle Storm in the north to San Diego Nomads in the south. Fashanu made quite an impact, scoring five goals in 15 appearances and being selected for the All-Star team from the Western Soccer Alliance at the end of the season, the Heat finishing fourth but winning more games than they lost. One goal in particular caught the imagination of the *Los Angeles Times* reporter who described it as 'a clue to Fashanu's past glories and possibly his future'. 'Fashanu', he wrote, 'took a long pass from Steve Sharp at midfield, galloped past defender, Jeff Stock, one-on-one and volleyed a rocket into the Seattle net from 20 yards out'.

He exerted an influence on the other players, on and off the pitch, as described by Billy Thompson, a talented young midfield player who was selected for the USA national team that season: 'Justin is very critical. He's European and that's the European way. It's kind of tough for a lot of players because they're not used to that. A lot of American players try to get away with doing what they think is right. Justin just won't accept that. He'll stop play and tell you. But as long as you realise he's just trying to make you a better player and don't take it personally, you'll be all right.'

Fashanu's season finished on a high note with the Heat beating the California Kickers 3–0 at home. The *Los Angeles Times* reported: 'Sunday's Warrior Stadium crowd was happy when Fashanu, the darling of the Heat's supporters, announced after the game that he would return next summer to resume his position as co-coach and forward. The fans had raised a chant of 'Just-in, Just-in' after two goals by the charismatic striker.' Head coach, John Britton, gave his verdict: 'Right now, everybody, including Justin, is gung-ho on his coming back. Of course, English clubs are interested. He showed pure professionalism this year. His vision on the field and his passing were uncanny. And he showed that he's able to play 90 minutes again.' It was beginning to look realistic for Justin to play in England over the winter and return the following spring.

Justin was enjoying life in LA. Looking back on his time there he told *Guardian* journalist, Cynthia Bateman: 'I was driving a five-litre Mustang Convertible with car phone, meeting all the right people and going to all the right places.' He became friends with Rod Stewart, himself a talented footballer who was once an apprentice with Brentford FC. Neil Slawson remembers gong shopping with Justin for a birthday present for him. They were wondering what they could possibly buy that he did not already have and then Justin came up with an idea: 'He was so pleased with himself when he decided to give him a Bible!', recalls Slawson. 'I looked at him out of one eye and said, "Ehhhh, are you sure?" He was truly proud of his gift selection and off to the party he went. When Justin came home I asked him how the gift went over, with the likes of George Michael and members of Duran Duran present. He chuckled and said, with a cheeky grin, "Not well I'm afraid". He described an uncomfortable silence over the room when it was revealed that Justin might be inferring that Rod needed to be saved. Justin later found the incident quite amusing, still pleased with his gift choice.'

Justin had evidently found a way of reconciling his Christianity with his materialistic lifestyle. 'God has always allowed me to live with style and panache', he told Bateman. While Justin was in LA Neil Slawson tried to help him to find the kind of church he liked: 'He kept looking for one which made him happy as he didn't want to attend a church where they looked or acted like "mummies"; he wanted a rocking, musical church with gospel singers.' On one occasion they went to a predominantly black church, their visit ending with Justin in conflict with an usher: 'Justin was approached by a very large muscular usher who told him to spit out his gum. Also when Justin saw that they had a gift shop inside the worship hall, he wanted to leave during the message. He was stopped by another very large usher who told him to go sit back down until the service was over as it would cause a distraction with the door opening and the light shining in from the hallway. It became quite a stand-off and Justin wasn't having it. I convinced him to come and sit back down on the nearest pew to the door until we could leave without incident. He was outraged by the conduct at that church.

Justin found the heavier side of US and LA life difficult to deal with. He sometimes accompanied Neil Slawson in his patrol car and Neil remembers that he 'couldn't believe how fast paced and dangerous our policing was here in the US – a bit more aggressive, I'm sure, compared to in the UK with the average bobby not carrying a weapon'. He was shocked by the suffering he witnessed: 'Justin was amazed at how "hard" the streets were here in the United States and always seemed to have such a look of concern on his face on certain calls for service, like he wanted to jump in and help the families in distress but understood now he was in my world and had to be the one to take a back seat and learn.'

Fashanu saw great opportunities opening up in US soccer. The USA had just won the right to stage the 1994 World Cup and one of the conditions was the formation of a national league. As someone who always wanted to do more than just play the game, he told the *Los Angeles Times*: 'The opportunities are vast in America for an individual who wants to work hard for an honest, professional program. On the other hand, a virtual fortune awaits me in England.' There were other attractions about the USA. It was not so unusual to be a black sportsman and a born-again Christian, and he was not tainted by his failure at Nottingham Forest. In fact, there was scope for a little reinvention. In his interviews with the North American press Justin claimed at various times to have played in the First Division for 10 years and to have won three international caps. It was more like the career he wished he had had or the career his brother was having. In those pre-internet days he could get away with these embellishments and no great harm was done. But he was setting himself up for some miscalculations when lying would get him into deep trouble on more than one occasion.

As for that fortune awaiting Justin in England, the man who signed him for Brighton, Chris Cattlin, was more realistic about his prospects: 'Since he's been overseas he's become a bit of a forgotten man. But if he comes back, he'll be judged on his merits.' Mel Machin was reminded of Justin when the *News of the World* sent out a reporter to write a story on his attempted comeback. Machin had been the reserve team coach when Fashanu was at Norwich and was the third man from that group of Norwich staff to manage Manchester City in the 1980s, after John Bond and John Benson. He contacted Justin and offered him a trial.

As the Heat's season wound up in July, Justin knew he still had work to do before he was ready for that trial. With the Canadian season extending to October, he headed north, to Edmonton, capital of the province of Alberta and home to soccer club, Edmonton Brickmen. The Brick Men were playing in the four-team Western Division of the Canadian Soccer League, and struggling. Fashanu was a welcome presence in the squad and, after one match, was appointed co-coach. All was going well as he scored five goals in 12 games but then, once more, Justin's knee was playing up, this time from a build-up of scar tissue. It was a major set back as he underwent surgery in Edmonton with Dr David Reid. During his surgery he picked up an infection and required two more operations.

* * *

It was not until after Christmas that Justin felt able to take up Machin's offer. Manchester City had spent the 1980s yo-yoing between the top two divisions and, when Justin arrived, were pushing for promotion from the Second Division. The *Manchester Evening News* announced his arrival with the headline, 'Thanks a Million', a reference to the club getting a player for free they had offered £1 million for when he was at Norwich. Justin told the paper he had made a mistake joining Nottingham Forest instead of City. He insisted his knee problem had disappeared completely. Mel Machin said: 'He is quick and good in the air as well as possessing the attacking aggression we so desperately need. He went into the wilderness for a while but I know he has class and quality and he could well provide the answer up front for us.'

Fashanu's first match was for the reserves against local rivals Manchester United on 3 January 1989. He got off to a great start, scoring with a header after 12 minutes, City winning 4–3. He was bursting with optimism after the game: 'This is just the start for me. The best is yet to come. I need at least two or three more games before I'm fully fit. I couldn't have had a better beginning with that early goal. It was just like old times. But I feel I have a lot to offer City in the future.' After another reserve match he declared himself ready for League football. But he was not fit enough, Machin knew it and Fashanu later admitted he had known it. Machin terminated his trial period after just three weeks.

Fashanu was still in demand in North America. Edmonton Brickmen president, Mel Kowalchuk, had been so impressed with him that he offered him the roles of player and head coach. The contract would be for two years at a rumoured 40,000 Canadian dollars a year. The money would be welcome. Medical bills and extravagant living had severely depleted Fashanu's funds. It was with the Brick Men rather than Los Angeles Heat that the 28-year-old signed up for the 1989 season, starting in May. In many respects, it proved to be one of the most satisfying seasons of his career. True, he was playing in front of crowds of only three to four thousand, in a stadium one report described as 'dilapidated', in a city whose sporting public was more interested in the Edmonton Oilers ice hockey team. But he played to a high standard, his knee lasted through the season and his coaching improved the performance of the team.

The Biography

One highlight was the 7–3 defeat of Winnipeg Fury in which he scored a hat-trick, his first three-goal return since the beginning of the 1980 season. A few weeks later he went one better, with four goals in a 5–3 win over Victoria Vistas, the Brick Men recovering from going 0–2 down. Justin's former fiancée, Julie Arthurton, was there supporting him and the *Edmonton Journal* reported that she modestly brushed aside any speculation that her presence was a factor. Justin introduced her to journalist, Joanne Ireland, as his girlfriend. Fashanu scored in an away defeat of Winnipeg in front of their record crowd of 10,109, which would have been a decent attendance at Notts County's Meadow Lane stadium. He even revived memories of earlier in his career by getting sent off. The *Edmonton Journal* reported: 'Fashanu – intelligent, co-operative, charming, talented and (usually!) disciplined – shattered the cardinal rule in his personal collection of coaching clichés. He lost his temper, kicked an opponent, got an early shower – and hurt the team.'

His role as head coach went way beyond coaching the players. He was more like a manager in British football; a big challenge for one so young. He explained: 'One of the things that attracted me here was that Mel was very keen on me being involved with the administrative work – how a club runs, from the finances to the PR to the players.' One July day, reporter, Ray Turchansky, caught up with Justin as he was out promoting the Brick Men. It was the annual Klondike Days parade, fair and exhibition (named after the Klondike Gold Rush). Justin had thrown himself into the event and was judging tray-carrying races in the 'Hotel Olympics' before getting ready to play ice hockey for the first time. Turchansky wrote: 'What counts is that Fashanu is out there selling soccer.'

The Brick Men enjoyed a successful season, finishing second in a five-team division before losing out in the play-offs for the Championship. Fashanu was second highest scorer in the division with 19 goals from 26 games. He was chosen for the All-Star Team of players from both the Western and Eastern Divisions of the Canadian Soccer League and as the League's most valuable player. Most importantly his knee had stood up well. He could return to England with more confidence this time.

Justin's experience as coach was more mixed. He had improved the team but was frustrated with the internal politics and the attitudes of his players. An organisation, The Friends of Soccer in Northern Alberta, had been set up to establish a grassroots connection with the Brick Men. There were positives – it secured a government grant to cover some of the club's costs, and provided volunteers to staff the stadium on match days. But Fashanu had to endure constant criticism for not including enough local players in the team including one whose parents were on the board. His frustrations with the players stemmed from what he saw as their lack of professionalism, 'the lack of willingness to commit, the physical, mental and social sacrifices that need to be made to make us a very competitive franchise'. The club was being sold, Mel Kowalchuk was leaving. Despite his positive contribution to the Brick Men, Fashanu was not expected to take up the second year of his contract.

In October 1989 he returned to Manchester City for another trial. He knew he was fitter and more ready than on the previous occasion but Mel Machin was not hopeful. His team had won promotion to the First Division and had better players. He had signed striker, Clive Allen, for £1 million. He admitted later: 'I really only agreed to let him come back again out of sympathy. I didn't really believe that it would work for him.' It took just two weeks for Machin to change his mind. Fashanu's first match was a reserve fixture against his old team, Notts County. He lined up alongside Clive Allen, who was coming back from a short-term injury. Between them they took the Notts defence apart, Fashanu scoring three goals and Allen two in a 5–3 win. After another appearance in the reserves, Machin awarded him a two-month contract and included him in the first-team squad to play a home fixture against Aston Villa. Fashanu was not guaranteed to appear on the pitch but his selection was a massive achievement. He had not played in English football for nearly four years and, in the First Division, for nearly six; his last appearance at that level being the fateful match against Ipswich when he injured his knee.

Justin had missed out on what should have been some of the best years of his career but through self-belief, perseverance and, as he saw it, the guiding hand of God, he was back. Anticipating the match he sounded excited, nervous and reflective. He told *The Guardian*: 'The biggest thing to combat is not my fitness but my lack of confidence. I still have fears; I still have doubts.' He added: 'When I get back to the First Division I don't know what my reactions will be. I don't know whether it's the fact that I'm playing or the road getting there that is important. I might probably retire the next day.' Mel Machin was impressed with him: 'He has worked hard and shown the guts and determination in trying to get back that he shows on the field. He is hungry and that is what I want.'

The match was played in front of over 23,000 spectators and the TV cameras. Fashanu was named as a substitute and came on after 70 minutes with City 0–2 down. He was greeted with a chorus of boos from the Aston Villa supporters. No doubt they remembered his confrontations with their defenders over the years. He was unable to influence the result but he had made it back. A few days after the match he spoke to Joanne Ireland at the *Edmonton Journal*, sounding reflective. 'It's not so much that I'm playing [First Division] football again but that I know myself better', he told her: 'I also recognise that I thoroughly enjoy coaching, the teaching aspect, and the next time round, I really think I can do a better job. Maybe I wanted to get back to England so much that I didn't really realise how I felt about things but I've put the ghosts to rest now.' Justin laughed when he caught himself asking her for news of 'home', meaning Canada. But the truth was he did not have a home. Once he left Los Angeles Justin seldom stayed in one place for more than a few months.

Justin had good reason not to sound too triumphant about his return to football at the top level. After the Aston Villa game the *Manchester Evening News* reported that he was 'clearly not ready for regular football', and he had picked up a minor hamstring strain during the match. It was a typical story of catch-22 for any player coming back after a long time out of the game at the top level. The only way to get 'match fit' is by playing regularly but in trying to earn a place in the team he strains his body and picks up fresh injuries. Back in the reserves, another hat-trick failed to convince Machin, though Fashanu was attracting the attention of other clubs. There was one more first team appearance as a substitute, in a 0-6 defeat at Derby. Manchester City were struggling and Machin did not see Fashanu helping the team. Half way through his two-month contract Fashanu was told he could leave.

*   *   *

Professional footballers are rarely sentimental about the clubs they play for, sometimes enraging supporters by signing for close rivals who offer more money or a better chance of winning trophies. Even so, Fashanu's trip to Second Division Ipswich to discuss a possible deal must have stirred up a few feelings in him. His games against them for Norwich were always played in a heated atmosphere, with a fair amount of racist barracking coming his way. Then there was the bust-up with Brian Clough which signalled the end of his career with Nottingham Forest and it was at Ipswich where he picked up the serious knee injury which still threatened to wreck his career in English football. His negotiations with manager, John Duncan, were to result in another unfortunate Ipswich episode.

Fashanu's agents were the World Sports Organisation, headed by a controversial character, Ambrose Mendy. A black man from an impoverished background in London's East End he had made a fortune in business, including sport, owning a Rolls-Royce when he was 19. He was perhaps best known for managing the careers of two other black men from the East End, footballer Paul Ince and Ince's cousin, boxer, Nigel Benn. Mendy had been imprisoned for fraud and was soon to be back in prison for a similar offence. He said, of life and business: 'You have to take as much as you can get in this world for as little as you can fairly give.'

Perhaps it was this philosophy which explains why Fashanu demanded a £300,000 signing on fee from Ipswich. Duncan was so outraged at the amount he was expected to pay that he went to the press with the story. Mendy demanded that Duncan be disciplined by the FA for leaking confidential information. The FA was not interested. Mendy insisted the figure was realistic, given that there was no transfer fee involved, but convinced no one. The *Daily Express* headline, '£1m flop Fashanu puts amazing price on his soccer comeback deal', was a cruel reminder to Justin of his reputation in England.

Having blown his chances with Ipswich, Fashanu signed a deal with another Second Division team. West Ham United, an east London club, took up the remaining month of his contract with Manchester City. West Ham were managed by Lou Macari who wrote of Justin, in his autobiography: 'He was a nice lad. I wanted to give him the chance to resurrect his career.' He told local paper, the *Newham and Docklands Recorder*: 'We need height and power in attack and we hope he can provide that.'

After a brief appearance for the reserves, Fashanu was selected for the squad to face Wimbledon in a home League Cup tie. Expecting to play against his brother for the first time in a competitive match, Justin told the paper: 'I love him to bits but we're both very passionate when it comes to playing football and I'm sure we'll each be doing what we can to help our teams win on the night.' In fact, John missed the game and perhaps it was just as well. It is mainly remembered for a punch-up between the players and the Fashanus might have found themselves torn between brotherly love and their commitment to defend their teammates. Justin came on with the score 0–0 and helped West Ham to a 1–0 win.

For the next match he travelled with the team to Blackburn, staying in a hotel the night before the game. Some players had realised Justin was gay and decided to play a prank on their mate, Mark Ward. He arrived later than the others having attended a funeral. When he checked in he was shocked to be told he was sharing a room with Fashanu instead of his usual roommate, Julian Dicks. In his autobiography Ward recounts (asterisks included): 'I left the key on the reception desk and started to pace up and down looking for help. Being asleep in the bed next to Justin? No f*****g way! I was panicking now, and started to hunt for someone to talk to – where the f*** was Alvin? He would sort it out. Just at that moment I heard lots of sniggering. I turned the corner and there, p*****g themselves laughing, were Alvin, Galey and Dicksy. [Alvin Martin, Tony Gale and Julian Dicks.] It was a good set-up and I was so relieved to hear that Justin was rooming on his own that night.'

The Biography

It is easy to see an incident such as this as a blatant example of homophobia and it may well be. Certainly Ward's open and unapologetic description of his own fear encourages that view. But Ward, not Fashanu, was the target for this prank. He was being teased for being homophonic rather than Fashanu being teased for being gay.

After Justin came out, one coach used the example of players joking about who was going to share a room with him as an indication of him being accepted. Justin may not have seen it that way, of course. But given the tensions were there, this sort of joking might have been the best way to dispel them, and appearing to take it 'in the right spirit' the price Justin paid to be accepted as 'one of the lads'. Assessing Justin's experience of being a gay footballer is sometimes clear cut, as with Brian Clough's bullying. But sometimes it hinges on interpretation of jokes and banter which may sound offensive when described but be intended to signal acceptance, depending on the subtleties of relationships, body language and tone of voice.

Fashanu played for the entire match against Blackburn, a 4–5 defeat, and for 65 minutes against Stoke City. But his hamstring injury was preventing him from training and, once again, not fully fit he was unable to prove his worth. Perhaps harshly, Macari also questioned his attitude. Macari and Fashanu were both staying in a hotel in Waltham Abbey, on the outer fringes of London, Macari being new to the West Ham job. He was unimpressed when, one evening, he asked for Fashanu at reception only to find he was out at The Embassy, a nightclub in central London popular with footballers. In his autobiography he admits Fashanu was not a drinker, and that he was polite and apologetic when challenged over it, explaining he had gone out because he was bored. But Macari still was not satisfied: 'It was not the best start for a bloke supposedly trying to restart his career. If I were fighting for mine I'd put off London for a few weeks until I got myself established.'

After leaving West Ham, Justin was back at Ipswich, presumably having made his peace with the manager. It was February 1990 when he turned out for the reserve team but that was as far as it went. Running out of options for his client, Ambrose Mendy approached Frank Clark, the manager of Third Division Leyton Orient. Clark knew Fashanu from his time as reserve team coach at Nottingham Forest and decided to offer him a short-term contract. They paid a lot of money for such a small club, Clarke hoping his reputation would bring in more spectators. With crowds averaging less than 4,500, Orient's fan base was not much bigger than the Brick Men's. The club was just a few miles from West Ham and the nearest professional club to Justin's birthplace in Hackney, and it was to Hackney that he moved, renting a flat. Justin signed up soon after his 29th birthday to a club at the lowest level he had played in England. Clark welcomed his arrival, telling the local paper: 'He has a lot of experience and could still be set for greater things.' But once again he was hampered by fitness problems, being restricted to coming off the substitutes' bench for his first two appearances.

Soon after moving to Hackney, Justin met Matthew Hodson, an occasion which highlighted the conflict he felt between his sexuality and his religious beliefs. They met at a gay bar, The London Apprentice. Matthew remembers it as being 'quite masculine' then, the sort of place where the men would be wearing white t-shirts, jeans and leather jackets. He was 22, 'looking cute'. He remembers Justin as 'very striking, tall and handsome'. Justin introduced himself. Matthew did not follow football but had heard of John and asked if they were related, to which Justin replied with his usual good grace, explaining his relationship with John. They went back to Justin's flat and Justin asked Matthew if he would like to listen to some music. But it turned out the only music he had was 'clappy Christian music' which Matthew describes as 'terrible' and 'not conducive to sex'.

They ended up talking about sex and religion. Matthew's parents were liberal Anglicans and he was interested in religion. He gave his view on Christianity and homosexuality in an interview with the magazine, *Boyz*: 'I was raised as a Christian…and still find much to admire in the teaching of Jesus, from a political and social perspective. Despite those Christians who seem to obsess about what us gays do in private, there's no record of Jesus saying anything about homosexuality. He had plenty to say about how wrong it is to charge interest on loans, and yet I've never seen Christians protesting against credit cards.' Justin's view was different. He told Matthew that God had made him gay to test him. He failed the test that night. Matthew found Justin 'charming and friendly'. The next morning they went to a nearby café, Justin tucking in to a full English breakfast.

Frank Clark and his physiotherapist, Billy Saunders, realised Justin was gay. Clark told www.tacklemedia.co.uk they were close to him and tried to persuade him to come out, feeling it would be better for him, especially as he was so scared about it leaking out. Clark's view was that there would be headlines but they would disappear. He was sure it would not be a problem in the dressing room – 'the lads thought the world of him'. But Justin was 'terrified' and would not do it. Of course, for him it was not just about coming out in the world of football but the possible reactions of friends and family and, perhaps most of all, his fellow Christians which scared him.

Fashanu's full debut for Orient was away to Tranmere, a match they lost 0–1. According to *The Times* report: 'There were times…when his contributions were too sophisticated for friend and foe alike.' Clark's assessment of his performances for

Orient is less flattering: 'The problem we had was that he wasn't a footballer, he was a battering ram. He was powerful and a good footballer in that sense but he didn't have a lot of skill.' Clark felt he was never the same footballer as before his injury: 'He wanted to play standing still but he wasn't good enough and we weren't good enough as a team.' Nor did he bring in any extra spectators. After two more goalless appearances Justin was dropped from the team. In six months of attempts to resume his football career in England Justin had enjoyed the highpoint of turning out for Manchester City in the First Division followed by a downward slide to being dropped by a Third Division team.

* * *

His prospects in Canadian soccer were not looking too good either. Under the rules of the Canadian Soccer League, players could be traded between clubs without having any say in which team they ended up. The new owners of Edmonton Brickmen decided that rather than have one star player in Fashanu they needed to strengthen the whole squad. In February, in a complicated three-way deal also involving Toronto Blizzard, Fashanu ended up with Hamilton Steelers. He was not pleased. The Steeler's owner, Mario DiBartolomeo, had a reputation as a volatile character with a tendency to lambast his staff and players in public. Despite Fashanu's previous success as a coach with the Brick Men, DiBartolomeo insisted he had acquired him for the Steelers as a player only. Fashanu threatened to stay away. If he sat out the season he would become a free agent. The stalemate lasted through March but, as Fashanu's Leyton Orient career subsided, he needed to play football somewhere.

In April, he flew to Hamilton to negotiate with DiBartolomeo. It took these two strong-willed characters three days to agree a deal and it was concluded in Fashanu's favour. He was made player-coach and, the *Edmonton Journal* reported, he was given assurances he would have control of the team on the field and DiBartolomeo would not continue his tirades. Fashanu agreed with Leyton Orient to terminate his contract to take up his duties with the Steelers. At least he was joining a strong team. The Steelers had won the Eastern Division the previous season. Making the most of the situation he found himself in, Justin told the *Hamilton Spectator*: 'I feel that this is possibly the best decision I've made in soccer outside England. I'm looking forward to working with the calibre of players we have here.' His truce with DiBartolomeo lasted eight games of which the Steelers won three and lost three. Fashanu then claimed they had agreed he should step down as coach, but DiBartolomeo announced he had been fired. After Fashanu failed to show up for the next match DiBartolomeo fined him 25,000 Canadian dollars and suspended him indefinitely.

During his enforced break Justin visited London, staying with John and his family in their Maida Vale flat. He had become a good friend of John's partner, Maria Sol, and adored his niece, Amal, who was just under two years old. It should have been an enjoyable stay but he found himself walking into a family row. Maria Sol had suspected John of having affairs for a couple of years. One had been reported in the tabloid press. The evening before Wimbledon's Cup Final appearance in 1988 a journalist from the *News of the World* approached John, saying his paper would be carrying a story about him cheating on his partner and asked for a comment. John was so furious he punched the door of his hotel room, seriously injuring his hand. There were fears it was broken and he would miss the most important match of his career and of Wimbledon's history but the club physiotherapist was able to bandage it up and declare him fit to play.

When Maria Sol challenged John with her suspicions that he was having relationships with other women he denied it. But just prior to Justin's visit, she had obtained proof of him having an affair with a woman she regarded as a friend. She decided to confront John and asked Justin to back her up. John insisted Justin should leave but Justin refused. Maria Sol made her allegations with Justin still present and then demanded that John left the flat. Later another row erupted. Justin had taken Maria Sol and Amal out in John's car and bumped into him outside the flat. John was furious to see Justin driving his partner and child around in his car, and staying in his flat when he had been thrown out.

After a month Justin was back with Hamilton, as a player only. DiBartolomeo had got his way. He played out the season determined it would be his last in Canada. He told the press: 'When the negatives outweigh the positives it's time to leave.' The Steelers finished third in the seven-team Eastern Division, won the play-offs for that Division and met Vancouver 86ers in the CSL Final where they were well beaten. Fashanu announced his plans. He would make a last attempt at a comeback in England. If it did not work out he would go into coaching but 'in a country where soccer is a predominant sport'. He had had enough of Canadian soccer. Eventually he would succeed in playing in England but not before enduring one of the most difficult years of his life.

Chapter 10

Coming Out

It was October 1990 when Justin received the phone call he had dreaded for nearly 10 years. A British Sunday newspaper had obtained compromising pictures of him in a gay bar and was going to run an article the following week.

In a panic he called John's agent, Eric Hall. He was a good choice. For a start he was relaxed about homosexuality. Before becoming an agent for footballers Hall had worked in the music industry. He had been a record promoter for Queen and a close friend of Freddie Mercury. Hall claims, in his autobiography, that Mercury had been in love with him and wrote the song, *Killer Queen*, out of frustration he could not have a sexual relationship with him.

He was also expert at handling the media. He knew the story could not be stopped but they could render it irrelevant by offering an exclusive interview to a daily paper which could be published before the Sunday paper's story, a practice known in the newspaper industry as a spoiler. It was damage limitation. Justin sexuality would still become public knowledge but at least he would have control over the content. There would also be the compensation of a fat fee. Hall persuaded Kelvin MacKenzie, editor of *The Sun* to part with £100,000. It says much for the British public's seemingly insatiable appetite for sexual gossip that the revelations of a footballer who had played only a handful of games in England in the previous five years could command such a fee.

But what also sold the story was the Fashanu name. John had become one of the best known footballers in Britain. His team, Wimbledon, had made a big impact on the First Division. Having been promoted in 1986, they finished sixth in their first season and stayed in the First Division for 14 years. Their greatest achievement was winning the FA Cup, beating Liverpool in the 1988 Final. The name, Wimbledon, might be associated with a leafy London suburb, strawberries, cream and lawn tennis but the reputation of the football club could hardly have been a bigger contrast. Relishing their underdog status and popularly known as the Crazy Gang, the team employed a style of play which was based on physically intimidating the opposition and getting the ball into their opponents' penalty area by the most direct means possible. There John Fashanu, Fash the Bash, would scrap for the ball to create scoring chances for himself or a teammate.

John was not all elbows and aggression and such was his effectiveness and goalscoring ability he was twice picked for the England international team in 1989. But his reputation was not confined to football. John had become a successful businessman, trading with Nigeria. He was a wealthy man. But he had also, through charity work, networking and prodigious energy become a prominent member of Britain's black community.

John still did not know Justin was gay. Rather than wait for him to find out through *The Sun*, Justin broke the news himself. John was appalled. He rang Eric Hall. In Hall's account of the incident John says: 'Can you imagine what it will be like for me when the fans read that my brother is gay? They'll give me hell.' Hall was not impressed by what he saw as John's selfish attitude and refused to answer his question about what Justin was being paid by *The Sun*. John found out from Justin and phoned Hall back, saying that if he pulled the story he would pay Justin the fee himself. Eric Hall had to explain that he had signed a contract with *The Sun* and, anyway, if *The Sun* did not run the story the Sunday paper would. But John was not listening. He told Hall that if the story appeared he would never work with him again, and kept to his word.

The Sun's fee was money Justin desperately needed to support his extravagant lifestyle. Since leaving Brighton his earnings had been sporadic and with the end of the Canadian soccer season he was facing a winter of unemployment. Finding himself in a situation not of his choosing, Justin was determined to extract as much financial reward from it as he could. *The Sun*'s New York correspondent, Allan Hall, met him at Toronto airport. Hall later accused Fashanu of borrowing his company phone credit card, noting down the 14 digit code and using it himself, running up a bill of £11,000 on Hall's account. When it comes to Justin Fashanu and *The Sun* it is difficult to figure out the truth. But when they arrived in London Justin definitely insisted on being put up in the smart and expensive Waldorf Hotel.

Determined to get value for its money, *The Sun* planned to run Justin's story over four days. But as Allan Hall worked with him on the story it became apparent there was not sufficient material. They resorted to regurgitating anecdotes about his football career. Realising *The Sun*'s readers may not be enthralled by tales of dressing room rows with John Bond, they started making things up.

*   *   *

The Sun was Britain's best selling newspaper, producing nearly four million copies a day. On Monday 22 October 1990 its readers were greeted with a headline which took up around half the front page: '£1m Soccer Star: I am Gay', the word Gay in letters three inches high. Following in much smaller letters was, 'Justin Fashanu confesses'. A photograph showed him outside the Houses of Parliament with Big Ben in the background. The caption was, 'Justin…Commons romps with MP'. Under the masthead, in small print, were the words, 'Thought: Justin Fashan-ooh'.

The story began: 'Soccer star Justin Fashanu confessed last night: "I'm gay – and I want everyone to know it".' It went on to report that Justin wanted to stop 'living a lie' and that he could not get back into top class soccer with it hanging over him. Justin said: 'It's taken a lot of soul searching to come to this but with God's help I know I've made the right decision.' News of John's horror at his brother's revelations was emerging and was included in the front page story. He disagreed that coming out would help Justin's career, claiming, instead, that he had wrecked his chances of a comeback, and 'no football club will take him now'. But he was still preoccupied with his own welfare, saying: 'One thing I don't want is newspaper boards all over the place with headlines saying 'Fashanu is gay' – because people might think it's me.'

The main centre page headline was, 'I Cheated on My Girl to Go Out with Men' with a second headline, 'I Found God in a Garage'. Past the front page hype and attention-grabbing headlines, what followed was an engaging, unsensational and reasonably truthful account of Justin's life as a gay man, including his visits to Part II, first with Julie and then on his own. Julie Arthurton had been contacted for a quote and refused to play the role of woman betrayed. She told *The Sun*: 'I still love Justin. He's a nice person and we're still friends.' Talking about the difficulties of being a gay professional footballer, Justin gave his versions of the incidents involving Pedro Richards and Simon Stainrod.

Justin told the story of meeting with Terry Carpenter to pick up his car and becoming a born-again Christian. *The Sun* reported: 'Mr Carpenter, 46, last night said Justin was letting down his religion: "He did not confess his homosexuality to me. If he has not kicked the gay habit, I think he needs to. I would like to talk to him again."' Justin confessed: 'I know that homosexuality is not right – not in the Bible anyway. I struggled with it and still do.' Readers disappointed with the absence of scandalous gossip were promised, 'Tomorrow: I slept with a married MP'.

In Tuesday's paper Justin claimed to have met a Conservative MP, who was married with a family, in the nightclub, Heaven. Justin said he had slept with him once and then 'resisted the sexual side'. He told a story of the MP taking him to the House of Commons where he sat on the Speaker's Chair, an act which, according to this story, nearly resulted in Margaret Thatcher sacking the MP. He also claimed to have had sex with 'someone in the pop scene' and another footballer when he was with Manchester City. Other stories were about meeting Peter Tatchell, and enjoying the gay scene in Brighton.

Wednesday's headline was: 'Clough told me to see a shrink'. Justin told the story of his rows with Brian Clough and said: 'I wish he had given me some advice. About the only time he did, he suggested I went to visit a psychiatrist. I honestly thought about it a few times.' There were accounts of his visits to Broadmoor hospital to see Ronnie Kray and crashing his car when leaving Parkhurst prison.

On Thursday the headline was, '"I'll have to quit Britain". That's what our kid John said when I told him I was gay'. In his response to John's comments, Justin said: 'I love my brother deeply, but along the way we have had countless bust-ups and fights. I don't think I'm being selfish when I say John is not the major issue here. He is not the child in the street with the dilemma about his or her sexuality.' He added: 'My sexuality is reality and, to be honest, I'm now asexual.' It was the first of a number of comments he would make over the next few years which downplayed his sexual relationships with men. On other occasions he spoke of being bisexual, claimed to be in a heterosexual relationship, and spoke of getting married and having children. This last instalment in *The Sun* petered out in an account of Justin's row with John Bond after headbutting Bristol City's David Rodgers.

*   *   *

The Biography

After these revelations little was heard from Justin for several months. No doubt his contract with *The Sun* prevented him from speaking publicly, a restriction which did not apply to John. The following Saturday Wimbledon were due to play away to their local rivals, Crystal Palace, and before the game John was interviewed for the TV programme, *Football Focus*. Speaking of Justin, he said: 'He's come out publicly and said his sexual preferences. You know, every footballer doesn't come out and say they like women or like men. That's no one else's business. So now he will have to suffer the consequences.' Then it got more personal: 'I wouldn't like to play or even get changed in the vicinity of it. That's just the way I feel. So, if I'm like that, I'm sure the rest of football is like that.'

John had been right in predicting to *The Sun* that he would be on the receiving end of homophobic abuse. The *Daily Mirror* reported that he: '…endured the roughest of rides from rival fans in his team's 4–3 defeat at Palace. They jeered and cat-called him mercilessly throughout the whole 90 minutes, every time he touched the ball or was involved in the action.' This may well have been the first instance of football supporters subjecting a player to abuse of this nature and, bizarrely, it was aimed at someone who they had no reason to think was gay. But John may well have brought it upon himself. He liked to portray an image of being, mentally and physically, the toughest player around but he had betrayed a weakness. He was scared people would think he was gay. No wonder some of the Crystal Palace fans latched onto it. The preoccupation of the more aggressive fans of any club is to wind up the opposition and, for some of them, getting to air their prejudices from the safety of a crowd is a bonus. John Fashanu's Wimbledon colleagues seemed to be experiencing their own form of homophobia that day. A fan remembers John scoring a goal and celebrating by pumping his fist into the air. His teammates, rather than running up and hugging him like they would normally, just shook him by the hand.

Sunday saw Marilyn Powell's revelations in the *News of the World* in which she linked Justin with her husband Tony. In *The People*, columnist John Smith had some strong words. It was this paper, under its former name the *Sunday People*, Justin had sued for libel in 1982 after it reported rumours he was gay. Smith wrote: 'I don't doubt that Joystick Justin received a substantial fee for finally coming out of the closet. But before this two-faced tittle-tattler starts congratulating himself on a healthy bank balance I should warn him that we plan to take steps to ensure he returns every penny of the cash he screwed out of *The People*.' Potentially Justin faced not only having to return the cash but, much worse, being charged with perjury but nothing more was heard of Smith's threat.

There was a marked absence of positive comment in the media and it certainly was not provided by weekly paper, *The Voice*. It was a paper specifically for and about black British people, their lives and their struggles. With a reputation for challenging mistreatment, especially of black people at the hands of the police, it was known for standing up for people's rights. But on this occasion it turned on a member of the community it claimed to represent. The first edition after *The Sun* articles led with the main headline, 'John Fashanu: "My Gay Brother is an Outcast" Voice Exclusive'. John was on a verbal rampage. But this was just one of five articles in this one edition in which Justin was attacked.

Justin had not done himself any favours by selling his story to *The Sun*, a paper widely seen as racist; its inclusion of concocted stories about Labour, 'loony left', local councils and their antiracist policies, intended to make them look ridiculous, being just one example. Though much of the content of his coming out story was genuine, engaging and nuanced, the tacky headlines, unconvincing gossip and general nature of the paper it appeared in gave critics scope for having a go at him.

The Voice editorial column was headed, 'Soccer Star's Own Goal'. It began with his £1 million transfer, praising him for showing black people in sport they could make it to the top. Then it put the boot in. Justin was accused of letting his family and 'the community' down with his 'tawdry revelation'. It took the line that his sexuality was his business but if he was going to come out he should not have done so by 'selling his soul to the highest bidder'. It finished with this resounding condemnation: 'Telling the world you're gay is one thing but claiming that your conscience and your faith in God led to the publication of such revelations is pathetic and unforgiveable.'

The religious theme was taken up by Christian columnist, Marcia Dixon. The headline for her column was, 'Why Justin's Story Should Sadden Us All'. She said his story was shocking because he had been a high-profile Christian but his Christianity had had no effect on his conduct. He has not completely accepted God, she wrote, and 'belongs to Satan'. Of course not all Christians take that line. For instance speaking about Christian attitudes towards homosexuality, Archbishop Desmond Tutu told the USA magazine, *Time*: 'For me there doesn't seem to be a difference at all with how I felt when people were being clobbered for something about which they could do nothing – their race. I can't believe that the Jesus Christ I worship would be on the side of those who persecute an already persecuted minority.' What Marcia Dixon said was consistent with some Christian beliefs, those associated with the types of churches Justin himself was attracted to. What made her article seem like an attack on Justin was its lack of compassion or perspective.

The Biography

Another *Voice* columnist, Tony Sewell, billed himself as 'the columnist who doesn't give a xxxx what people think'. (The 'x's were his.) His line was that gays were their own worst enemies and: 'We heteros are sick and tired of tortured queens playing hide and seek around their closets.' The next headline was 'Nigerians Shocked Over Soccer Ace's Confessions'. *The Voice* reported the Nigerian High Commissioner in London saying: 'In Nigeria we treat homosexuals with utter contempt.' It told its readers that homosexuality was illegal in Nigeria but no longer punishable by death.

In an article, 'Homophobia and Postcolonialism', on the website www.english-e-corner.com, Mica Hilson puts this sort of attitude in context and warns against, 'Western biases that may depict postcolonial nations as being less advanced and inhumane'. He writes about how it has been argued that colonialism erased many native ways of thinking and it has been suggested that postcolonial people have constructed mythologised depictions of their cultures before colonisation. This may include the idea that homosexuality did not exist in these societies. For example, the psychiatrist and influential writer and thinker on decolonisation, Franz Fanon, developed a theory that homosexuality was a sign of psychological distress exclusive to western peoples.

There is another strand of history which also contributes to the kind of attitude expressed by the Nigerian High Commissioner. Laws against homosexuality were introduced to African countries, and other colonised countries, by the British. As these countries became independent they incorporated them into their own laws. Add in the influence of European-based Christian churches and, arguably, it is homophobia rather than homosexuality that western people introduced to Africa.

Unlike Justin, John had made and maintained links with Nigeria which he saw as important in understanding and connecting with his heritage. He had also embraced the black family of his birth more strongly than Justin. It is significant that when, after Justin's death, he sought to explain why he had made such hostile comments about his brother's sexuality, which he later regretted, he described himself as 'an African man'.

The main headline for the interview with John was, 'Fashanu Family Shocked by Justin's Gay Love Confessions'. This was followed by, 'My Gay Brother has Shamed the Family Name' and 'John Fashanu Blasts His Brother's Public Coming Out'. John said: 'If I saw him now I couldn't be responsible for my actions.' He continued by saying he was bitter Justin did not confide in the family. He claimed he would not have condemned Justin for being gay but Justin had been selfish to 'do it this way to his family and the black community'. He added: 'I have no wish to contact Justin whatever. He is a stranger, an utter stranger. The real Justin Fashanu can walk into my office anytime but this person is not the same person I grew up with.' Finally he brought the argument back to his own position in British society: 'How can I be sitting on the board of the national curriculum with politicians such as Ian McGregor and Angela Rumbold, deciding on the future of school kids when my brother does this to me?' Slipped into the interview was a comment from 'a top British manager' saying no team in Britain would ever sign Justin after these revelations.

*   *   *

The Voice's demolition job on Justin Fashanu's character did not go unnoticed. Nor was it an isolated instance of its hostility to gays and lesbians. The previous week's edition had featured a headline, 'Why Gays and Lesbians aren't Fit to be Parents: Bishop Speaks Out Against Councils Which Allow Homosexuals to Adopt'. Although the article was more balanced than the headline, *The Voice* was getting a reputation for giving space to homophobic rants.

The paper had been somewhat reliant on support from left-wing and publicly funded organisations since it was launched with the help of a grant from the Ken Livingstone-led Greater London Council. Trade Unions advertised for members and employers with equal opportunities policies, such as voluntary sector organisations and Labour-controlled councils, made use of the job opportunities pages. They did not want to be associated with a newspaper perceived to be homophobic and threats were made to withdraw advertising. Gay groups and indignant readers wrote in with complaints and began to organise a boycott.

The Voice was in trouble and reacted quickly to appease its critics. The following week's editorial made no reference to Justin Fashanu but said: 'Black people know only too well what it's like being treated as second class citizens. Unfortunately, the experience of racism has not given us a greater degree of tolerance or understanding when it comes to accepting those who are different from ourselves. The treatment of gays and lesbians within our own community is proof of this. The black community is generally hostile and damning of its gay brothers and sisters, displaying the sort of narrow-minded ignorance we normally associate with bigots and racists.' It concluded: 'Can we morally demand equality and respect if we are denying the same to members of our own community?'

Subsequently *The Voice* included a positive article about black gay men and an apology, of sorts. Printed on the front page it said: '*The Voice* has received a number of complaints from the gay community, who have suggested that our coverage of the recent

The Biography

Justin Fashanu story was irresponsible and gave the impression that *The Voice* is anti-gay. It goes without saying that *The Voice* is opposed to all forms of prejudice against any group in society because of their race, sex, religion or sexual orientation. We have examined our treatment of the story in question and we accept that in some respects it could be interpreted as homophobic. This was not our intention and we therefore regret any offense that may have been caused.' Three months after the Fashanu issue editor, Steve Pope, was replaced. According to *The Guardian*, he left 'under a cloud', following a row over coverage of Justin Fashanu declaring his homosexuality. *The Voice*'s new editor, Winsome-Grace Cornish, went on to develop an editorial policy and code of practice intended to improve coverage of lesbian and gay issues.

The most visible sign of changing attitudes at *The Voice* was the interview with Justin Fashanu in May 1991. The front page headline was, '"The Toughest Time of My Life" Gay Soccer Star Justin Fashanu Speaks Out'. The headline for the centre page spread could not have been a greater contrast to those from the previous October: 'Those Who Say You Can't Be Black, Gay and Proud Are Ignorant'. In the interview Justin talked about the reaction from his family and the frustrations of his football career but spoke most passionately about his struggle to reconcile his sexual orientation with his Christian beliefs.

Justin revealed he was staying with his sister, Dawn, in Hertfordshire. In an article he wrote a couple of years later he called her 'a rock' who was always totally supportive. He said Pearl, who he called his real mother, was cool about it but he had not spoken to his foster mother, Betty Jackson. He felt she needed to make the first step to re-establish contact. He and Phillip had not spoken. Of John he said: 'It's heartache when you have a reaction like that from a brother you love. It would be easy for me to be unforgiving to my brothers, John and Phillip, but I love them.' About the reaction to him coming out, but avoiding referring specifically to *The Voice*, he said: 'I was naïve. I didn't anticipate the ferocity of the attack on me from certain quarters. If I knew what I know now I could have prepared myself better. I am afraid every day, every minute. But when you decide to come out, you have to take on the responsibility.'

In interviews Justin tended to choose his words carefully, being diplomatic and looking for the positives in any situation. Occasionally, though, he let his guard down and was more spontaneous and emotional. There was his outburst when he could see Norwich City were heading towards relegation. He was equally ardent here when talking about his relationship with Christianity. He revealed that he has not entered a church since he came out: 'I haven't wanted to embarrass, or rather put pressure on, the minister and congregation. In the Bible it states that when someone carries on living in sin he should be asked to leave the church and since they may feel I'm living in sin, well…' He talked about how hard it was because he needed to go to church and read the Bible, and he was no longer reading or praying: 'The saddest thing has been the disruption of my relationship with God.' Justin said he has not decided yet if his sexuality was sinful: 'I've read the Bible. I've read it all and don't understand a lot of it. I think that some of its precepts override others and the main things are truth, love and obedience to what you think is true.'

Then he put caution and tact aside: 'I think, basically, that if God wants to deal with me and I go to hell, then at least I can look him in the face and say, 'I didn't pretend to be something I wasn't'. But so many people who are in high-spiritual positions, so many of them are ducking and diving and doing the same things in private. I think we're going to be surprised at some of those who make it through the Pearly Gates. And I think the fair Christian qualities like compassion and kindness have been missing from those who have criticised me the strongest.'

Talking about his future Justin sounded like the teenager he was when journalist, Mick Dennis, described him as more desperate for fame than anyone he had ever come across. If he could not resurrect his football career, Justin told *The Voice*, he may pursue a screen career in the USA: 'Football is a means to an end to me. It was never the whole cake. I'm fiercely ambitious and I want to succeed on a global basis.'

In coming out Justin Fashanu became one of the few openly gay black British public figures and arguably the most visible. His coming out, the coverage in *The Voice*, the campaign against it and the paper's positive response were of great significance to black British gay men and lesbians. For the book, *Stonewall 25: The Making of the Lesbian and Gay Community in Britain*, Olivette Cole Wilson and Clarence Allen wrote: 'Justin Fashanu's decision to come out…brought dramatic change. It highlighted the fact that black gay men exist, something the wider community was loath to recognise; and just as, if not more, important, it showed that gay men exist within the black community. Equally it forced people to realise that not all gay men are effeminate and petite. We are everywhere.'

* * *

Not all gay people were as positive as this about Justin's coming out, because of the way he did it and what he had to say. *The Sun* was loathed by many gay activists. His motivation was open to question, and his guilt and confusion about his sexual identity and religious faith was not the message many wanted to hear.

The Biography

Justin set about explaining himself in a series of interviews and his own contribution to *Stonewall 25*. Wanting to be seen as in control of the situation, he told a story which appeared credible but was some way from the truth. He presented himself as a man who had carefully thought through his decision to come out and his choice of paper. He said he knew a gay teenager in Canada who had been rejected by his family. He became a rent-boy on the streets and ended up killing himself. Justin told *Gay Times*: 'That was when I thought that everybody, especially those with a high profile, should accept the responsibility of being truthful. If more people said, "Now listen, homosexuality is everywhere", then we will be saving lives.' He claimed to have chosen *The Sun* because it was the sort of paper football fans read: 'When I became a million pound player, a born-again Christian or when my problems with Brian Clough happened, it was all depicted in *The Sun*. They've followed my career for the last 15 years. In any case, if I had gone with a serious paper then *The Sun* would have picked it up and hounded me for the rest of my life.' Soon he was admitting the more gossipy stories had been fabricated.

As for his Christianity, he continued to speak frankly about his beliefs and doubts. It was one area of his life where he did not yet seem to feel the need to present a carefully worked out story. He said to *Gay Times*: 'The importance of Christianity as I see it is how much we care and how much we love. I don't think inherently that having anal or vaginal sex is right or wrong. What we need to be aware of are the thoughts behind what we're doing. What's important is for gay people in high profile positions like the Government to come out and show there's a bigger percentage of homosexuals than people realise. Not enough people are being honest so that everyone can see that homosexuality isn't a sin, or if it is, then millions and millions of people are going to go to hell.'

In this *Gay Times* interview, a few weeks after Justin's interview with *The Voice*, he indirectly acknowledged the rough ride the paper had given him: 'Although I'm somewhat cocooned in a celebrity world I've certainly found that people who you would expect to be understanding and sympathetic to minority groups are often the most bigoted, prejudiced and judgemental people themselves. There's no question that the black community needs to wake up to the fact that homosexuality is not the white man's disease but something that also hits their families and their lives. Just because you're gay doesn't mean you've let anybody down.' But he was full of praise for *The Voice*'s new editor, Winsome-Grace Cornish, who he described as fabulous.

Justin was, inevitably, becoming a spokesperson for gay people. His charm and ease with the media, his desire for publicity and his identities as black, Christian and a professional sportsman, meant he was made for the role. In May 1991 Justin appeared in a TV programme, *Byline: 'A Kiss is Just a Kiss'*. It was a hard-hitting documentary presented by the actor, Michael Cashman, about his own and others experiences of being gay in a hostile world. The title, a line from the song, *As Time Goes By*, was chosen because, Cashman, in his role as Colin Russell in *EastEnders*, had kissed Barry Clarke, played by Gary Hailes. It had been the first gay kiss in a British soap and a controversial moment. In his contribution to *Byline*, Fashanu took the line that if people like him were out it made it easier for other gays and challenged stereotypes.

Justin was finding his place as an openly gay man in the public eye. But the rest of his life was not going so well. The effect of his struggle with his religious beliefs and practice was profound. His brothers and sister, separated from each other as young children, were again separated, this time by their responses to Justin's sexuality and the way he had shared it with the world. His football career was in the doldrums. John Marshall and Terry Deal, who had interviewed Justin for *Gay Times*, wrote: 'It is not yet clear whether his story will end in triumph or tragedy.'

Chapter 11

Coming Back

Justin's first media appearance after coming out was on the TV chat show, *Wogan*, in February 1991. Sitting in for the usual host, Terry Wogan, was Clive Anderson. It was not a great interview, with Anderson firing provocative questions at him, about *The Sun*, his brother John, and Brian Clough while Justin tried to talk about football and homophobia. He claimed his efforts to make a comeback in the English game had been hindered by rumours about his sexuality, saying he felt he might as well be open and honest about it but still could not find a club: 'I'm fit and strong but the doors aren't opening because of my sexuality.'

His comments drew criticism from sports writer, James Lawson, in the *Daily Express*. He pointed out that Fashanu had played for several English clubs the previous season and they had let him go because he was not fit enough. Lawson suggested it was time for him to acknowledge his career was over as so many other players had to do because of injury, adding: 'By his blanket charge against soccer he does nothing for himself nor for genuine victims of prejudice.' Lawson had a point. It was not unusual for footballers to retire early because of injury. Kevin Reeves and Peter Mendham, two of Fashanu's contemporaries at Norwich, had both given up the professional game for this reason while in their mid-20s, around the time Brighton were paying off Fashanu. Frank Clark, Fashanu's most recent manager in England could not have been more supportive. He had invited Justin back to Leyton Orient to train with the reserves even though he did not feel he was good enough to play for the first team, which suggested Lawson was right. There was another good reason to suggest it was time Justin called it a day. His appearance on *Wogan* came the day before his 30th birthday. Thirty is generally seen as the age at which footballers begin to go into decline rather than the age to resurrect a career.

A few weeks after *Wogan* Fashanu did find a new club, Southall FC, in west London. It was a club with a strong tradition and once nearly 20,000 fans had crammed into its Western Road stadium to watch a third-round FA Cup tie against Watford. But that was in 1936. The club Fashanu joined was in the Isthmian League Division Two South, known as the Vauxhall League after its sponsor, and playing in front of a handful of spectators. Fashanu was appointed as player-coach until the end of the season. Speaking to the *Southall Gazette* the chairman discounted the potential for friction between Fashanu and the other players because of 'the lurid stories of last year', saying they respected him as a player and for all he had achieved in the game.

While Fashanu was with Southall, film was shot for inclusion in a TV programme, *Them and Us*, with Craig Charles as the presenter. It showed the players speaking up for Fashanu. One said 'I don't mind sharing the showers with Justin'; another said he respected Justin for his football qualities. These comments were contrasted with a clip of John in his *Football Focus* appearance, saying he and other footballers would not want to get changed near a gay teammate. Gordon Taylor, of the Professional Footballers' Association, who had supported Justin in his dispute with Brian Clough, spoke up for him: 'We're in this business as an association to try to get rid of any discrimination.' The Tottenham Hotspur scout, Ted Buxton, had been to watch Fashanu play, commenting: 'He's done things tonight which show a touch of class.' Buxton felt Fashanu could progress if a Fourth or lower Third Division club offered him a chance and he could play for a season and get fit. He added: 'If he's playing well the crowds will forget his private side.' But later in the programme he contradicted himself: 'If a top class player in the First Division came out and said they were gay they would have to pack up the game.' Justin was still claiming he was not being given a chance because of his sexuality: 'I've come out and said what I've said. It's hindered my career but on the positive side it will hopefully help other gay people involved in football because, believe me, there are many.'

* * *

The Biography

When Justin's unhappy season with Hamilton Steelers had ended he thought he was finished with the club and with Canadian football. But he needed to be playing, he needed to prove himself. His abilities were still appreciated in Canada. In June he was back with the Steelers for the 1991 season. The *Edmonton Journal's* John Kernahan caught him in upbeat mood after he had scored both goals in a 2–0 win for Hamilton over North York Rockets: 'Three things excite me here. First, I'm happy. Second, I have a lot of respect for the coaching here. And third, I'm impressed with the players we have here.' Fashanu added that he wanted to show people he could play and 'after what happened here last year' wanted to leave Canada 'on a good note'. Kernahan described Fashanu as easily the most skilled player on the pitch and the Steeler's manager-coach, John McGrane, enthused about his headed goal: 'The ball must have been 11 feet in the air. He looked like Michael Jordon out there. And wait 'til he's fit enough to play the whole 90 minutes full out.'

In Canada there were no headlines about Justin being gay but it was an issue within the club. McGrane and owner, Mario DiBartolomeo, spoke about it after his death, giving contrasting versions of events. McGrane thought having an openly gay player had not been a problem: 'I told him I wasn't homophobic and all I wanted from him was 100 per cent play. The other players and Justin would actually joke about it. We'd give a yellow jersey to the player who had a bad practice and I said the player who got two yellow jerseys in a week had to room with Justin on our next trip. We all laughed at that, it was right out in the open.' This kind of joking may have been tiresome for Justin but perhaps indicated some sort of acceptance. Talking about dressing room banter the cricketer, Andrew Flintoff, once said: 'The funny thing is that when no one's taking the piss out of you, that's the time to worry. It's almost like a form of endearment to have it directed at you.'

Halfway through the season Fashanu was suddenly transferred to Toronto Blizzard. No explanation was given at the time but evidently owner, Mario DiBartolomeo did not share his manager-coach's positive view of Fashanu's integration into the squad. When he eventually explained Fashanu's move he said: 'He was very destructive to our team and unfortunately we had to part. He was living a dual life and some of our younger players didn't know how to handle a homosexual in the dressing room.' He described Justin as a 'mixed up guy' and said he was often seen in the company of 'young boys'.

It is clear from the comments of people who knew him in Canada that although Justin was often charming and good company he could also be infuriating. Mary Morris, described as the mainstay of the Steelers' front office, remembered one of the better times: 'It was 1990 and we were flying to Montreal for an important game. Justin learned that it was my granddaughter's birthday. He found a woman on the plane who played the bagpipes and got her to play *Happy Birthday* for Megan. Then he bought her a toy seal at the hotel and asked her what else she would like. She said she wanted him to score a goal for her. He did, and the Steelers got to the League Final.' But Mary Morris was not always so enamoured with him: 'He wouldn't practice like the others, work hard and sweat. It was "I am Justin. I don't need to".' There was a story that he walked into a florist and ordered 400 Canadian dollars worth of arrangements for himself, putting it on the Steeler's account. Another time he lent a vehicle, which had been leased by the Steelers, to a boyfriend who wrecked it. Fashanu just left it in the soccer club car park.

Until Justin's enforced coming out it was difficult to find anyone who would say a word against him, with the notable exceptions of Brian Clough and Larry Lloyd. Afterwards there were still plenty of people who liked and admired him but he also came in for criticism, for his unreliability, his obsession with money and his carelessness with other people's, and his dishonesty. There has to be an explanation for these changes in his behaviour. John McGrane felt that Justin never came to terms with his sexuality and, in his mind, it got tied up with his failure to make it back to the top level of English football: 'It ate at him like a right denied.' Justin had told *The Voice* of 'the disruption to his relationship with God'. He told John Kernahan, 'I'm a happy man, I'm contented, I'm at peace with myself'. But it was never that easy for him.

Fashanu got off to a great start with Toronto Blizzard scoring both goals in a 2–1 win over Montreal Supra. But the following week there was another run-in with DiBartolomeo when Toronto played Hamilton Steelers. After 60 minutes Fashanu was sent off for 'cutting down a player with his elbow'. As he left the pitch, DiBartolomeo could be heard shouting at him. A furious-looking Fashanu changed course and headed towards the press box where he was seated. A Blizzard official managed to persuade Fashanu to turn away, preventing a confrontation. DiBartolomeo was President of the Canadian Soccer League which made his behaviour even more unacceptable. After the match Fashanu told the *Toronto Star*: 'When the league president shouts obscenities across the field in front of everybody that is totally disgraceful and unacceptable behaviour. I was only going to tell him what I thought of him.'

Fashanu was sent off again and contributed only one further goal, although he did play some games in defence. (His total for the season was seven: four for Hamilton and three for Toronto.) It was a good season for the Blizzard. The Eastern and Western Divisions of the CSL had been combined into one division. Toronto finished second, qualifying for the four-team play-off for the Championship and making it to the Final against Vancouver 86ers. Just as he had been with the Steelers the previous season, Fashanu was on the losing side, Toronto lost 5–3 in what proved to be his last match in four eventful seasons of Canadian football.

* * *

With the 1991–92 season underway, Justin found himself back in England without a club, Southall's financial problems preventing them from re-employing him. Although his failure to prove his fitness may have been sufficient reason in itself, prejudice did not help. When his agent phoned one club the manager asked, 'You mean that queer?'

Ossie Ardiles was a manager with a different attitude. A World Cup winner with Argentina in 1978, at Tottenham Hotspur he had become one of the first foreign players to make an impact on the English game. He had just been appointed manager of Newcastle United who were playing in the Second Division and aiming to get back to the First. Ardiles knew something about hostility based on factors you can do nothing about. The Falklands War coincided with his spell with Spurs. Realising he would provoke abuse from English crowds for being Argentinian and from people back home for playing in England, he felt obliged to go on loan to the French club, Paris Saint-Germain, until it was over. In his autobiography Ardiles wrote: 'I'm not interested in the age of players, their skin colour, their nationality, their sexual orientation. I'm only interested in whether or not I like the way they play football.' Arriving at Newcastle he noticed all the players were white. When he signed the black player, Franz Carr, there were people asking, 'How can you bring a black player to this club?' To Ardiles he was simply a good footballer.

He knew Fashanu through Christians in Sport and offered him a trial. Fashanu signed up on 24 October. It was a big opportunity with Newcastle attracting crowds of over 20,000. His debut came in a League Cup tie at Peterborough where he had played his last game for Brighton nearly six years previously. Since then he had started only five matches for English League clubs, with a handful of appearances as a substitute. Fashanu came on with 20 minutes to go but failed to prevent a 1–0 defeat. The Newcastle players' disappointment was compounded when they returned to the dressing room to find money and jewellery had been stolen. Justin lost £500 cash but told reporters, 'At least they didn't get my £7,000 gold watch'. Shortly after, Ardiles ended his trial, Fashanu claiming he was not given an explanation.

An internet post, by someone using the initials WB, gives an insight into the world of Justin Fashanu at this time. They met in a Newcastle pub and WB, having no interest in football, did not know who Justin was even when he introduced himself. Justin explained why he was there and why he was accompanied by two bouncers, to fend off intrusive journalists. He made quite an impact on WB: 'I was transfixed by the man. I had never before met his like. He was charming, generous, interesting, masculine and startlingly good-looking.' They became lovers and this unemployed young man, in his early 20s, found himself in a world of celebrity. Justin invited him down to London where they had dinner with Michael Cashman and his partner. Justin talked of them both becoming models and discussed with him if he could deal with the press attention if they went public as a couple.

WB wrote that as they spent more time together 'a few rather odd traits began to surface'. One was Justin's habit of only referring to gay people and black people in the third person, 'they' rather than 'we'. Then, there was his obsession with money, 'with what he could have had if things had been different, or how much more someone else was making'. Justin 'seemed to have no appreciation of the cost of things'. He would phone up WB asking him to get a plane to wherever he was at the time: 'I was on the dole and, even though he always promised to reimburse me, I never could make him understand that it would take more money than I got in a month for me to achieve such a distance at such a speed.'

Their affair petered out after a month: 'In my short time with Justin I saw many sides of him, the proud achievements, the sense of loss, the strong businessman and the childlike need to be liked, the skilled and confident footballer, and confused little boy needing a direction…I quickly grew tired of his confused and changeable states of mind, one day chatty, likeable, loving, talking of long-term plans…another time he'd be bizarre, vindictive, in denial of his own identity, bitter at his lot, shallow in his needs and flippant of mine.'

An anonymous internet post may not always be the most reliable source but, written a few days after Justin's death, W.B.'s account has an air of sincerity and authenticity about it. Perhaps what also emerges from this episode in Justin's life is his difficulty in sustaining relationships of all types when he was so often on the move. He did maintain some friendships – Maria Sol Acuña became an even closer friend after her split with his brother, John – but there were long periods when he did not see them and his friends seldom met or even knew of each other's existence. He stayed in touch with people he met through football – such as former Notts County manager, Howard Wilkinson, and the goalkeeper who stayed with Justin in Nottingham, Les Cleevely –

but their contact was sporadic and eventually petered out. Before email, texting and social media it was so much harder to stay in touch across distance and time zones.

Fashanu's attempted comeback took him next to Leatherhead in Surrey, a complete contrast to Newcastle. Even with his presence bringing in more spectators, the biggest home attendance was 211 during his spell there. Like Southall the team was in the Isthmian League Division Two South, known after its new sponsor as the Diadora League. And like Southall, Leatherhead had known better days. Notably in the 1974–75 season they reached the fourth round of the FA Cup, going 2–0 up away to First Division Leicester City before losing 2–3.

The *Leatherhead Advertiser* reported his signing as 'the greatest transfer coup in Leatherhead's history'. First-team coach, Micky Byrne, had met Fashanu when coaching in the USA and was delighted to have signed him. Justin, who was still hoping to play at a higher level said: 'I'm looking forward to having a few matches with less pressure and controversy.' He made his debut at home against Barton Rovers on 5 November 1991, missing a penalty as Leatherhead won 1–0. He played the next seven games, scoring four goals and taking Leatherhead to the top of the league. His brief spell there is fondly remembered. In Goff Powell's history of the club, *Up The Tanners*, he wrote: 'To watch his skills was a pure delight. If only he had stayed longer!'

*   *   *

'A meeting of a desperate footballer and a desperate club', was how Torquay United fan, Nick House, described Justin Fashanu joining his team, in *When Saturday Comes*. In May 1991 the club had enjoyed one of the best days in its history, winning the penalty shoot-out of a Play-off Final at Wembley, earning promotion to the Third Division for the first time in 19 years. But the 1991–92 season was proving a disappointment. When Fashanu was signed Torquay were in bottom place. Chairman, Mike Bateson, had sacked the manager, John Impey, and put injured player Wes Saunders in temporary charge. With the club in financial difficulties and the 28-year-old Saunders already on the payroll, it at least kept the costs down.

Bateson was slashing costs all round. The full-time groundsman was dispensed with, the Youth Training Scheme abolished and players' contracts were being paid off. Bateson was trying to sell his most promising player, defender Matt Elliott, who eventually played for Leicester City and Scotland. To add to the sense of despair around the club, Bateson was at odds with his players and the supporters. He publicly accused some of the players of not training enough and drinking too much. The supporters were unhappy because he was planning to move the club from its Plainmoor stadium to a new site some distance from the town. Attendances were falling, from over 4,500 on the opening day to under 2,500 for the most recent home game.

Something had to be done. Recruiting a player who had consistently failed to prove his fitness to play in the English Football League and paying him huge wages was not the most obvious move but it was the gamble Mike Bateson decided to take. As usual Fashanu drove a hard bargain. His wages were to be £1,000 a week, thought to be at least three times those of the other players. He was to be put up in a hotel with all expenses met. This was no trial; Bateson gave Fashanu a contract to the end of the season. There was even a transfer fee, Leatherhead receiving £2,000. Bateson's thinking seemed to be that Fashanu would score goals and, as a 'big name' with a bit of controversy surrounding him, attract more spectators. He felt Justin would have been playing at a higher level if he had not come out as gay.

Torquay United had a modest history having never been higher than the Third Division. With the town situated on the south Devon coast Justin could contemplate many long coach journeys to away grounds. A smaller, quieter version of Brighton, the town was well away from the centres of celebrity life he liked to inhabit. But it did offer full-time professional football and an opportunity to show he still had what it took.

The transfer was announced at a press conference on 5 December. Bateson and Fashanu both sought to make light of the 'gay issue'. Bateson commented: 'We will have a chat with the players. There is bound to be a bit of ribaldry at first.' He joked that the best way for the teetotal Fashanu to be accepted by the other players was to learn to drink 15 pints a night. Fashanu said he expected taunts about his homosexuality and colour by their opponents' fans and suggested he only had to be Jewish and he would have 'all three of them'. About the Torquay fans he said: 'They have got to decide whether they support me or are embarrassed by me. I hope they support me but it's up to them.'

Fashanu was introduced to the fans at the next home game, signing his contract on the pitch at half-time. Nick House wrote: 'The tannoy announcement that this was 'our first million pound signing' provoked much merriment and a few high-pitched catcalls which, more significantly, gave way to a round of applause for the new boy.' Most Torquay supporters were more worried about whether Fashanu would improve their team than who he slept with, and they had reason to be concerned. Saunders realising Fashanu was not fit enough, delayed his debut while he came in for extra training.

The Biography

Two weeks after signing, Fashanu's first appearance came in a home match against Preston. He made quite an impact. 'Fash is star of the show', was the headline in the local paper, the *Herald Express*. Reporter, David Thomas, wrote that Fashanu 'visibly lifted United's young team in a debut full of promise'. Nick House noted: 'This one performance alone endeared him to the Plainmoor fans and homophobic remarks were few and far between.' Having beaten Preston 1–0, Torquay travelled to Fulham – there were some big clubs in the Third Division that season. Fashanu was sent off after 80 minutes, having been booked twice, as Torquay lost 2–1. He was in the habit of complaining that his sendings off were unfair and this time he might have had a point. He was supported in his view by his manager and chairman, and Jimmy Hill in his role as a TV pundit. Fashanu had been given a hostile reception by the Fulham fans. His physical style of play and tendency to retaliate already got him in trouble with referees. There was a real danger that the extra, unwelcome attention he was getting as an openly gay player would mean he would miss half the season through being suspended.

Fashanu's next notable moment came in a New Year local derby against Exeter City. In front of 5,700 spectators, Torquay's biggest crowd for eight years, he scored the only goal of the match with a shot from 10 yards. It was his first goal in English League football for six years. When David Thomas interviewed him Fashanu was feeling optimistic. He said that when Bateson had made his offer he wondered if he was fit enough and hungry enough: 'Despite being out of the game all those years I know after a few games that I am still good enough and strong enough to stay in football for a considerable time yet.' As usual he saw himself in a mentoring role: 'I have had a lot of experience not just of football but of life. There are plenty of young players at Torquay and if you want to learn and progress in the game you need to have somebody who's been there to talk to and learn from.'

Three days after the Exeter match Torquay played West Bromwich Albion at home. They were the club Fashanu had made his first-team debut for Norwich City against 13 years previously. On that occasion he just failed to score with a header. This time he did better. One fan remembers him winning a corner in front of the packed away end and while waiting for it to be taken the West Bromwich fans sang, 'He's bent, he's queer, he takes it up the rear, Fashanu, Fashanu'. The corner came over, he scored and you could have heard a pin drop among them. David Thomas remembers Fashanu's intimidating power as he flung himself at the ball, giving the tough defender, Graham Roberts, no chance. Another 1–0 win and Torquay were 17th and out of the relegation zone.

Fashanu's comeback was turning into a classic story of triumph over adversity, and Torquay's season from one of despair to one of hope as the fans found a new hero. And a more profound story was also emerging from the action. Fashanu crashed the ball into the net and, in that one moment, the Torquay fans felt a little less bashful about their gay player, the West Bromwich fans a little less scornful. A stereotype was subverted. A brave man was pushing back prejudice.

Justin's teammates seem to have been relaxed about the presence of an openly gay man among them. He did make it easy for them. He kept his gay social life well away from the club and spared his colleagues from potential embarrassment by getting changed for training sessions in a separate room. He replaced Matt Elliott as team captain because he was already doing most of the talking on the pitch.

With this bright start Fashanu was attracting the attention of scouts from bigger clubs with Mike Bateson saying he would let him go if he received an offer of £250,000. His every move was reported in the *Herald Express*. 'Fash Finds Millionaires Row Pad', was the headline of a story of him moving from the hotel to rented accommodation. Another report noted he had advertised for a 'live-in assistant' in several magazines, including *Gay Times*. The post went to Dominic Hurd who Justin described as an actor who did TV and PA work: 'He's going to be a great help because I'm involved in so much work, with Torquay and outside.' A front page photograph showed him with the teenagers who interviewed him for the magazine, *Who Cares?* Then there was a report of his appearance on *Open to Question*.

In this TV programme Justin was questioned, sometimes aggressively, by a group of rather stony-faced young people. He kept his cool throughout, even when asked: 'Rather than being proud of your sexuality haven't you used it as an emotional crutch to justify a career that's sadly over?' He replied that he thought he was proving himself and would not have made a comeback if he felt he was going to make an embarrassment of himself. It would not have been worth it given the taunts and aggravation he was subjected to. When asked about the taunts he said they did affect him but the show must go on and he had to have broad shoulders. He still insisted that coming out had adversely affected his football career: 'For someone who has the pedigree and background that I've got I found the door closed. Friends who I'd known for many years who'd become managers and coaches and chairmen and directors – suddenly the doors shut and I couldn't get a job.'

About his sexuality he said: 'I had lots of girlfriends and still do and I love women and think they are beautiful creatures. But I found I am attracted to guys as well. Does that make me gay? I don't know. I'm going through a situation where I'm trying to find out who I am and what I am and I'm still young now, I'm only 29…In five years I may be married and have kids.' Justin was actually heading for his 31st birthday but he had solved the problem of being over 30 and looking for a contract by knocking a year off. For the rest of his career in England and Scotland his age was always given as a year less than it was.

During the programme Justin revealed he had been given an Aids test as part of his medical before joining Torquay. He used the opportunity to point out that it was among heterosexuals that Aids was on the increase and talked about the African American basketball player, 'Magic' Johnson. Johnson had recently announced he was HIV positive and was using his own example to emphasise the risks to heterosexuals. Soon after the *Open to Question* programme Justin appeared on *Tonight with Jonathan Ross*. It was a more relaxed occasion and he came across as charming and good-humoured while still speaking seriously about Aids, the dangers to promiscuous heterosexual sportsmen and the need for everyone to be aware of its threat.

Fashanu continued to shine for Torquay. In one match, away to Swansea, he drew praise from the opposition manager, Frank Burrows, who said how impressed he was with Justin, having come back from a bad injury, and how much he had enjoyed his physical contest with Swansea's centre-half, Mark Harris. David Thomas wrote that Fashanu was playing the Swansea defence on his own. This was the problem for Torquay; they simply did not have a strong enough squad for the Third Division and were back in the relegation zone.

Mike Bateson brought in a new manager, Yugoslavian, Ivan Golac. He had played with Fashanu at Southampton and they got on well. Wes Saunders had recovered from injury and was back in the team. Soon after Golac's appointment, Torquay were away to West Bromwich. Two minutes from the end Fashanu was sent off for a challenge on a defender as they went to head the ball. Saunders was so incensed he started an argument with WBA's Darren Bradley and they were both sent off too. David Thomas reported that Fashanu had had to endure 'some oafish close-quarters abuse' from one of the WBA substitutes as he left the pitch. Both Golac and Fashanu insisted the WBA players had been trying to get him sent off. The club appealed against Fashanu's sending off but was unsuccessful. Having been suspended for one game after his dismissal against Fulham, Fashanu received a four-game ban for this one. He was so disillusioned that, before his suspension, in a home game against Wigan, he produced what he described as his worst ever performance confessing, 'I admit I was feeling sorry for myself'. David Thomas wrote: 'He had a hang-dog look about him all afternoon as if just waiting for his suspension to take effect.' Fashanu was feeling the pressure of being an openly gay footballer. He told Thomas: 'Every time I walk outside my front door I feel I'm under the spotlight and have to justify myself.'

Fashanu continued to seek and enjoy a high profile in the media. In April he was a signatory to a letter published in *The Times*, with actors Dora Bryan and George Cole, and politicians Joan Lester and David Steel. They were marking 100 years of the charity, National Children's Home, which offers support for families with adopted children, and making a case for greater government funding. Some publicity was less welcome. *The Times* reported that he was banned from driving for four weeks and fined £265 for speeding and failing to produce his driving license. He was driving a Jaguar XJS with a personalised number plate, A9 JSF. He presented the pilot of a radio series, *loud and proud*, which was aimed at young lesbians and gay men and their friends. The programme was taken up by BBC Radio 1 but Justin was disappointed to be replaced by a different presenter, DJ Paulette.

Justin continued to keep his gay personal life well away from the football club. So successful was he in doing so that people who got to know him well, such as Mike Bateson and David Thomas, seriously wondered if he was, in fact, gay. Rather than socialise on the Torquay gay scene Justin would drive 20 miles up the road to Exeter. Boxes on Tuesday, held at the nightclub, Boxes, offered what he was looking for. Many of the people who went there were not out and wanted to protect their privacy. Cameras were not allowed. The event was not openly advertised but became known throughout the gay community, making it the best attended one-nighter in south-west England. The DJ was Alan Quick who recalls that Justin turned up most weeks: 'At Boxes he could be himself, meet like-minded people and have a good time without prying eyes. He enjoyed music, dancing and meeting new people, often bringing friends with him.' He would request particular tracks, a favourite being *A Deeper Love* by Clivilles and Cole. Alan got to know Justin well and remembers him as 'witty, considerate and charming'.

Justin was struggling with his Christian beliefs. He was interviewed for the magazine, *The Face*, in May 1992. Asked if he was religious he replied: 'I believe strongly in a spiritual world and in Jesus Christ. I'm not sure if I believe in the philosophies that many of the established religions talk about. They're out of touch. The church is not a good ambassador for getting across spiritual things to people who need them. At the moment I'm just a member of my own church.' He sounded more positive when he visited a south London comprehensive school where he divided his time between football coaching and speaking to GCSE sociology students. The following notes from his talk were taken by one of the pupils, Sarah, and included in the book, *Challenging Lesbian and Gay Inequalities in Education*: '"I am comfortable with who I am." Justin is a born-again Christian and he feels that his religion helped him to realise he was gay and "come out of the closet". Justin said, "The Bible is a wonderful book to live your life by". Justin is very open and caring. He said he's come out because "I don't want to go to my deathbed and not have lived". Justin has helped me to understand more about homosexuality and to accept it.'

*   *   *

Following his suspension Fashanu picked himself up and kept knocking in the goals. Despite arriving halfway through the season he ended up as Torquay's top scorer with 10 goals in 21 games. But it was not enough to save the team from relegation. Golac departed and Fashanu had to decide whether to stay with the club which had treated him well but would be playing in a lower division. He had to abandon plans to spend another summer playing in Canada because he needed an operation to remove growths on his toes. While he was recuperating he contemplated his options. There was some interest from Exeter City managed by Alan Ball who, like Golac, had played with Fashanu at Southampton. The previous season Exeter had just avoided Torquay's fate of relegation from the Third Division. Then Mike Bateson made an offer. Having appointed another player, Paul Compton, as manager he offered Fashanu the role of assistant, with the expectation he would also carry on playing.

Fashanu thought about it for two weeks before accepting the post. The front page of the *Herald Express* carried a photograph of him standing between Paul Compton and Mike Bateson, his arms round them and planting a kiss on Bateson's cheek. The headline, 'Fash Kisses Top Job Hello!', was a little misleading – it was not the top job – but the photograph and headline nicely conveyed the club's relaxed attitude towards appointing the first ever openly gay man to hold a managerial post in English football. Justin was erroneously reported to also have become the first black man to enter soccer management in England. The honour should probably go to Tony Collins who played for a host of clubs in the 1950s, including Norwich and Torquay, before managing Rochdale from 1960 to 1967. But there had been few since and his appointment was still notable in that respect.

Justin's football career was back on track but away from the pitch he continued his habit from Hamilton Steelers, of running up debts and behaving in ways which alienated people. For his summer holidays he arranged to go to Lanzarote in the Canary Islands through a company which advertised in *Gay Times*. On his first attempt he was turned back when it was discovered he had altered his date of birth on his passport. Terry Deal, who had interviewed Justin for *Gay Times* and helped him set up the holiday, wrote: 'I learned later that the holiday was never paid for and that he had left a trail of debt in his wake.' David Thomas spoke of Justin 'running out of financial and emotional credit' by the time he left Torquay.

There was no international pre-season tour for Torquay. With the exception of a match against Watford, friendlies were played against local opposition. A fan remembers Justin before one of these games. He was wearing a white suit and shoes but kicking a ball around with some youngsters, not at all worried about getting dirty. It is an image which captures some of the character of the man with, as Les Cleevely put it, 'a film star's aura but a great sense of humility'.

The 1992–93 season could hardly have started better for Fashanu. He scored in each of the first four matches. He missed out in the next and then came a home fixture against Cardiff City. It was played in a heated atmosphere, Cardiff brought 1,000 fans and there were 100 arrests, mainly outside the ground. Justin scored with a header. Then, in the 81st minute, he and Cardiff defender, John Williams, jumped together trying to head the ball. Fashanu caught Williams in the face with his elbow and was sent off. Elbows in the face were controversial. They could finish careers. It happened to Torquay defender John Uzzell whose cheek bone and eye socket were fractured in a clash with Brentford's Gary Blissett. Torquay were taking the case to court, with Blissett charged with grievous bodily harm. He was eventually found not guilty, highlighting the difficulty of proving intent. Fashanu claimed: 'I was using my arms to protect myself. You have to do it. There was no intention to injure him.' Paul Compton defended Fashanu with a different line of argument: 'There was a lot of intimidation against him on the pitch and from the crowd. A person can only take so much.'

All three of Fashanu's sendings off while with Torquay were associated with him being wound up by opposition supporters and, in at least two instances, opposing players. On this occasion he was suspended for three games. It seemed to sap Fashanu's enthusiasm and his goals dried up. Word seemed to be getting around that players could provoke him into getting sent off. There was a home game against Chesterfield in October. Playing for Chesterfield was Mick Kennedy who was notorious for baiting opponents and his tough tackling. He was winding up Fashanu and then caught him with an over-the-top tackle. At half-time Fashanu hid in the players' tunnel and leapt out at Kennedy swinging his fist. Fortunately for both of them he missed.

A few weeks later Torquay were away to Halifax. Among their opponents was Jimmy Case who had been in the Liverpool team when Fashanu scored his famous goal for Norwich City. This was a less glorious occasion, captured by extracts from David Thomas's match report: 'Case alleged that Fashanu had stamped on Luckette – not even Luckette had the cheek to go along with that…Fashanu's booking for a barging challenge in the 74th minute was followed by a ridiculous incident moments later when right-back, Dudley Lewis, blatantly tried to provoke Fashanu into a scrap that would have ensured his dismissal. Fashanu pushed him away and walked off, getting only a lecture from the referee.'

It is impossible to know what was being said to Fashanu on these occasions but a glimpse into the abuse some players were prepared to dish out comes from a court case from 1993 involving the Stoke's black player Mark Stein. Stein appeared in court charged with assaulting Stockport County defender, Jim Gannon. But the case against Stein was undermined when Gannon, as a prosecution witness, admitted to having called Stein 'a short, ugly, black, bean-headed twat', his lawyer arguing that it was 'the language of the football park'. Although the judge found Stein guilty, he gave him a conditional discharge because he had reacted to 'extreme provocation'.

Things got worse for Fashanu and Torquay. He was involved in what was reported to be 'a training ground bust-up' with Dennis Salman, defender and Youth Development Officer. Salman was sacked from his post as Youth Development Officer and dropped from the team though he was retained as a player.

Justin had made his comeback but, having dreamt of getting back to the top, found himself struggling in a struggling team in the bottom tier of the Football League while having to deal with abuse from opposing fans and players, and even within the club. He wanted more from life than this. He came up with a plan. It would make money and headlines. It might even silence the taunts about being gay.

Chapter 12

Diamonds and Hearts

It was a Friday evening match, 11 December 1992 at Colchester, and Torquay's assistant manager was nowhere to be seen. The mystery of his whereabouts was solved the following day. Newspapers reported that Justin had been 'canoodling' with the actress Julie Goodyear, who played Bet Gilroy in *Coronation Street*, at the TV show's annual Christmas party. Further details emerged from 'close associates'. Apparently they had been friends for five or six years but 'now they are a couple'. It was a story made in PR heaven.

The young Julie Goodyear shared Justin Fashanu's desperation to be famous. In her autobiography she tells the story of how after her first appearance in *Coronation Street* she walked up and down Manchester's main shopping street hoping to be recognised. She had to give up after a passer-by took her to be a prostitute. Her personal life had been what tabloid papers called 'colourful'. It included relationships with men and women. Briefly, in 1966, and then continuously from 1970 she played the character Bet Lynch, who married and became Bet Gilroy. This flirty but cynical character with her dyed blonde hair and leopard print clothes was a gay icon. As Susan Irvine put it in *The Independent*: 'Bet dresses like a drag queen and drag queens have returned the compliment. But it's her diva qualities in the face of tragedy that make her a gay heroine in the mould of Judy Garland.'

Justin and Julie's age difference added more intrigue to their relationship. Julie was 50; 19 years older than Justin. The papers loved it. Once again, Justin was all over the front page of *The Sun* and once again not everything was true. The headline was 'My Bet On The Side: Gay soccer star tells of affair with Julie' Justin shared with readers that he had fallen in love with Julie and explained he had told her of his past affairs with footballers and a Tory MP: 'She is very philosophical. She understands it is individuals that matter, not a way of life.' Contacted for a quote Julie Goodyear offered: 'Justin's a lovely man. He's adorable, yet also very sensitive.' The story continued inside with the headline, 'I Never Thought I'd Fall For Girl'. Justin revealed that he first met Julie when he was playing for Southampton. They lost touch but he called her up when he was with Manchester City and their friendship grew. Then seven months ago they had become lovers. He usually drove up to Manchester after the game and they would stay in the Queen's Suite of the Midland Hotel. He said that when he came out she was 'a real brick' and 'a warm shoulder to cry on'. 'I loved her for it.' The age gap did not worry him: 'I enjoy her experience of life. It is mixed with a youthfulness of spirit and physical beauty.' He was not prepared to talk about what happened between them in bed: 'That is a very private matter.' Saying they had not decided whether to wed he described Julie as 'his perfect woman'.

Desperate to get in on the story the *Daily Mirror* went after Julie Goodyear's version of events but was told she did not have anything to add. It resorted to producing a mock script for *Coronation Street* featuring a Justin Fashionable. Readers were invited to continue the script, the best entry winning a weekend for two in Manchester including a tour of Granada TV, home of the TV soap. Next was an announcement that Julie Goodyear would be attending a match at Torquay. She would meet Justin's teammates and pull pints in the social club, like her character, Bet Gilroy. *The Sun* reported: 'At half-time she toured the Plainmoor Ground, prompting a cheeky chorus of 'Get your t**s out for the lads!' and a mass humming of the *Street* tune.' Not every fan was pleased to see their match against Shrewsbury turned into a tabloid pantomime and it was perhaps fortunate for his reputation with the fans that Fashanu laid on the goal for a 1–0 win. According to the *Daily Mirror* Julie Goodyear jumped up and hugged chairman Mike Bateson as Sean Joyce slammed the ball into the net. *The Sun* had bought exclusive rights to pictures of

Goodyear celebrating with champagne in the dressing room with Fashanu and the other players, the local *Herald Express* taking great delight in barging in and taking its own pictures.

A couple of months later their relationship made more headlines. This time Fashanu revealed to *The People* that their affair was over. Under the headline, 'Fashanu Dumps 'Old' Julie', he explained: 'I love Julie more than I've ever loved anyone. And all the ingredients were right except her age. If she'd been ten years younger, I'd probably have married her.' The problem was: 'My dream is to have a big house and fill it with lots of kids. I couldn't see that sort of future with Julie.' He described how they cried together when he broke the news to her. Apparently what they did in bed was no longer private as Justin shared: 'Julie makes love like she is...warm, giving and interesting.' There was more, as Justin described how she had reawakened his interest in women, and he did so using a particularly unfortunate metaphor: 'When you have curled the ball into the back of the net once, you can do it again.' Julie Goodyear had had enough and decided it was time to tell the truth about Justin: 'The reason he makes me laugh a lot is he makes vast sums of money for fantasising about me.' Their friendship had been real and the rest was made up. Justin sent her a bunch of roses and an apology.

The reality of Fashanu's football life was proving as surprising as the fiction of his love life. By this time he was with a new club and looking forward to playing in front of 40,000 spectators.

*   *   *

Distracted, and disillusioned with Torquay United, Fashanu's form had deserted him. Coming into the New Year he had scored once in 16 games. Paul Compton was faced with the unpalatable situation of having to drop his assistant from the team. A year and a day after he had marked his renaissance with a goal against Exeter Fashanu found himself sidelined. After another defeat, Compton felt his presence had been missed and he was back for the next match. There was one more goal, Fashanu's seventh of the season, giving Torquay an away win at Northampton and ending a run of five losses.

Then, with Compton struggling as manager, Bateson took some unorthodox action. He brought in Neil Warnock as an unpaid consultant. Warnock had just left his managerial post at Notts County and was negotiating a pay-off. Meanwhile he was willing to work for free so as not to jeopardise it and became temporary manager in all but name. The disgruntled Fashanu felt he should have been offered the job and promptly walked out saying: 'I cannot go along with some of the things that are happening at the club and I feel it is the right time to leave.' A few days later he was more conciliatory, saying there were no hard feelings: 'I am not at loggerheads with anyone at the club and I want them to do well and haven't fallen out with Mike Bateson.' Several English lower division teams expressed interest in signing Fashanu but he was looking for a new challenge. He took up an offer from the Scottish Premier Division club, Airdreonians, or Airdrie. Fashanu secured a contract until the end of the season and Torquay United received a transfer fee of £5,000.

Having made such a positive impact on his arrival at Torquay, Fashanu's poor form towards the end of his stay, and his obsession with money and celebrity, left a journalist, a fan and the chairman feeling disillusioned. Journalist, David Thomas, got to know Justin well and they became 'friends of a sort'. Describing him as 'someone you couldn't help liking', he felt Fashanu was intensely lonely and did not let people get close to him. Instead he surrounded himself with younger admirers, male and female, and acted the 'small town superstar'. He was critical of what he called Justin's 'exploitative nature'. This was not only about extracting every last pound from the club that he could but also about relationships. David Thomas felt that nobody was prepared to challenge his inconsiderate behaviour and once did so himself. Justin knew a young woman had gone to a great deal of trouble to get them both tickets for a concert but casually stood her up. David Thomas told him exactly what he thought of his behaviour and felt that by taking that stance he strengthened their relationship.

Thomas recalls Fashanu the footballer as formidable when he put his mind to it but you never knew which Fashanu would turn up. He thinks it was no coincidence that one of his best performances came early on against West Bromwich Albion. He had told Fashanu he was being watched by a scout from First Division Coventry City. Thomas describes him as 'lazy' a comment which echoes that of Mary Morris from Hamilton Steelers who criticised his commitment to training. In a piece written by Juliet Jacques for the website, inbedwithmaradona.com, Thomas talks about the time Justin asked him to help write his memoirs. He decided to test Justin's commitment by suggesting he drafted a rough plan and was not entirely surprised when it never materialised. He was also relieved saying: 'I would have spent a lot of time nailing the truth about his life. Justin would have produced a version of events according to Justin, which wouldn't necessarily stack up.'

Nick House wrote a follow-up piece for *When Saturday Comes*, his early enthusiasm for Fashanu having faded from the time he prioritised the *Coronation*

Street Christmas bash over Colchester away. He concluded that Mike Bateson's money might have been better spent on 'a dour, non-celebrity, yet proven manager'. By the end of Justin's stay Mike Bateson might have agreed with Nick House. He told Simon Freeman of *The Guardian* that signing Fashanu was a big mistake: 'We paid him a grand a week, which was just silly. Nothing to do with him being gay. He just didn't perform for us.' In the TV documentary, *Shot Down in Flames*, Bateson described him as 'charming, arrogant, demanding, persuasive, selfish, a liar and a selfish liar'. He spoke of his desperate desire for money: 'Every time you talked to Justin you had to be very, very careful. He wouldn't physically take money out of your wallet but he'd try to do it by any means he could. If he talked to you for more than a few minutes it would always lead to some idea that Justin had got for making a few bob. No matter what you gave him – if you gave him a million pounds – he'd spend a million plus a hundred thousand and he'd still be in debt.'

Once Justin told him he was being pursued by 'very heavy people' for money he owed. He said if he did not come up with £8,000 he would have to flee. Faced with losing his player Bateson lent him the money. He never saw it again. Legal attempts to reclaim it after Justin left the club came to nothing when it became apparent he simply did not have the money to pay back. Despite all the difficulties Justin caused, Mike Bateson clearly retained some affection for him. Their relationship was not all about money. He and his wife, Sue, even tried, without success, to help Justin restore his relationship with John. In declining to be interviewed for this book Bateson called Justin 'a strange, likeable rogue'.

*   *   *

Fashanu was exuberant when he phoned David Thomas from Scotland. Having made his debut for Airdrie in a 0–0 draw away to Motherwell he was about to face that 40,000 crowd at Ibrox, home of Glasgow Rangers. He told Thomas: 'I'm back in the big time and it's going to give me a bigger buzz than ever. I'm playing for the Wimbledon of Scottish football and I'm looking forward to performing on the big stage again. The Ibrox faithful are bound to give me a tough time. It won't worry me; it will motivate me even more.'

Like Torquay, when Fashanu signed for them, Airdrie were fighting relegation. The club had been promoted to the Premier Division for the 1991–92 season and finished seventh out of 12. They even made it to the Scottish Cup Final, losing to Rangers but qualifying for the European Cup-Winners' Cup (Rangers having also won the League title). But 1992–93 was proving more of a struggle. Having lost to Sparta Prague in the first round of European competition they had spent most of the season in the bottom two places of the division, with two to go down. Situated 15 miles east of Glasgow, Airdrie were competing in the same division as its two huge clubs, Celtic and Rangers. Rangers were dominating Scottish football, in a run of winning nine consecutive League titles and with players such as Richard Gough, Trevor Steven, Mark Hateley and Ally McCoist in their squad.

Under the managerial duo of Alex MacDonald and his assistant, John McVeigh, Airdrie were playing in a direct physical style, prompting Justin's comparison with his brother's team, Wimbledon – the Crazy Gang. Scotland's tabloid press called Airdrie the Beastie Boys, although it was an image the club resisted. But Fashanu loved it, and the leniency shown by Scottish referees. McVeigh recalled Fashanu's contribution to the match against Rangers which resulted in a great result for Airdrie, a 2–2 draw. McVeigh told journalist Tom English: 'I remember Alex McLeish and Brian Irvine clattering him. His eyes were rolling about his head. "Come off, Justin," I said, "You're all over the place, son." He said, "No, gimme 10 minutes". He went back on, threw the elbow into the two boys, absolutely rapped them, and said, "Right, I'll come off anytime now".' The *Airdrie and Coatbridge Advertiser* reported that Fashanu was given 'a rough and rousing welcome from the Ibrox faithful' and 'showed some great touches throughout'.

Airdrie's nickname, The Diamonds, led to the obvious jokes about him being the Queen of Diamonds but not even the most prejudiced onlooker could find anything effeminate about this gay man's performances. Such was Fashanu's contribution to the fight against relegation he became a cult hero. The fans' song for him went: 'He's black, he's gay, he plays for Air-da-ray, Fashanu, Fashanu.'

Airdrie chairman, George Peat's motivation for signing Fashanu was much the same as Bateson's. He wanted a personality, a striker who would bring in the crowds and give his team a chance of avoiding relegation. Tom English wrote extensively about Fashanu's year in Scotland in an article, 'A Player to the End', for *Scotland on Sunday*. Peat told him: 'We agreed a thousand quid a game but he was always coming in looking for more. I got to thinking that he must have gone home every night and sat down and said to himself, "Right, now how can I make an extra five hundred quid tomorrow?".' McVeigh remembered taking him to the Ford garage to pick up his sponsored car: 'It was supposed to be an Orion. Everybody had an Orion. Justin says: "I'm not an Orion kind of guy". So he goes in to see the manager and he obviously talks him round his little finger because the next thing I know Justin has driven past me in this sports car, this flash soft-top going like the clappers out of the garage and down the street.'

Fashanu's early departure from the Rangers game represented the only minutes he missed from Airdrie's spirited but unsuccessful attempt to avoid relegation. He kept clear of injury and suspension, only a dispute about money threatening his participation. Dorothy Martin, Airdrie's commercial manager, was forced to deny she was acting as Fashanu's agent and had advised him not to turn up for a game as he pursued a better contract. She was later sacked. Fashanu was criticised by James Traynor, in *The Herald* who wrote that he should have been dropped: 'The last thing Airdrie need right now is an inflated ego feeding off past exploits and milking them for more than they are worth. Twice pointedly referring to him as 'the Englishman', Traynor suggested Fashanu's form, 12 matches and only two goals after joining Airdrie, had been unimpressive. It was not a view shared by McVeigh who rated Fashanu's contribution so highly he claimed that if he had joined a month earlier Airdrie would have stayed up.

Justin seems to have been popular with his teammates. Kenny Black told Tom English: 'He was a very, very bright guy, very sharp. You couldn't outfox him. He was open about his sexuality; it wasn't a taboo subject at all. We'd call him a big poof and he'd say, "Hey, Blacky, don't knock it till you've tried it". Justin was playing alongside Owen Coyle who joined Bolton at the end of the season. Soon after, Coyle got married and invited his ex-teammates to the wedding. He told *The Sun* that one of his best memories was of Justin's enthusiasm for the singer who performed during the service: 'She started the ceremony with a beautiful number and as she finished Justin Fashanu was out of his seat shouting "Magnificent girl, magnificent". Also interviewed for *The Sun*, goalkeeper, John Martin recalled: 'You get the big shots coming to the club but he wasn't at all like that, he got involved with all the boys and had a laugh.'

The predictions made by John and others that Justin had ruined his prospects of ever playing professional football again by coming out as gay had proved to be ill-founded. Footballers were not all virulent homophobes after all. Nor were they unable to cope with the delicacies of sharing the physical intimacies of their professional lives with a gay man. Just as Fashanu was subverting stereotypes of gay men, perhaps his teammates were subverting stereotypes of straight footballers. Justin did not necessarily enjoy the banter about his sexuality as much as it appeared but he knew how to deal with it and how to make himself popular in the dressing room. Harder to deal with was the conflict he was unable to resolve between his Christian beliefs and his sexual orientation. By this time he was keeping quiet about his faith but had found his way back to the church. After his move to Scotland he became a member of the congregation of the Whitburn Pentecostal Church.

A new attack on gays was coming from the Jamaican music scene. A ragga artist, Buju Banton, released a single, *Boom Bye Bye*, with lyrics advocating shooting gay men – 'battyboys'. Anecdotal evidence from the streets of Britain suggested an increase in violent attacks by straight black youths on black and white gay men, some accompanied by gestures of shooting guns and reciting of the song's lyrics. The organisations, OutRage!, and Black Lesbians and Gays Against Media Homophobia, campaigned for the record to be banned. Another Jamaican recording artist, Shabba Ranks, defended Banton on TV show, *The Word*, quoting from the Bible when doing so. The issue was creating tensions between antiracist activists and gay activists, putting black gay men in a situation of feeling they had to choose sides. For example, Ted Brown, a member of Black Lesbians and Gays Against Media Homophobia, was quoted in *The Guardian*, saying that the campaign against black homophobia was in danger of turning into black baiting: 'The press has given the impression that lesbians and gay men were doing fine until these blacks came and started beating them up. It's no wonder black lesbians and gay men are refusing to come forward and protest against homophobia. They can see a racist element in the way the issue is being treated.' Throw in the Christian element as well and Justin might well have decided not to get embroiled in this particular dispute. Instead, undaunted, he put his name to a statement from the Anti-Racist Alliance which described the views of Buju Banton and Shabba Ranks as likely to 'divide our communities and harm the real lives of lesbians and gay men'.

Back in Airdrie, Justin's popularity with fans stemmed not only from his performances on the pitch but his approachability. Gary Stewart remembers an incident after a home game with Rangers. Airdrie's defeat virtually condemned them to relegation and ensured that Rangers won the League. After the game some fans of both teams gathered in front of a shop selling TVs to watch other results coming through. By this time Justin had changed and was walking through the shopping precinct wearing headphones. Spotting the fans he went over and spoke to them. He was even friendly to the Rangers fans, who had given him a tough time during the game, shaking hands, giving them high fives and congratulating them on the result. Gary Stewart wrote: 'It says it all about the man. He was a gentleman and always had time for the fans.'

His last game for Airdrie was a 1–2 home defeat to Motherwell, Fashanu scoring Airdrie's goal, his fifth in 16 appearances. In front of just 3,000 fans he gave the match a sense of occasion, throwing his shirt, boots, shorts and socks into the crowd before departing in his briefs. Seven months after leaving he looked back on his spell with Airdrie. Interviewed by Bob McKenzie of the *Daily Express* he told him: 'If a computer had been asked to make that match it would probably have blown up. Yet amazingly it was a match made in heaven. Here I was with my reputation, Flash Harry, turning up in my Armani or Versace or whatever. They were down to earth guys who had been with other clubs, were expected to be relegated and said "everybody hates us". Airdrie is not the most fashionable place on earth but I had a fantastic time because everybody took me at face value. The manager, Alex MacDonald, took the chance and was only interested in my football ability. The fans were great and I was sorry to leave.'

* * *

Airdrie were eager to sign up Fashanu for another season but with several Scottish Premier Division clubs showing interest it was inevitable he would move on. There was a brief summer interlude where he turned out for the Swedish club, Trelleborgs FF. Then he returned to Airdrie to train with them while he negotiated a move. After talks with Partick Thistle and Motherwell it was the Edinburgh-based club, Heart of Midlothian, Hearts, which he signed for. The attraction was obvious; by finishing fifth the previous season Hearts had qualified for European competition, the UEFA Cup.

Hearts were short of money and manager, Sandy Clark, had to sell their centre-forward, Ian Baird, to Bristol City for £200,000. Clark had been a similar player to Fashanu and admired the qualities he had shown with Airdrie. He represented a ready-made replacement for Baird and did not cost a transfer fee. Fashanu came with a recommendation from Hearts new reserve team coach, Walter Kidd, who had played with him for Airdrie: 'He came to Airdrie with a big-name reputation but worked as hard as anyone. There are some players who would have looked at Airdrie as a way of making some easy money but Fashanu is not that type.'

Through his choice of club Fashanu had given scope to the jokers who could now call him the Queen of Hearts. But the big issue in this move was not sexuality but race. Compared with England it was taking longer for black players to become established in Scottish football in significant numbers and the attitudes of fans were more like those of English fans in the 1970s and 80s. Paul Elliott, who played in England and Italy before signing for Celtic in 1989, said racial abuse in Scotland was far worse than what he had experienced before. Hearts fans were considered to be among the worst in this respect, notorious for having pelted Rangers' black player, Mark Walters, with bananas. Soon after Fashanu joined the club the head of Scotland Yard's Football Intelligence Unit identified Hearts supporters as among those targeted by the racist British National Party to promote their criminal activities. Regarded as the first black man to play for Hearts, when Fashanu told the *Daily Mirror* he was confident of 'winning over the boo-boys', he was referring to racism rather than homophobia.

Not that his sexuality was off the agenda. One supporter wrote to the *Edinburgh Evening News* claiming that Fashanu would bring ridicule to Hearts and the thought of him playing in the maroon jersey turned his stomach. He was challenged in a letter written by a J. Robertson, who suggested that, if that was his attitude, this person should not consider himself a true Hearts supporter. This letter writer did not draw attention to his status but was actually the Hearts forward, John Robertson, coming to the defence of his new teammate. (This John Robertson should not be confused with the former Nottingham Forest player with the same name.)

Fashanu's time with Hearts got off to the worst possible start. In a behind-closed-doors friendly with Stenhousemuir he aggravated his old knee injury. It was to blight the whole of his brief stay there. Hearts went to Germany for a pre-season tournament, Fashanu missing the first two games. He was introduced to the home fans at Hearts' Tynecastle stadium before a friendly match against Everton, John Robertson noting, 'he received a great welcome from the fans'. After Justin's death, John Colquhoun wrote a warm and perceptive article about him for *The Scotsman* and recalled this occasion. Colquhoun had just rejoined Hearts, his home-town club, and he and Fashanu were standing next to each other in the players' tunnel waiting to go out onto the pitch: 'I had never felt so physically inferior as I did that evening. Comparing myself to this superb specimen of lean, muscular athleticism I was, indeed, forced to admit that never before had I felt so squat, peelie-wally and downright Scottish'. He explained that whereas the rest of the squad ate rolls and sausages after training: 'Justin would produce a series of Tupperware dishes from which he would eat the healthiest and most unappetising looking lunch I had ever seen.' Colquhoun concluded: 'We all get the physiques we deserve.'

The first competitive match of the 1993–94 season was away to Rangers, Hearts losing 2–1 in front of over 42,000 fans. Fashanu was substituted in the first three matches and told the *Edinburgh Evening News*: 'I'm not happy with my form. My best is yet to come. When my knee is right and I shake off a slight ankle injury I will be more mobile and the fans will see the real me.' They did not have long to wait. The next match was a home fixture against local rivals, Hibernian, and Fashanu put in what was probably his best performance for Hearts in helping his team to a 1–0 win in front of over 17,000 spectators. A Hibs fan, posting on the internet, was so ashamed of the racist abuse directed at Fashanu in this match that he listed it as one of his lowest moments supporting his team. Another fan also remembers racist abuse directed at Fashanu. Dan Gerrard has a black Zimbabwean father and white Scottish mother. In an article for *The Scotsman*, in 2011, he wrote about watching Hearts as a 13-year-old: 'The experience was enough to put me off going to games for life. As the only non-white face in the crowd, I was horrified and scared by the barrage of chants that were aimed at Fashanu. For the first time, I felt ashamed to be Scottish.'

Three games later and Hearts were home to Partick Thistle. Fashanu scored his first and only goal for the club with a deflected shot putting them 2–0 up in the 37th minute. Early in the second half he left defender, Grant Tierney, lying prostrate on the ground after an off-the-ball incident and the referee sent him off. TV cameras showed Fashanu had elbowed him in the face. Clark was furious and said he would be fined heavily.

Hearts had drawn Athletico Madrid in the UEFA Cup, the first leg being played at Tynecastle on 14 September 1993. Fashanu's participation was a tremendous feat, a vindication of his efforts to come back from the knee injury which had occurred nearly 10 years previously. It had been a long hard road since Brighton terminated his contract in 1986. Less determined and stubborn footballers would have given up. This match also represented a short-term change of fortune. It was less than a year since he had been dropped from the Torquay team.

Hearts won the tie 2–1, the first goal coming from John Robertson after the goalkeeper failed to hold Fashanu's header. In the next match this combination worked again when Fashanu headed to Robertson who scored to give Hearts a 1–0 home win over Celtic. It was a morale-boosting win in a season which saw Hearts struggling towards the bottom of the League table. Opinions on Fashanu's contribution to the team were sharply divided. David McCarthy, writing in the *Edinburgh Evening News*, said this goal showed how important Fashanu was to Heart's game plan. But he also suggested he had become too important with Hearts only tactic being to find him in the penalty area with a high ball for him to head on to Robertson or Colquhoun. Other reporters were scathing about his lack of mobility and inability to score himself.

* * *

Once again Justin appears to have been popular with his teammates. In *The Scotsman* John Colquhoun wrote: 'In the company of footballers he was a natural raconteur enthralling the lads with unbelievable tales of his past – some of which actually turned out to be true.' A fan, nominating John Robertson in a vote for Hearts' cult heroes, contributed this memory: 'I'll never forget a hilarious interview with Robbo and the late Justin Fashanu…which was littered with double entendres such as "I'll try to get on the end of his long balls from the back".' Robertson felt comfortable enough to joke about Justin in his column in the *Edinburgh Evening News*: 'Big Fash is taking stick for allowing his new home to be featured in a newspaper. Having a pink bedroom does not seem to embarrass him in the slightest and he just laughed off our attempt to wind him up. An investigation is now underway to discover why he insists on having white lilies in every room.'

Steve Hodge wrote of the perils of not conforming to dressing room culture at Nottingham Forest, citing Fashanu using his own towel instead of the one issued by the club. He hardly conformed at Torquay, Airdrie and Hearts but perhaps had developed the self-confidence to carry off his non-conformity with more aplomb. And the players at these clubs may have been more open-minded than those at Forest where Brian Clough set the tone. Perhaps a lesson from examining Fashanu's experiences in professional football is not to generalise, about players, managers, supporters or anyone else.

Colquhoun tackled, head-on, the delicate issue of the presence of a gay teammate in the dressing room: 'If I say to people within the macho testosterone-laden game of football that I played with Justin Fashanu one thing is certain, there will be more nudge, nudge, wink, winking going on than in a whole series of *Carry On* films…We had to endure the usual cracks from fans about the after-game bath but it was never a subject that was a problem for anyone at the club. The very fact that we had to endure that kind of ridiculous nonsense permitted us a tiny glimpse of the pressure with which Justin Fashanu had to deal.'

Around this time Justin was writing 'Strong Enough to Survive', his contribution to *Stonewall 25: The Making of the Lesbian and Gay Community in Britain.* He used the opportunity to give vent to his feelings of disappointment and frustration with the lesbian and gay community while trying to balance his criticisms with some positive statements of hope and belief. Aware that he was addressing a predominantly lesbian and gay readership he allowed himself to express grievances he would never have talked about in his media interviews. Having said he was bisexual, he accused the gay world of wanting people's sexual identity to be fixed just as much as the heterosexual world: 'Lesbians and gays feel very threatened by bisexuality. They seem to say that you can only be gay or straight. Some of my biggest critics are the people who you would have thought would understand what prejudice and intolerance is all about – blacks and gays.'

He wrote: 'When I came out I thought I would meet my true family. Sometimes I would listen to transsexuals and they would talk about how they were trapped in a body that wasn't theirs. I knew exactly what they meant. I felt I was living my life as a lie. I thought that when I came out all my problems would be over; all I would have to do was stand firm and I would be welcomed into the gay community. But it didn't happen like that. I felt isolated and alone and none of the people who could have helped me did. I felt used and abused by the gay machine, which seemed to say that I was just another celebrity to be exploited for the cause.' He added: 'Coming out for me was incredibly, almost suicidally, lonely.'

In this most intimate and honest portrayal of his struggles Justin still felt unable to admit that he had not wanted to come out. There was still a gap between the truth about his life and what he chose to share. But he was not covering up the difficulties he was experiencing with his religion: 'I am a born-again Christian and coming out has made me look at my faith very hard. I got no support from the church and so really had to think about the place of God in my life.'

Justin was still able to find an upbeat note to end on: 'Lesbians and gays are so creative, so dynamic, so loving and caring and spiritual that together we can create a joyous, rich environment. Lesbians and gay men have so much potential; with a little bit more courage, dignity and pride we will be absolutely great.'

Justin's disillusionment may explain how he responded to two young gay men who contacted him. Tony Dickenson was an Englishman living in the USA, playing soccer on a scholarship and struggling with being gay and a footballer. Then he came across an article about Justin in *BLK*, a magazine for lesbian, gay, bisexual and transgender African Americans. Contributing to an internet blog, Tony wrote that after reading the article, much of which was about *The Voice*'s coverage of Fashanu's coming out, he wrote to Justin and was amazed when Justin phoned him from Edinburgh to thank him for the note which he said he deeply appreciated.

Troy Fairclough, met with Justin around the same time. He is a younger brother of footballer, Chris Fairclough, who was at Nottingham Forest with Justin, and first met Justin when he was about 10 years old and Chris invited him to the family home. Troy talked to journalist, Hilary Whitney, for www.theartsdesk.com when he was publicising his play, *Justin Fashanu in Extra Time*: 'I was struck by his charisma…he charmed the whole family.' When Justin was at Hearts, Troy was at university in Scotland: 'As a young gay black man I wasn't exactly inundated with role models and my brother Chris suggested it might be a good idea if I met up with Justin…It was very strange and I kind of regretted it in a way because he was very different to the

The Biography

Justin I had met when I was younger. He was very distant, very guarded and there were lots of long pauses in the conversation. We didn't really engage with the whole coming out thing. We touched on just about everything else, about Chris and how the family were doing, but we never really addressed that. I'm not sure what I was looking for but whatever it was, I didn't get it.'

In the gay world of Edinburgh it seems that what David Thomas called 'the exploitative side' of Justin's character came to the fore. Writing in *The Scotsman*, immediately after his death, two journalists were scathing about his behaviour. Their tone was in marked contrast to that of John Colquhoun whose article was in the same edition. Conal Urquhart wrote: 'While he lived in Scotland he built up an image of a charming and suave gentleman. But the reality was a cynical manipulator who bled dry anyone with whom he became involved.' Gillian Glover had good reason to feel aggrieved. She was the latest person Justin had approached to help with his autobiography. She agreed to do so only for Justin to pull out of the project on the day the contract was due to be signed, saying he had a change of heart after praying. She wrote: 'He was immensely urbane and charming. It was difficult to believe he was actually a serpent wrapped round a tree which, on reflection, he was. Everyone who got close to him was shafted. With me it was only my time but with others it was an awful lot more.'

Evidently they knew of some seriously bad behaviour but did not feel able to be more explicit. Ten years later, in 2008, another journalist, Tom English, felt able to say more in his article, 'A Player to the End': 'He targeted wealthy gay men and charmed vast sums of money out of them. There's the tale of the wealthy businessman who was infatuated with Fashanu. To the footballer, this was an opportunity too good to miss. This businessman funded Fashanu's lavish lifestyle on the apparent promise of an affair that never materialised. Those who observed the scene said it was cruel, that Fashanu had taken his admirer for five figures, had abused his affections to a scandalous degree.'

As usual Justin was operating on many fronts and twice appeared on TV programmes talking about racism in football. On the Scottish TV show, *Trial by Night*, he argued that racism was worse among Scottish football fans than south of the border. In *Will to Win* he spoke about stereotyping of black footballers as unable to cope with the mud and cold of British winters. This stereotype was one he and other black footballers had done much to dispel but Ron Noades, the chairman of Crystal Palace, had brought it up again in 1991, saying on the TV programme, *Critical Eye*: 'When you're getting into mid-winter you need a few of the hard white men to carry the black players through.' His comments were particularly ridiculous because Crystal Palace were enjoying their most successful spell ever with black players such as Mark Bright and England internationals, Andy Gray and Ian Wright, in the team. Fashanu did not specifically refer to Noades but said: 'The first thing was that I felt really angry about it. Then I felt really disillusioned because these people saying these things were successful businessmen. They were people who had made money, who had got credibility. Presumably they had been around a little bit and it was scary to think these so-called models were thinking like that.'

*   *   *

Fashanu's participation in the first match against Athletico Madrid may have demonstrated how far he had come in his attempt to resurrect his career. But the return leg, two weeks later, marked the beginning of his decline. In the build-up to the game the Spanish press were critical of Fashanu, accusing him of going out to deliberately injure players in the first match. Fashanu predicted 'a torrid time' from the Athletico Madrid defenders. He needed to stay calm and not react to provocation. He failed to do so and was booked in the seventh minute. Clearly being wound up by the opposition players, he committed several more fouls. Fearing a red card, Sandy Clark felt obliged to take him off at half-time. Hearts lost 3–0 in front of 35,000 spectators and were out of the competition. In the league, Hearts were not scoring enough goals. A 1–0 defeat away to Raith Rovers in mid-October left the club third from bottom, the *Edinburgh Evening News* awarding Fashanu a rating of just three out of 10 for his performance. Something had to be done and Clark brought in striker Mo Johnston whose former clubs included Celtic, Rangers and Everton. Fashanu was dropped from the team.

Around the time Johnston arrived, Justin was giving an interview to Alex Bellos of *The Observer*. Headlined 'The Iconoclast Happy at Last' the piece painted a picture of a sophisticated man who had learned from his struggles. One paragraph read: 'Relaxing in his plush flat in Edinburgh's historic New Town, he is philosophical about the good his ordeal has done him. "I have had all the cars, the flash homes. Now I realise it is all so empty. Now I am hungry for new experiences. I go to operas, I go to classical recitals, I dine with politicians. I have an interest in the not-so-fashionable charities". He claimed his knee injury was not troubling him at all.

There were managers in Scotland who still believed in Fashanu. One was Premier Division Dundee United's Ivan Golac who had played with him at Southampton and managed him at Torquay. He described Fashanu as 'the best target man in Scotland next to Mark Hateley' and 'one of the best professionals I've ever worked with'. Golac put in a bid of £60,000 which was accepted by Hearts. Clark had some kind words for Fashanu: 'Justin is a good player and I'll be happy to keep him if he doesn't go. Things haven't worked out for him so far but there is no way our poor form recently is down to him.' Fashanu was ready to leave but the deal was vetoed by the Dundee United board with no explanation being given.

With Fashanu stuck in the reserves another offer came in, this time from Dundee FC, also in the Premier Division. Fashanu turned it down, saying he thought he could still make a contribution to Hearts. Dundee's player-manager was Jim Duffy. In 2006 he wrote about gay footballers for *Scotland on Sunday*. He did not mention having tried to sign Fashanu but did refer to him as 'a gem of a bloke'. Duffy wrote: 'Within the squad unit, the bond between players is powerful. You need only hear the Airdrie and Hearts guys who played with Fashanu talk so fondly of him to recognise that a person having a different sexuality need be no obstacle to them establishing a camaraderie with their fellow professionals.' He continued: 'I would not hesitate to sign a gay footballer and would never take any interest in a player's outside activities as long as they do not break the law or compromise their physical wellbeing. Equally, though, I would not hesitate to leave a gay player out if the barracking he received from the stands – which initially would be extreme – adversely affected him and threatened team morale.' Duffy's view was that any negative reaction to a gay player coming out in the 21st century would be from fans rather than players. It could be during matches or on the internet: 'Can you imagine how an openly gay footballer would be treated by frenzied opposition fans on all these bilious websites and fanzines?'

Out of the team and presumably in denial about his knee, Fashanu decided to seek advice from athletics coaches on how to improve his speed. He generated some headlines about entering Edinburgh's famous Hogmanay Dash but then withdrew. Justin did make a rather different public appearance in the festive period. It was in the TV show, *Camp Christmas*, with Julian Clary, Stephen Fry, Quentin Crisp, Sir Ian McKellen, Martina Navratilova, Pam St Clement and a host of other gay celebrities.

Fashanu was performing reasonably well in the reserves and the first team had failed to improve in his absence. Eight weeks since his pervious appearance in the first team he was named in the squad for a match away to St Johnstone. It was played on 18 December 1993, Fashanu coming on as a substitute as Hearts lost 2–0 in front of 4,600 spectators. It was his 15th and final game for Hearts and his last in British football.

Chapter 13

Changing Fortunes

Fashanu's last few weeks with Hearts were among the most eventful of his life. No longer in the team he was pursuing other interests. With a business partner he secured the lease to the City Café in Edinburgh's Blair Street. The *Edinburgh Evening News* reported that he intended to restore the 'trendy café' which had gone into receivership. Justin told the paper, 'it has a very subtle clientele'. He said he was settled in Edinburgh and, whatever happened in his football career, he wanted to stay there.

Into the New Year, Justin's ability to train and play for the reserves was restricted by his knee injury. But Scottish clubs were still interested in signing him. He turned down an offer from First Division Dumbarton because they could not match his wages. In February Airdrie tried to take him back to help with their promotion push. It looked like the perfect move but Justin had other things on his mind. Whatever he was saying in public he must have known his days as a professional footballer were numbered and he would soon lose any form of regular income. He had done well out of the tabloid press. There was the out-of-court settlement for his libel case against the *Sunday People*, his fee for coming out in *The Sun*, and the money he had made selling stores of his relationship with Julie Goodyear. Each had involved some degree of invention or deception. An idea began to form in his mind. If all went to plan it would earn him a fortune – and bring down the Conservative Government.

The Biography

John Major had succeeded Margaret Thatcher as Prime Minister. Leading up to the party conference in October 1993 the Conservatives were suffering in the opinion polls. In an attempt to boost his own and his party's popularity Major delivered a speech which emphasised his belief in what he perceived to be traditional British values: 'It is time to return to core values, time to get back to basics, to self-discipline and respect for the law, to consideration for others, to accepting responsibility for yourself and your family – and not shuffling it off on other people and the state.' The phrase, 'back to basics', was interpreted by some party members as a stand against moral decline and especially extra-marital sex. The Conservative Party was then embarrassed by revelations of several married MPs having affairs. Notably, in January 1994, Tim Yeo was forced by his constituency party to resign as a Government Minister after it emerged that a woman this married MP was having an affair with was expecting a baby.

Newspapers were eager for more stories about Conservative MPs' sexual indiscretions and this was the background against which Justin Fashanu hatched his plan with agent, Scott Hardie. At the beginning of February they approached the *News of the World* with their story. Fashanu was claiming to have had 'three-in-a-bed' sex sessions involving two senior members of the Government. They demanded £20,000 up front and a further £300,000 on delivery of the evidence which would enable the paper to run the story. They told the *News of the World* reporters it was the story of the century but failed to convince them it was true.

Next they tried *The People* and persuaded their reporters to pay for Fashanu to fly to London, stay in an expensive hotel and give him £1,000 for his time. He was demanding a further £300,000 if they used the story. When Fashanu met reporters, Mark Thomas and Phil Taylor, it was clear to them he could not back up his claims. But they realised without paying Fashanu any more they could write a story about him trying to sell this story to them.

It was published on Sunday 6 February and began: 'Bi-sexual soccer star, Justin Fashanu, claims he had three-in-a-bed gay sex romps with two senior members of the Government. And he is trying to peddle the sensational story for £300,000. "This will topple the Government", bragged Fashanu, the ex-lover of Julie Goodyear. "I had sex with two leading Tory MPs but I would never vote for them. The hypocrisy of these people makes me sick. How can they preach back to basics when they are leading a double life?"' The report also had a dig at 'the money grabbing player', saying that after being put up in a top hotel he complained: 'My room is like a broom cupboard. I live in a £250,000 house and I don't expect treatment like this.'

Fashanu had been out-manoeuvred and embarrassed. He was also in trouble with his club. On Monday 7 February Hearts announced he was being fined and suspended for missing training without permission when he was in London meeting the reporters. Chairman, Walter Mercer, said it was not the first time he had had to speak to Justin about missing training. On the same day, news was emerging that a Conservative MP, Stephen Milligan, had been found dead in his home. He had a plastic bin liner over his head, an electric flex round his neck and was wearing only a pair of women's stockings and a suspender belt. It was suspected that he died while practicing erotic asphyxiation which involves restricting the oxygen supply to the brain in order to heighten sexual arousal. It was not clear if anyone else was implicated in his death.

Having missed out once, Fashanu and Hardie sensed another money-making opportunity. They started contacting newspapers suggesting that Fashanu had the inside story on Stephen Milligan. To give credibility to the story they also contacted the police who were investigating Milligan's death. On Tuesday 8 February, Fashanu was quizzed by the police for two hours. The next morning, the *Daily Express* carried a front page report under the headline, 'Gay Soccer Star's Quiz on Dead MP: Probe into reports of sex ring at Commons'. Fashanu told the paper that he knew Milligan, knew he was gay and that he was not the strong and confident character in private life that he was in public. Fashanu added: 'There are many Tory MPs who are gay, more than people imagine.'

Significantly the *Daily Express* also reported that Fashanu had not been able to help the police. For the second time in a week he was at the centre of a story which did not appear to add up. Newspaper, radio and TV reporters gathered outside his house, eager for quotes and Fashanu ended up giving an impromptu press conference outside his front door. He started by telling the truth: 'I have never met Stephen Milligan…I have never, ever had any sexual relationship with an MP.' Then he tried to explain how the stories had got into the papers and did so by blaming the reporters: 'Like vultures you wanted to believe there was a relationship with a footballer and MPs with kinky sex.' He confessed that as – according to him – they already believed these stories to be true he saw the opportunity to make 'some easy money'.

Fashanu had not only damaged his credibility trying to sell gossip to the newspapers but, more seriously, had involved himself in a police investigation into the suspicious death of public figure. One of the many headlines about him in Thursday's papers was in the *Daily Mirror*, 'Fash the Trash: He wasted our time say angry cops'. A police officer had told the paper: 'We were led to believe he had important information that could help us clear up some of the unanswered questions but it turned out he had nothing to tell us. He said he didn't even know Mr Milligan. Some of our colleagues think he should be charged with wasting police time.'

Later that day Hearts issued a carefully worded statement. The directors said that Fashanu's contract would not be renewed at the end of the season and they would negotiate bringing his current contract to an end through the Scottish PFA. Sandy Clark said that Fashanu had continued to be absent from training and would not be selected for the first team again. He added: 'Recent press reports suggest that the player told lies in an effort to gain in financial terms. Hearts think such conduct is unbecoming for a professional.' Some press reports referred to Fashanu being sacked, which was not strictly true. In fact, Fashanu effectively dismissed himself. By the end of the day he was on a plane to Los Angeles.

Some unflattering profiles and opinion pieces appeared over the next few days. The most scathing came from Tom English, this time writing for *The Sunday Times*, who described Fashanu's recent behaviour as 'the most distasteful and sleazy episode in the history of Scottish football'. About the press conference he wrote: 'Fashanu did not look like a man that had lied through his teeth to prise "easy money" out of a tabloid newspaper…He did not look embarrassed, humiliated or defeated, just resigned to the fact that no matter what he said, people would take it up wrong, warp his words and land him in trouble again. It is the logic that created him and will ultimately destroy him.' He latched on to Fashanu's obsession with money: 'Becoming so highly paid at such a young age was the worst thing that could have happened to him. He wasn't ready for riches but slowly, as his form dipped and he couldn't live up to his price tag and his reputation, they became everything to him.'

English claimed that Fashanu's celebrity status as an openly gay man, rather than his ability, was the reason he had been able to stay in football so long. He wrote: 'This is the man who sensationally announced his homosexuality and immediately clubs clamoured for his signature thinking he would drag the punters through the turnstiles like some kind of bizarre travelling circus act.' Fashanu saw things rather differently. A week after his last game for Hearts, he told a *Daily Express* reporter he could be playing at a higher level, in the English Premier League (formerly the First Division) if he was just judged on his ability. English got his facts wrong. Clubs did not 'immediately clamour for his signature'. It was not until a year after he came out as gay that Fashanu was offered a trial by a British full-time professional club, Newcastle. Fashanu's argument that he could be playing at a higher level than the Scottish Premier League was equally fanciful. A thorough examination of how Fashanu actually performed on the pitch after coming out as gay suggests he probably played at the level his ability and fitness allowed.

Subsequent newspaper stories gave some insight into Justin's lifestyle and spending habits while living in Edinburgh. The *Edinburgh Evening News* reported that he had often held showy dinner parties in his flat and quoted a former friend: 'Justin enjoyed being part of the in crowd and tried very hard to impress everyone with his wealth. Little did we know he was bouncing cheques left, right and centre.'

He was reported to have left a trail of debts: cleaners, a flower shop and laundry were among businesses he owed money to. He left nearly 30 boxes of personal possessions in storage including racks of Armani and Boss clothes, and antiques. Three years after Justin left Edinburgh the storage firm revealed that, having failed to recoup the £2,500 he owed them, they were entitled to sell his possessions.

*   *   *

Justin's knee injury and the mess he had made of trying to make money from selling stories to newspapers had rendered him virtually unemployable in Britain. North America still offered possibilities but it was over a year before he was working and earning again. He tried once more to resume his football career in Canada. In May, Hearts were in Hamilton for a tournament with Aberdeen and Celtic to commemorate British week. Some of the players were sitting outside a café, soaking in the afternoon sun when, as John Colquhoun recalled: 'A large white car drew up and the big man jumped out and told us to wait while he got changed.' But they never saw him again.

Trying to track Justin down was journalist, Mark Honigsbaum, who was writing a feature on John Fashanu for the magazine, *GQ*. But he was equally interested in Justin, the relationship between the two brothers and their contrasting fortunes. Everything seemed to be going right for John. He had married Melissa Kassa-Mapsi, born in Ivory Coast and the niece of a former president. Journalist, David Thomas (not the reporter who covered Torquay United) described her as, 'coming from an African family of enormous wealth and political influence'. John was hosting the popular Saturday evening TV show, *Gladiators*, with Ulrika Jonsson. Honigsbaum captured his jet-setting lifestyle: 'On Sunday he was in Zambia delivering medical supplies in his capacity as a roving ambassador for Unicef. On Tuesday he flew back to London to entertain some clients from Nigeria. Then today, Wednesday, he was up with the lark to open a new youth opportunity centre in Acton, followed by another business meeting with clients from Sierra Leone.' John was reluctant to talk about Justin, at one point threatening to end the interview if Honigsbaum pursued his line of questioning.

Honigsbaum eventually contacted Justin through James Thompson, the restaurateur who had been buying the City Café with him before Justin made his sudden exit from Edinburgh. According to Thompson Justin was playing for the Canadian team, Toronto Italia, but although he signed a contract it was cancelled when he failed to show up for training. Justin would not speak to Honigsbaum but sent him a statement which Honigsbaum described as, 'rather rambling and apologetic' but also, 'defiant and rather moving'. It ended: 'I believe we have one life to learn and to grow and, if you fall, the outward journey gives you enormous strength. Nobody has been physically, mentally, spiritually, intentionally hurt. The thought I leave you with is love has to be unconditional.' Honigsbaum wrote: 'This last sentence, especially, seems to be pregnant with meaning. In the end Justin appears to be speaking directly to his brother.'

Justin was keeping a low profile but in January 1995 a *Daily Express* reporter tracked him down to a council estate in Harthill, a village halfway between Edinburgh and Glasgow and a few miles from Airdrie. He was staying with Susan Arnott, described as a 36-year-old factory worker. She told the reporter: 'People think it's strange him living here with me. We are not having a relationship or anything like that. We are just good friends. I have known Justin for years.' She said they attended church together every Sunday and Justin spent a lot of time with the local children who saw him as a big brother type figure. All Justin said was: 'I'm living here and I'm feeling good.' Airdrie fan, Gary Stewart, remembers playing on a local five-a-side pitch wearing an Airdrie top. As he was leaving he heard someone singing an Airdrie song. He turned round and was surprised to see it was Justin. They chatted for a while. He remembers: 'Justin was there with some guys from Whitburn Pentecostal Church.'

The *Daily Express* made much of this 'sad riches-to-rags story', saying it was, 'a poignant contrast to the glittering millionaire lifestyle of younger brother John Fashanu'. But, soon after, John experienced some setbacks. At the beginning of the 1994–95 season he had moved from Wimbledon to Aston Villa for £1.35 million but was injured in February and never played again. Then in March he and his wife were among several people arrested over allegations of match-fixing. Melissa Kassa-Mapsi was not charged but John was together with the Southampton and former Liverpool goalkeeper, Bruce Grobbelaar, Wimbledon goalkeeper, Hans Segers, and Malaysian businessman, Heng Suan Lim. After the first trial the jury was unable to reach verdicts and it was necessary to hold a second. It was not until November 1997 that this trial was concluded, the defendants all being found not guilty.

But John Fashanu, who exercised his right to silence throughout, still came out of the saga with his reputation and his bank balance severely dented. Having been found not guilty he expected to have his legal costs reimbursed from the public purse. But when his solicitor applied to the judge he refused to allow it. According to David Thomas in his account of the trials and the events leading up to them, *Foul Play*, the judge said this was because John came into the category of a defendant who had brought proceedings upon himself and acted in such as way as to lead the authorities to believe that the case against him was stronger than it actually was. Challenged by John's solicitor the judge was more specific: 'He chose to receive very considerable sums from the Far East in the names of other people and that can only have led the prosecution to believe the sums were obtained nefariously, coupled with the total absence of any indication of business activities that could account for the proper use of these monies.' John Fashanu's legal costs were believed to be £650,000. He also lost work including his *Gladiators* contract, the total cost to him of these trials coming to around £1 million.

*   *   *

While it was John's turn for his financial dealings and integrity to be under scrutiny Justin was quietly rebuilding his life. In August 1995 he moved to Georgia in the southern United States to play for Atlanta Ruckus. He found himself in a city with a rich history as a centre for the American civil rights movement, the birthplace of Martin Luther King and with over half the population African American.

North American soccer had gone through organisational changes since he last played in Canada in 1991. Atlanta were in the six-team A-League, which included three Canadian teams and was the second tier of North American soccer.. It was well into the season when he made his debut on 11 August in a home match against Seattle Sounders in front of 2,425 spectators. He made an immediate impact, scoring in the 10th minute. The game finished 1–1 and, with no draws allowed, went to a sudden death shoot-out, won by Atlanta. Interviewed for the *Atlanta Constitution*, he could not resist being less than truthful about his recent career: 'I've been playing at the highest level of soccer for 16 years and when you do that you just need to take time off.' He claimed to have played for Hearts for three years, to have been one of the Scottish League's top scorers, and said he had not played competitively for eight months when it was actually a year and eight months.

The Ruckus finished fourth in the A-league, qualifying for the play-off semi-finals. The first leg, on 14 September, was at home to Montreal Impact but Fashanu was nowhere to be seen. He had been suspended by the club. It was another difficult episode in his professional life but his move to Atlanta would still prove to be a success. Justin was volunteering with the soccer coaching programme run by the YMCA (Young Men's Christian Association) in Buckhead, a district of Atlanta. He arrived to find a volatile situation. The popular director of soccer activities, Bizham Vesali, had been sacked after a criminal background check revealed a drug conviction from many years previously. Parents who volunteered on the programme were campaigning for him to be reinstated. Meanwhile the YMCA had to run coaching sessions for up to 2,800 young people. Chief executive, Phil Noble, explained: 'That's when Justin came on as a volunteer. Once we saw what we had we asked him to come on full-time.' Justin was put in charge of the whole fall programme and did so well he was given the job for the following two years.

He was able to enjoy some rare stability and guaranteed income while demonstrating talents which would enable him to continue to earn a living from football after he retired from playing. One of the coaches, Sean, who worked with Justin in 1996, recalled the experience in an internet post: 'He was a really nice, humble guy who all of the coaches I knew really liked and respected. We had a coaching clinic one weekend and the guy running it played a tape of the 100 greatest goals in Premiership history and I was shocked to see Justin had one of the goals. He never mentioned he was a professional footballer.'

But that summer Fashanu had to survive a threat to his job when stories of his past reached Buckhead. The *Atlanta Constitution* reported: 'The leader of Buckhead YMCA [Peter Noble] says he was unaware that its new sports director had been a favorite topic of sensational tabloid news reports in Britain. Tabloid newspapers in London and Scotland drew unflattering portraits of Justin Fashanu in 1994 and 1995, linking him to scandal, alleging financial problems and reporting troubles with the last team for which he played in Britain. There were no reports of unlawful activity.' Fashanu declined to comment but was supported by Noble. He admitted not having known about Fashanu's reputation in the British newspapers but said the YMCA had carried out a criminal check which had extended to Britain. He continued: 'Justin's doing very well. His performance has been very good. He's poised, professional and he knows his job.'

New forms of communication were making it harder for public figures to keep unpalatable information away from an interested public, a development which would ultimately get Justin into serious trouble. In November 1996 the internet made possible a more light-hearted incident, prompting the headline in Norfolk's *Eastern Daily Press*, 'Fashanu 'plot' uncovered by BBC'. It reported: 'The BBC yesterday ruled out the possibility of Justin Fashanu becoming the unlikely winner of their prestigious Sports Personality of the Year award.' Fashanu had been the recipient of hundreds of votes cast using email in what the BBC said was an organised attempt to hijack the award. The votes were to be discounted. The *Eastern Daily Press* suggested Justin may have been seen as the perfect antihero by those looking to upset the status quo, being 'both black and a homosexual'.

By this time he was in New Zealand, playing for Miramar Rangers in the National Summer League. The club had links with Norwich City; Peter Mendham and John Fashanu having both played there in the early 1980s when they were signed with Norwich and seeking to regain fitness. The season for the Summer League was November to March, fitting in well with Justin's responsibilities with Buckhead YMCA. New Zealand soccer was amateur but in practice players could be paid for taking on additional responsibilities. Fashanu was given a role of promoting the club, one to which he was ideally suited. A recording of an interview with Derek Walker on *The Football Show*, on radio station, The Point 1476, showed him in fine form, bubbling with positivity. A typical comment on New Zealand soccer was, 'There is lots of talent that just needs to be nurtured and brought along.' He was running training camps for young people, promoting them with the slogan, 'Come and play soccer in the sun'. Asked about his future he did not talk of playing but about coaching youngsters: 'I'm pleased with taking things slowly and seeing what happens.'

Walker was familiar with Fashanu's playing career in Britain and asked him a series of questions about the different clubs he had played for. Fashanu said his fondest moment was signing for Norwich City. He admitted things had not worked out with Nottingham Forest, his voice tightening up as he spoke. But when Walker asked, 'Brian Clough; was he a decent chap?' his quick wit came to his rescue, replying, 'He thought so, next question'. He sounded most enthusiastic when talking about his time with Airdrie which he described as phenomenal: 'We had a superb following. The crowd was very partisan and loyal and it was very aggressive. People didn't want to play at our place.' Listening to him, you could forget they had been relegated.

Soccer in New Zealand was behind rugby and cricket in popularity. Miramar, a suburb of the capital, Wellington, were attracting crowds which were usually under 1,000, though 2,000 watched the home game against Wellington United. The standard of soccer was a level below the North American A-League and one at which Fashanu could still excel. One fan remembers: 'He was pretty heavyset and slow when over here but was a good target man, had a good lay off, and the odd really classy touch which set him apart from the average player. He was pretty useful with his elbows too.' He was still capable of the occasional special moment: 'I watched him score an absolutely fantastic volley reminiscent of the goal he scored against Liverpool.'

An article in *The Dominion* summed up the impact he was making on and off the pitch. Miramar had won their first four matches with Fashanu scoring three goals: 'Pacesetting national league soccer club, Miramar Rangers, are enjoying Justin Fashanu's influence off the park as much as on it. Coach, John Cameron, said, "He offers quite a lot at practice but he doesn't do it in a way that undermines the coaching staff. The younger guys think he's marvellous taking them for a little extra practice". Fashanu's abilities have given Miramar a new attacking dimension, and helped divert attention away from Miramar's other potential goal scorers.'

Kevin Thompson played with him in the Miramar forward line and says: 'I must say I liked Fash, he was a nice guy, maybe a little mixed up. There was no drama about him being gay; a bit of banter between the lads. He had a good sense of humour.' Justin was in a sexual relationship with a man he met in Wellington but, as usual, he kept his personal life well away from football. A favourite memory Kevin Thompson has of Justin was the time he invited him to a party at his flat: 'Justin rolled in at about 10pm wearing tight black leather trousers and a body-tight pink singlet. This huge black man in the lounge was quite a sight – he carried it off well and the ladies thought he was a "right geezer".'

Miramar's form dropped away and the team ended up fifth in a 10-club league, Fashanu scoring an impressive 12 goals in 18 games. Having left Hearts in disgrace and Atlanta Ruckus suspended by the club, his spell with Miramar went relatively smoothly, perhaps more evidence of Fashanu settling down and carving out a new, quieter and controversy-free life for himself. But he may not have completely put his carelessness with other people's money behind him. It seems that he ran up some hefty bills in the name of the club which he left Miramar to pick up after his departure. And he appears still not to have accepted the need to pay parking tickets despite the best efforts of Ronnie Brooks, at Norwich City, and then Brian Clough.

Justin returned to his job with Buckhead YMCA and, in June was tempted back to Atlanta Ruckus. The Ruckus had nearly gone out of business in 1996 before being rescued by local businessman, Vincent Lu. He moved the club to Roswell, an old High School stadium in an area with a growing Hispanic community and, with this in mind, the club recruited a number of players from South America. The coach was the experienced Angus McAlpine, who had previously coached the USA national Under-20 team. But the club was under-financed and disorganised. The build-up to Fashanu's first match illustrated the chaos McAlpine was operating in. The squad was about to embark on a 5,000 mile round trip to play Seattle Sounders and Vancouver 86ers. But two players, from Nigeria and Mexico, had not secured visas and two Brazilians were flying in to join up in Canada by no means sure they would be allowed in. A long injury list guaranteed the out-of-condition Fashanu a starting place against Seattle who thrashed the Ruckus 7–0.

Angus McAlpine remembers that Fashanu 'was tripping over his feet and struggling terribly', and 'one yard behind in his pace and in his mind'. Fashanu was having a tough time with the Brazilians complaining that he should not be in the team because his ball control was so poor. In turn, Fashanu criticised them for turning up late for training and away trips. He told McAlpine, 'You should crack the whip, like Brian Clough'. McAlpine could see Fashanu had something to offer and persisted in playing him, believing his game would pick up as he got fit. He felt vindicated by Fashanu's performance against El Paso Patriots, a few weeks after his debut, when he scored his first goal of the season: 'He was on his own against a goalie and a defender. He was at too much of an angle to score so he kicked the ball back towards his own side. He turned, looked up and then booted it and scored. From then on the Brazilians were happy. They said, "Alright you should keep him".'

But shortly after this match McAlpine resigned after a row with Lu who, he felt, was not investing enough in the club and did not understand soccer. McAlpine had wanted Fashanu to be his assistant coach, and Fashanu begged him to stay, saying they could work together. McAlpine went back to Lu but it was too late and McAlpine and Fashanu both ended up leaving. McAlpine thought he was the only person at the club who knew Justin was gay but according to Lu: 'Everybody knew who he was and what his life had been like but nobody here had a problem with him that I know of.' Fashanu's record with Atlanta Ruckus over 1995 and 1997 was 11 matches and two goals, scored on his first and last appearances. It was not only his last appearance for the Ruckus but his final match as a professional footballer.

*   *   *

Around the time Justin was leaving the Ruckus Graham Daniels met him at Buckhead YMCA. It was Daniels who had invited him to talk about Christianity to his teammates at Cambridge United during Fashanu's Notts County days. He had brought over from Britain a group from Christians in Sport and was surprised to find Justin working there. They had a long conversation over breakfast one day. Justin talked about how difficult it was being catapulted into the public arena as a Christian and then wrestling with his sexual identity but feeling he could not talk about it. Daniels recalls that the conversation was serious but Justin did not seem weighed down by the world. In public he was 'extremely articulate and effervescent'.

At the end of August 1997 Justin made an emotional return to Norfolk for the funeral of his foster mother, Betty Jackson. John missed the occasion because he was on a business trip to Nigeria and Justin spoke for both of them to the *Daily Mirror*: 'I know John feels the same way as I do. We know it was Mama Jackson who gave us the strength of character and foundation we needed in life to make our assault on football. She was faithful, loyal and loving.' Betty Jackson's son, Edward, recalls Justin viewing her body and getting upset because she did not look like the Betty he remembered. While in Norfolk Justin was able to spend time with Ronnie Brooks who had been a father figure to him when he signed for Norwich City.

After Betty Jackson's funeral, Edward and his family visited Justin in Atlanta. Betty had not left a will and Edward and his sister, Susan, decided they wanted to share their inheritance with Justin and John: 'We thought that was what she would have wished for.' They also wanted to talk to Justin about his future. Edward told the *Eastern Daily Press*: 'We hired a motor home and visited him in Atlanta where he was staying with a family. We tried to convey the idea that we were always there for him if he needed us. We were worried about his career because he seemed to be determined that his career was in football. He had had this knee problem and we were saying that maybe someone was trying to tell him something. He was always very good with people and would have made a good TV presenter, but he wouldn't let go of football.'

Back in Britain the *Pink Paper* decided to celebrate its 500th issue by polling its readers on which public figures had made the most impact on lesbians and gay men. Princess Diana was easily first. Justin Fashanu came in at 98. It was some acknowledgement of the courage he had shown in playing as an openly gay footballer and his willingness to confront homophobia. On the other hand he had alienated some lesbians and gay men with his evident unease with his sexual identity and his attempts, successful and unsuccessful, to sell gossip to the tabloid press.

Meanwhile, it seemed as if there was no need to be concerned about his future. Fashanu was no longer pursuing playing contracts and was completing his third year heading up Buckhead YMCA's sports coaching programme. But he was ready for a new challenge. A friend of his was starting up a new franchise to play in the A-League. With his playing experience, coaching skills and flair for PR, Fashanu had a lot to offer.

Chapter 14

January – May 1998

In January 1998, Justin moved into a rented apartment in an exclusive development in Ellicott City, Howard County, an affluent area between Baltimore and Washington DC. He had been hired by A.J. Ali, a young entrepreneur from Baltimore, to be coach of a new franchise, Maryland Mania. His job in the first year was to build up the Mania at all levels as preparation for participation in the A-League in 1999. Attracting the interest and involvement of young people was crucial and on 26 February the *Baltimore Sun* announced: 'The Columbia-based Maryland Mania, which is to begin to play next year in pro soccer's A-league, and the Soccer Association of Columbia, will offer a free two-hour clinic starting at 10am 7 March at Hawthorn Park in the village of Hickory Ridge. This clinic is specifically aimed at children from low-income families who are not registered with a soccer club. Girls and boys between six and 13 years old are welcome. Justin Fashanu, Mania coach and former English Premier League player, will lead the clinic.'

Justin found a gay scene in Washington DC. A gay man told Scottish paper, the *Daily Record*, that Justin particularly liked a club, Mr Ps. Another described him as a party animal who was always kind and helpful, never did drugs and was never into anything dangerous. Meanwhile A.J. Ali, who was a friend of Justin's introduced him to the church he attended, the Bridgeway Community Church in Columbia.

The Biography

On Saturday 21 March A.J. Ali took Justin along to a men's Bible study class led by Lonny Wortham, a pastor at the church. Wortham had not met Justin before and did not know he was gay but, as it happened, gave him a passage to read from the Bible which dealt with 'sexual purity'. Justin expressed some disagreement with it which led to a discussion between them after the class. They arranged to continue their discussion the following Tuesday but when Wortham phoned he did not get an answer.

Justin had his mind on other things. Through his role with Maryland Mania, he was meeting local teenagers and began inviting them to his apartment. That Tuesday, 24 March, four young men and two young women, all between the ages of 16 and 18, gathered at his home, drinking beer and smoking marijuana. Maryland state law only allowed people under 21 to consume alcohol if they had their parent's consent. Journalist, Brian Deer, investigated what happened at Justin's apartment that evening for an article published in the *Mail on Sunday* in July of that year. According to Deer's account, Justin, who was 37, told these teenagers that he was 28 years old. He also said he could offer them office jobs with the Mania at the improbably high rate of $200 a day. One of the young men was DJ, a 17-year-old who had a job delivering dishwashers and cookers. (DJ was the name he gave in interviews.) He arrived around 6 or 7pm. Over the evening, night and next morning several incidents occurred which resulted in him phoning the police to complain he had been sexually assaulted by Justin. Less than six weeks later Justin was dead.

*   *   *

There are differing and sometimes contradictory accounts of what occurred that night; the actions and intentions of the Howard County Police Department; and how and where Justin spent his last few weeks. What follows is the most complete, accurate and unbiased account which could be put together from both existing and freshly obtained information. It shows how misunderstandings have arisen and been perpetuated, so much so that some articles about Justin Fashanu assume there is no doubt that he was guilty of serious crimes whereas others are equally sure the police had no interest in him.

DJ accused Justin of three instances of unwanted sexual attention. The first involved touching; the second, anal sex; and the third, oral sex. There are three main sources of information about DJ's accusations: the TV documentary, *Fallen Hero*; Brian Deer's article, 'End Game' for the *Mail on Sunday*; and newspaper, *The Scotsman*.

DJ gave an account of the first incident to *Fallen Hero*. He said that about 9.30pm he asked Justin if he could ring his girlfriend, Laura and his mother. Justin said he could use the phone in the bedroom. DJ described what happened next: 'Justin followed me into the bedroom and I was sitting on the edge of the bed and Justin sat behind me while I was talking to Laura. Justin reached around me and was sort of fondling me. And I quickly told Laura there was something wrong and I had to get off the phone…I hung up on her, got up, I turned around and told Justin I wasn't gay and I preferred women. He said he was sorry, nothing would happen again. Could we let the night go on as it was? I said it was fine with me. I was having a good time, I'm not afraid to admit it, and I did want to stay to party.' Deer's account of this incident is broadly similar but Justin's action sounds more aggressive: 'He made a grab for his [DJ's] groin'.

Deer takes up the story. DJ then phoned his mother who told him to come home. DJ did not have a car and his mother, who had been disabled in a traffic accident, could not come and collect him. His father, a salesman and former policeman, was away on a business trip. DJ refused to leave. His mother accused him of drinking and they had a row. DJ put down the phone and went back to the party. Around 11pm, four of the group departed, leaving Justin, DJ and one other young man. Justin suggested to DJ that they should get some more beers and they drove to the Allview Liquor Store in his borrowed Mercedes before returning to the apartment.

There are three versions of the second, most serious alleged incident. In Deer's article he described DJ feeling tired soon after midnight: 'He felt a strange, hazy feeling, not easy to explain. It was not a feeling he was at all used to. He had only drunk three 22oz beers [just over three pints in total] and the marijuana didn't pack that sort of punch.' According to this version, DJ told Justin he was too drunk to go home and asked if he could sleep on the couch which Justin agreed to. Deer wrote: 'DJ fell asleep. The other kid left. Time moved on to 2am.' Choosing his words for maximum impact Deer continued: 'Soon after, Fashanu seized his chance. He would not take rejection a second time. At some dimly-lit level DJ knew what was happening. But his struggle to stop it failed. Fashanu's power was briefly regained. The ex-star raped the boy.'

DJ's own description of this second incident was somewhat different. Speaking in *Fallen Hero* he said he remembered falling asleep on the couch but the next thing he remembered was waking up in the bedroom. He added: 'But earlier in the night, it was almost like a dream, I can remember seeing Justin behind me, and it seemed so much like a dream I didn't even bother with it.' DJ made no mention of a struggle.

A third version of this second incident was reported in *The Scotsman* on 5 May. It claimed to quote directly from papers lodged with the court. According to this account, DJ told the police: 'I crashed on his sofa and the next thing I remember was waking up with him attacking me. I mean on top of me with his hand on my neck. I tried to scream but he pushed my face down. I was humiliated and in pain. When he had finished I was sobbing. I slipped out of the apartment when he was in the bathroom.' Not only was this version substantially different from the other two but, if it was accurate, the third incident could not have occurred. (Unfortunately this biographer's attempt to verify *The Scotsman*'s account was thwarted when he was denied access to the court papers on grounds of the age of the alleged victim.)

The third incident DJ described occurred in the bedroom. He said in *Fallen Hero* that he woke up to find Justin performing oral sex on him. According to Brian Deer's account, this happened about 8am: 'DJ said he yelled, "No", struggled up, got dressed and immediately left the apartment.'

DJ walked a mile home and after he spoke to his mother they phoned the Howard County Police Department reporting a sexual assault. The police took them to the emergency room at Howard County General Hospital for tests. There a doctor found a tear in DJ's rectum with bleeding. Samples were taken for analysis. Later that day DJ was interviewed by Detective First Class Glenn Case. He told Case he thought he had been drugged.

No one can say what went through Justin's mind after DJ left. Was he expecting a visit from the police? Did he decide in advance what he would say? Justin was used to not telling the truth. He had felt forced to lie about his sexuality and succeeded in keeping it out of the public arena for a long time. He had made money out of lying to newspapers. He routinely exaggerated the story of his British football career when he was in North America. Lying had also got him into deep trouble. His attempts to sell stories about Conservative MPs had gone badly wrong and he could have been charged with wasting police time. When these stories surfaced in Atlanta and threatened his position as head of youth coaching, he might have realised that the internet had ended his ability to move continents and leave his past behind.

On the morning of Thursday 26 March, Detective First Class Glenn Case drove to Justin's apartment to question him about DJ's allegations. He had worked out a strategy. He would give Justin an 'out'. He would ask him if he had had consensual sex with DJ. If Justin said he had, there was little the police could do. There were no witnesses and the case would probably not have gone to court. The age of consent being 16, if the sex had been consensual nothing illegal would have occurred. The marijuana and alcohol were relatively trivial matters in comparison.

Justin answered the door. Glenn Case explained why he was there and Justin agreed to answer some questions. Case asked him about DJ. Justin said DJ had slept in his apartment but nothing of a sexual nature had occurred. He said he had heard the door close when DJ left to go home. Brian Deer reported what happened next. Glenn Case explained to Justin that he was not under arrest but he wanted to ask some more questions. Justin said he was willing to answer them. In response to these questions he told Case he was not gay; that he had not taken DJ to buy beer; and that he was willing to take a lie detector test and provide a blood sample. Deer noted: 'Case left the apartment puzzled by Fashanu's self-assurance. Given the possibility of a rape charge, self-assurance was an incongruous demeanour whether he had committed the offence or not.'

Justin was feeling far from self-assured. Soon after Case left he phoned Lonny Wortham who remembers him sounding 'very panicked'. He told Wortham he had had consensual sex with DJ who asked for money the next morning. When Justin told him he did not have any money to give, DJ threatened him, saying if he did not give him something he would tell what happened. He said he was frightened, that DJ had gone to the police and he thought he was going to be charged. Next Justin phoned his friend Maria Sol Acuña in London. Managing to sound relaxed he told her he was missing England and had decided to return. Would it be OK if he stayed with her until he found somewhere to live? She was about to set off on a two week holiday but said he was welcome to use her flat and she would leave the keys with the porter. The next time Wortham heard from him was later that day or the next day. Justin phoned from the airport to ask him to pick up the car he was leaving there. He was on his way to London.

Unaware of Fashanu's absence, Glenn Case continued to investigate the events of the night of 24 March. He spoke to other people who had been at the party and obtained witness statements saying Fashanu had taken DJ to buy alcohol. He interviewed DJ for a second time and DJ told him Justin Fashanu had been a famous sports star in England. When Case got back to the station, out of curiosity, he put Fashanu's name into an internet search engine. It took him to two websites which named him as an openly gay soccer player. Fashanu had lied to him at least twice. Tests had shown the presence of semen in the sample collected from the hospital. It could provide conclusive evidence that Fashanu did have sex with DJ.

The law in Maryland made anal sex between anyone, gay or straight, illegal. Known as the Sodomy Laws, this legislation had been introduced across the USA in 1916. Additionally Maryland had legislation which specifically made oral sex between lesbians or gay men illegal. But these laws were being challenged by the American Civil Liberties Union. The Sodomy Laws were being repealed across the USA. In Maryland this legislation and the law relating to oral sex had fallen into disuse. Within a year they would both be repealed. In practice, if Justin was going to be prosecuted it would be under legislation which did not discriminate between homosexual and heterosexual acts and did not forbid consensual anal or oral sex. Whereas in England the age of consent for gay sex was still, at 18, two years above that for heterosexual sex, this distinction did not apply in Maryland. The age of consent was 16 in all instances.

As the evidence against Justin mounted, the police were getting ready to charge him on three counts: They were: first degree assault – having the intention of forced sodomy; second degree assault – which related to unwanted touching; and second degree sexual assault – anal rape. If found guilty he faced a prison sentence of up to 20 years although it would probably be about 10. It was not until Thursday 2 April, eight days into the investigation, that the police obtained a search warrant and went to Justin's apartment. They found he had gone, taking clothes and personal effects with him. The next day they obtained an arrest warrant.

*   *   *

Soon after arriving in England Justin phoned Lonny Wortham. It seemed that he had never resolved the conflicts between his faith and his sexual orientation in his 16 years as a gay born-again Christian. He had not gravitated away from churches which saw homosexuality as a sin, nor had he tried to modify his sexual behaviour. The accusations he faced had brought that conflict to crisis point. Wortham describes him as having 'a soul in torment'. Justin called every few days, though not saying where he was calling from. Their conversations lasting from 15 minutes to an hour. They would talk theology, about the Bible and homosexuality, and also about how Justin should deal with the accusation of sexual assault. He was terrified of going to jail but Wortham pointed out there might not even be a trial and he could not stay on the run for ever. Justin and Lonny Wortham were able to engage in discussion about whether homosexuality and Christianity were compatible; Wortham believing that it was not, Justin arguing that God had made him gay but being willing to reconsider his position. They talked about him getting involved with a Christian organisation called Exodus international which 'offers hope and help to people seeking freedom from homosexuality'.

Justin spoke to at least two more people about his fears giving them the same version of events he had given Lonny Wortham. He called his friend, Neil Slawson, who had become a police officer in California and asked him for some informal legal advice, especially about extradition. Justin told him he was not confident he could prove the sex had been consensual. He turned up unannounced at Ronnie Brooks' home in Norfolk. He was upset and scared. They hugged and Justin burst into tears.

Brooks, the magistrate, had once told Justin he had to pay his parking tickets. This time there was far more at stake and he could see no alternative other than to advise Justin to go back to Maryland and face the possible charges.

Ten years previously, when his knee injury was threatening his career, Justin had visited a community of Cistercian monks in a Catholic monastery, Mount Saint Bernard Abbey, set in Charnwood Forest, Leicestershire. He contacted the monastery again, booking himself into an Easter Retreat. He used the name, Justin Lawrence, this surname being his mother's maiden name, but gave his real name when he arrived. There, with other guests and the monks, he attended mass seven times a day starting at 3.15am. He was befriended by an Irish woman, Rita Condon, who told *The Sun*: 'He was so nice and seemed a happy man but there was a sadness in his eyes.' Once he told her he was tired and asked her to pray that he would stay in England. She said he spent much of the time walking in the grounds on his own. He did not tell Rita Condon what had brought him there but did talk to the monks about it, continuing with them the discussion he had with Lonnie Wortham. Father Rufus was interviewed for *Fallen Hero* and said: 'I never had a sense that Justin was in any way condemnatory, at all, as regards the individual in the States and the accusations and so on. He seemed to be very understanding. But there was no doubt in my own mind that that was the catalyst that had got him to this very rock bottom…To the fore of his mind was the awareness that throughout his life there had been a conflict between his faith and his sexuality. He was struggling to come to some understanding and to know how he could move forward because he was so very aware that he hadn't dealt well with that in the past. In his own words, that it had been a very destructive force in his life.'

Justin stayed in touch with Lonny Wortham, speaking to him for the last time one to two weeks before his death. On that occasion Justin asked him: 'What happens to a Christian who commits suicide? Does he go to heaven?' He asked Justin if he was thinking about suicide. Justin assured him he was not; it was a general question; he sounded convincing on that point. Wortham told him: 'God does not want you to sin.' It was understood between them that sin could be forgiven; 'Jesus died for our sins'.

Some further information about Justin's movements was revealed at the inquest into his death. According to the coroner, he made a brief trip to the USA though no further information has emerged about where he went or who he saw. He was clearly frightened by the situation he found himself in, and in turmoil about what to do. Yet he was able to convince at least two people that he had no problems at all. Soon after arriving in London Justin answered an advertisement from Kaveh Abadani who was looking for someone to share his flat in Swiss Cottage. Justin moved in with him.

The Biography

Kaveh Abadani told the inquest that Justin was 'positive, friendly, very confident, starting a new life in London, happy.' Justin told him he was going to make a pilot of a TV programme.

After Maria Sol Acuña returned from her holiday they saw a great deal of each other over the next few weeks. She found him happy and pleased to be back in England. He did not mention the trouble he was in to her. There are perhaps two explanations for Justin's apparently positive state of mind. One is that he was adept at keeping things to himself. He had managed to keep his gay life secret from close friends, housemates and family for many years. But also, as time passed and he heard nothing about being wanted by the police, perhaps he relaxed, thinking the investigation had been dropped.

On Thursday 30 April Justin spent the evening at the home of Maria Sol and her daughter, Amal, who was nine years old. Justin adored Amal and the feeling was mutual. Writing for the Justin Campaign website in 2011 Amal said 'I remember the day as if it happened minutes ago'. She came home from school and was delighted to find him there. She remembers them having 'a strawberries and cream war' with their dessert. Then she sat on his lap while she did her homework. Amal dreamt of being a singer and Justin knew somebody who owned a recording studio. He offered to take her there on the Saturday. Maria Sol remembers Justin was happy and smiling when he left that night.

*   *   *

In Maryland attempts by the police to find Justin had not succeeded. When they discovered he had been living in Atlanta they spoke to the police there who confirmed he had not been accused of any crimes in the State of Georgia. Rather than leave the case open they put out a press release in the hope someone who knew where Justin was living would contact them.

The news was made public the day after Justin visited Maria Sol and Amal. A short bulletin from the US-based news agency, Associated Press, was released at 9.12am Eastern Time on Friday 1 May. In London the time was 2.12pm. Under the headline, 'Justin Fashanu sought by police in sexual assault', the news item outlined the charges he faced and reported that the Howard County police believed he had left the country. The UK-based Press Association picked up on the story. Using the headline, 'Police Hunt Soccer Star Over Gay Assault Claim', it gave more detail including a quote from a Sergeant Morris Carroll: 'Right now we are asking Mr Fashanu to return to Howard County, Maryland, voluntarily. That is what we are hoping he will do once he hears that the arrest warrant exists, but if he does not we will extradite him.' A PA journalist had contacted John Fashanu who said he had not spoken to Justin for more than seven years: 'I have not got a clue where he is. It does not interest me one iota what he does.' The story was also taken up by the *Baltimore Sun*. It reported that 'a source' said detectives had alerted federal and international agencies about the charges facing Fashanu. In a more considered response John told the paper: 'No one knows where he is. I am greatly concerned and saddened by these allegations and pray to God they are not true.'

There was to be a great deal of confusion about the actions and intentions of the Howard County Police Department. Firstly, Justin was entirely within his rights to leave the USA when he did and there was no warrant out for his arrest at the time. He may not have known of the warrant until these news reports on 1 May. Secondly, the Howard County police had not yet initiated an international search. The *Baltimore Sun* was wrong in this critical respect. Thirdly, although police threatened to extradite Justin if he was found to be living outside of the USA whether they would have done was questionable. When interviewed for this book, Glenn Case was doubtful if his department would have invested the effort, time and money required. It was not 'the crime of the century', he said.

Much of the information about Justin Fashanu's last hours comes from contemporaneous notes taken by *Times* journalist, Dominic Kennedy, at the inquest on 9 September 1998. About 15 minutes after the Associated Press bulletin was released Justin hailed a cab in Kingsway, central London. He asked to be taken to Fairchild Street in Shoreditch, just north of Liverpool Street railway station. After being dropped off he went into Chariots, a health spa for gay men. It was about 3.15pm. John Pickford was working in reception. He half recognised the tall black man who entered the club and, in a light-hearted exchange, Justin gave his name, explaining he was one of the two Fashanu brothers who played football. Pickford said Justin appeared to know his way around the club. At about 6pm Justin borrowed some shaving foam from a friend of Pickford's who also worked at the club. Around 6.30pm Pickford saw him making a phone call and about 7pm noticed he was fully dressed and about to leave. Justin gave him a key he had used and John Pickford said, 'Thanks, see you later.' Justin replied, 'Thanks, I've had a good time in here today', and left. Pickford told the coroner that Justin did not appear distressed.

If anyone saw or spoke to Justin after he left Chariots they have never come forward. At around 12.30pm the next day, Saturday 2 May 1998, he was found dead, in a lock-up garage close to Chariots. No time of death was established, the coroner saying he might have been dead 'for a matter of hours' before he was found. Between leaving Chariots and taking his life Justin presumably became aware of the news story that he was wanted by the police, as it was picked up and broadcast by the British media. But there was no evidence showing what he heard, saw or read; whether for example he was still alive when the Saturday morning papers went on sale.

The garage, in Fairchild Place, was built into a railway arch. Although the doors were locked a piece of corrugated tin had fallen down and Justin climbed in through the gap. He was carrying a black holdall containing a large burgundy filofax. He took a mirror from the wall and propped it up on a sink in the toilet. There he cut his right wrist three times, the longest cut being 7cm. The wounds were described by a pathologist as superficial although there was a lot of blood. Pieces of blood-soaked tissue littered the floor. He may have been mopping up blood so he could write the suicide note which was found in his filofax. He wrote:

> 'Well if anyone finds this note hopefully I won't be around to see it. But let's begin at the beginning. What a start. Everything going so well then I felt that I was abandoned, left alone without anybody to turn to. Being gay and a personality is so hard. But everybody has it hard at the moment so I can't complain about that. I want to say that I didn't sexually assault the young boy. He willingly had sex with me and then the next day asked for money. When I said no he said you wait and see. If that's the case, I hear you say, why did you run? Well justice isn't always fair and I felt that I wouldn't get a fair trial because of my homosexuality. (Silly thing really but you know what happens when you panic.) The blood is from my wrists cut because I want to die rather than put my friends and family through any more unhappiness.
>
> I wish that I was more of a good son, brother, uncle and friend but I tried my best. This seems to be a really hard world. I hope the Jesus that I love welcomes me home. I will at last find peace!!
>
> Please let Maria Sol and Amal know that I love them with all my heart and to know that I was the person they knew me as. Please send my love to John, Phillip, Dawn, (Aatu), Remi, Delli, mum and Daniel. Special thanks to Edward, Rachel, Jemima, Simeon and the boys. Love to my friends in the US and say that I had the best time of my life there. Love!!'

After writing the note Justin made his way through the garage and found some tyres and electric flex. He used some combination of the tyres and a chair to climb up, tie the flex round a rafter and hang himself. Justin Fashanu's life was over, but the story of his life was not.

Chapter 15

Aftermath

Saturday 2 May 1998 was the first day of the bank holiday weekend, the London weather cloudy and mild. Justin Fashanu featured in the British morning newspapers for the first time for over four years, when he had made the claim about knowing Stephen Milligan and departed from Hearts in a hurry. As usual, *The Sun* packed the most information into the fewest letters with the headline, 'Sex Rap Gay Fash Vanishes'. Not unusually in its stories about Justin Fashanu, its reporting was not entirely accurate, claiming 'Interpol has been told to watch out for him'. *The Mirror* used the headline, 'Fashanu Hunted For Sex Assault On Boy, 17'. It claimed 'an international police hunt is underway' and 'Interpol were alerted as Fashanu fled America'. These, and other reports, gave a misleading impression of how far advanced and how active the Howard County police were in their search.

Stephen O'Connor lived in a flat next to the lock-up garage in Fairchild Place and had an arrangement with the owner to keep his car there. His car was parked in the street outside. Just before 12.30pm O'Connor spotted an approaching traffic warden and decided to open up the garage to move his car into it. There were two padlocks on the double doors which he unlocked. As he pulled opened the doors he saw a man's body hanging from a rafter. He checked that the man was dead and called the police. They were there within minutes. They found a passport in a rear pocket of his jeans. The name in it was Justin Fashanu.

The Biography

That Saturday was the last day of fixtures in the bottom two divisions of the Football League. For some teams promotion and relegations places were still at stake. The day's matches were their most important of the season. Torquay United had been stuck in the lowest tier of the Football League since being relegated in 1992, Justin's comeback season. They were playing Leyton Orient, in east London, with promotion a possibility. The fans, who had made the long trek up from Devon, were to be disappointed. Their team lost 1–2: they had missed automatic promotion and would have to take their chances in the Play-offs. Around 5pm the Torquay fans trickled out of Leyton Orient's Brisbane Road stadium. Turning on their radios for the other scores they heard the startling news of their former player being found dead. They remember the shock of realising this was a real matter of life and death, something far more significant than a football score. That Justin had also played for Leyton Orient and had died a few miles from where they had been watching the match somehow made it worse.

Phone lines were busy as the news was relayed among families, friends and colleagues in Britain and North America. Those in the public eye had to deal not only with their own feelings but think of something suitable to say to the media. This was going to be a big story.

The tributes and obituaries showed how Justin divided opinion, as was illustrated by a newspaper for gays and lesbians claiming his death had little to do with homophobia and a canon in the Christian church claiming it did. Also noteworthy was the contrast between the comments made by football people who knew him in the early days and those who knew him after he came out.

Justin's two managers at Norwich City both spoke. John Bond told the *Eastern Daily Press*: 'This is a very sad day. What a waste of a life. He was a real talent and a handful for every defender he played against.' Ken Brown added: 'He was a great fellow and a great player. I am very sad.' Norwich City played their last match of the season on Sunday 3 May, a meaningless fixture in the second tier of English football. It was away to Reading, who were already relegated, the Canaries finishing in mid-table. There the Norwich fans paid their own tribute, reviving a chant not heard from them for 17 years: 'Keep on scoring Fash-a-nu.'

Justin's death was particularly painful for Ronnie Brooks who agonised over whether he could or should have advised Justin differently and whether it would have made any difference. He was full of emotion when filmed for the TV documentary, *Shot Down In Flames*. Ronnie Brooks had never been comfortable with Justin's sexual orientation but had never stopped loving him. Tearfully, he said: 'I hope people remember him as the kindly, happy, exuberant young man who was destined to make his mark in whichever of the two sports he'd taken on, and he certainly did that.'

People from the world of football who knew him later in his career were also complimentary but their comments demonstrated an awareness of his struggles and his flaws, with some not entirely surprised his life ended this way. Tony Shepherd worked for Ambrose Mendy's World Sports Organisation and knew Justin from the late 1980s when they represented him. He said: 'I just found him very, very good company. He was very charming – it was a case of the proverbial birds out of the trees. He seemed very enigmatic. He knew he had this X factor. But I don't know if anyone got close to Justin. He was a larger than life character, a loner; he never had a close circle of friends.'

John McGrane, Justin's manager at Hamilton Steelers, said that much as the news shocked him 'you knew at some point something would happen with him. He alienated all the people in his life, hadn't talked to his brother for four years. In the end there was no support structure there. It was like some kind of self-destruction.' He described Justin as a 'well-mannered man who was pleasant and courteous' and 'played so unlike the pre-conceived notion many have of homosexuals. He was hard-nosed and very aggressive.'

Mike Bateson, chairman of Torquay United recalled: 'Everything was quite amicable when he was here. We never had any problems except because of his ego/personality he sometimes thought he was bigger than the club. He was charming, articulate and interesting. He could also be very selfish. Sometimes he wouldn't do anything unless there was some benefit to him. The supporters will be sad. They liked him. He was a damned good footballer. His death shook me but it didn't surprise me. It was fairly inevitable it would end this way. He seemed to be always stumbling around doing it his own way refusing to listen to advice.'

One of his managers at Torquay, Paul Compton, said: 'I think when Justin came out he struggled to live with it and now it has come to an unfortunate end. He never hid anything and found it quite easy to talk about it. But coming out is something that, at times, he probably regretted. He was always being chased by the women. He had that charisma and he was a nice fella.'

David Thomas who reported on Torquay United wrote: 'If I've got a lasting memory of him it would be of him emerging from the scruffy, peeling paint dressing room of tumbledown Belle Vue, Doncaster, after the match. He looked terrific. He smelt like he'd just had a long session in a high class beauty parlour. And he was ready to meet his public. There you have him. A man for whom the public was no problem but the private was a lonely nightmare.'

The Biography

Julie Goodyear expressed sympathy for his family but not for Justin: 'He obviously ran out of lies. He told a lot of lies about me for money. The only relationship I ever had with Justin was one of friendship but he claimed it was a sexual relationship which wasn't true. I maintained a dignified silence but I do think these things catch up with you.'

The comments of Airdrie club secretary, George Peat, reinforced Justin's own comments about his brief time with the club being particularly enjoyable, with fewer problems than he experienced at other clubs in the later part of his career. Peat said he had never met anyone like Justin Fashanu: 'He was a larger than life character. He was totally unpredictable. He was extremely popular with everyone at the club and got on very well with the staff. He was a person who was so full of fun but you always suspected he was up to some sort of scheme or other.'

Heart's teammate, John Colquhoun's article in *The Scotsman* was a warm contrast to those written by the journalists, Conal Urquhart and Gillian Glover, for the same paper but he was clearly aware of Justin's tendency to exploit people. Calling him 'a likeable rogue', Colquhoun wrote: 'He believed he needed to lead a luxurious lifestyle that his footballing ability could no longer provide. Only one other asset could produce the funds to maintain his high living – his charm.'

The allegation of sexual assault and the controversial events of his life meant there was an element of scandal associated with Justin's death, one that could be exploited by media avid for sensational stories. *The Sun* got stuck in with its headline, 'Shame of Fash'. It began with his visit to Chariots. Trevor Mapp, the owner, turned down a £25,000 offer from an unnamed tabloid newspaper for the inside story of Justin's final hours there, in order to preserve client confidentiality. That did not stop *The Sun* creating its own improbable version of events. Under the headline, 'Gay Fash's last night of lust', it claimed he 'spent six hours romping naked with other men before disappearing into a back room with an oriental looking lad'.

More serious was the possibility Justin had been a sexual predator. The issue was raised by Tobias Jones in *The Independent*: 'Whether he wanted to cast himself as the paternal figure he had so often admired in others, or whether he was motivated by darker forces, Fashanu's attachments in the last three years of his life were largely to youth projects.' In *The Sun*, Allan Hall recalled interviewing Justin in the Waldorf Hotel in 1990 for the articles in which he came out as gay. He claimed to have found Justin in bed 'with a boy not a day over 15'. He did not explain how he got into Justin's room in these circumstances or why, if he thought a serious crime was being committed, he did not report it to the police. The *Pink Paper* reported that a man had told them that, as a 17- year-old, he was sexually assaulted by Justin in a Torquay hotel after being interviewed for the job of his PA. It also claimed 'there is a welterweight of rumour around Fashanu and very young men'. Tabloid newspapers were searching for negative stories about Justin's sex life and financial inducements were offered for victims to come forward but nothing else on this theme was published at the time.

The *Pink Paper* staff's beliefs about Justin's behaviour may explain its decision to publish an editorial which challenged Peter Tatchell's claim that Justin was killed by homophobia. Tatchell's argument was set out in a long press release from his organisation, OutRage!, a shorter version of which was published in *The Guardian*. Tatchell described their friendship and outlined Fashanu's life story which he saw as a series of rejections which began with him being put in care and continued with his experience of homophobia from football, the black community and the church. He wrote: 'Becoming a born-again Christian screwed up his life. With his church damning homosexuality, he became very confused and unhappy about his sexual feelings. Desperate attempts at relationships with women failed. His longing for the love of men never went away. While publicly proclaiming Christian celibacy, he ended up resorting to furtive gay sex. That made it impossible for him to have a stable gay relationship. Caught between God and gayness, he suffered terrible emotional and psychological turmoil.'

Writing of Justin's later years he admitted: 'There is no denying that he progressively disappointed many people who put their hope and trust in him as a role model. He became trapped in a downward spiral of declining football performance, bad debts, false claims about sexual affairs with leading politicians, unreliability and desertion of long-standing friends.' But he concluded: 'Justin Fashanu was a bright shining star – not a flawless star – but a star nonetheless. And I am proud to have counted him as my friend.' The *Pink Paper* editorial argued that although Tatchell had written 'what many of you want to hear' and 'it may suit you to graft the big issues of sexuality and race on to Fashanu's death but they are trace elements, not touch paper – or the cause'. His death, it said, 'has a soapy, pathetic inevitability'.

In *Gay Times*, Terry Deal recalled interviewing Justin in 1991. He wrote of Justin's courage and generosity in readily agreeing to the interview, saying that *Gay Times* was often refused interviews with out gay stars from 'far less contentious arenas than soccer'. Deal, who became a friend of Justin, continued: 'Justin oozed what appeared to be genuine charm and self-confidence, brightening up any room or gathering with his huge presence and big beaming smile. He was one of those people who spoke to you in such a way that you were made to feel he was really happy to be talking to you.' But he also saw another side of Justin: 'Somewhere behind the charming façade there was something more complex than just the slightly desperate loneliness he occasionally exhibited.' He went on to describe Justin's troubles with his passport and the travel company when he was with Torquay United. Reading similar stories from former friends and acquaintances he was left wondering if Justin was not just someone with serious debts but 'some sort of compulsive con man'. Deal concluded by reminding readers of something Fashanu had said in the 1991 interview: 'There are many people who would love to come out, not just in sport, who will be looking to see what will happen to me. If I can get back on the field and do what I do best and score goals and be accepted, the way will be open to other people. But if Justin Fashanu is buried and gone, and the blockade continues, then I think it will put back – by a long way – the chances of other people in sport coming out. It's as important as that.'

* * *

The day after Justin's body was found a post-mortem was conducted but proved inconclusive. Although the cause of his death appeared to be suicide by hanging, the blood on his wrists caused some confusion. The bloody scene in the toilet, and Justin's holdall were only found on Tuesday 5 May when garage owner, Norman Keane, arrived at 7am. He called the police who opened up the holdall and discovered Justin's suicide note.

The note was shown to the Fashanu family and some of its content was reported in the press. It was widely reported to include: 'The first I heard I was a fugitive was when I turned on the television news. I realised that I had already been presumed guilty.' *The Voice* reported that he had written, 'Judging by the hysterical reports in the newspapers I was never going to be allowed a fair trial'. According to *The Mirror* and other papers Justin had written that DJ had, 'boasted to pals about Justin's rich brother in London and said that unless he obtained a substantial amount of cash from John Fashanu he would accuse Justin of sexual assault'.

These first two extracts gave the strong impression of Justin reacting to the tone and content of TV and newspaper reports. The third gave substance to his claim of being blackmailed. The theme that Justin may have killed himself because of exaggerated and misinformed reporting in the British media was taken up by *The Voice*. It quoted 'a source close to Justin and the Fashanu family': 'There was total misinformation and that is what killed him.' Some of the reporting was misleading. It suggested there was already an international search underway. But it was not baseless. The Howard County police did want to arrest Justin and had said they would extradite him if necessary.

Justin's suicide note was read out at the inquest in September, and is reproduced in chapter 14. None of these three supposed extracts were in it. It seems unlikely that they were accidently omitted. It has to be assumed they were fictitious. Their existence has added to the confusion about the circumstances of Justin's death.

The impact of his death was being felt in Ellicott City. A *Baltimore Sun* journalist broke the news to DJ. It reported that he lit a cigarette and remained silent for a few moments before saying: 'I have a lot of mixed feelings. I feel bad that he did it to himself. But I'm also disgusted about what he did to me. I'm upset that I didn't get to see him go through trial, see justice. I didn't get to confront him, ask him why he did it.' Shortly after, it was widely reported that DJ had taken an Aids test which proved negative. Another *Baltimore Sun* article revealed that DJ had been tested for the date rape drug, Rohypnol, but the test had proved negative. DJ and his mother told Brian Deer the test had been delayed and the drug could have left his system. Rohypnol, a powerful sedative, offered a possible explanation for him being barely aware of the alleged anal sex at the time and his hazy memory of it. The *Baltimore Sun* reported that nurses and police who examine rape victims for signs of physical trauma were being trained to identify the effects of date rape drugs which, it said: 'Knock victims unconscious and wipe away their memories.' However research has revealed that the majority of people who believe they have consumed these drugs are suffering from the effects of alcohol.

DJ did not have the opportunity to confront Justin in court. Instead, like many alleged victims of sexual violence, he found his own behaviour under scrutiny. Deer wrote: 'Since word had got out about his ordeal there had been ugly, whispered speculations. Surely this kid [who lifted weights] was too strong to be raped. Maybe he was gay and just didn't know it yet. Why the hell did he stay overnight?... They conjectured that the kid must have changed his mind. He must, really, have asked for it.' He was able to give his version of the events of the night of 24 March to Brian Deer and for the TV documentary, *Fallen Hero*. In this programme he was asked about Justin's allegation of blackmail and replied: 'I don't exactly know where those came up from. I do know, yes, we hired a lawyer afterwards to protect ourselves, to protect myself...But I never intended at any time to blackmail him. I never intended at any time to sue him. I just wanted justice to be served.'

In the week after Justin's death, the Howard County police were called to the apartment he had stayed in after the building manager found it unlocked with no sign of forced entry. It had been ransacked with broken glass from a picture frame on the floor and items scattered around. Carved into a wall with a knife were the words: 'I can't help it. I'm gay. I'm sorry. Goodbye.' The mystery of whether Justin had returned to the apartment or it had been done by someone else was never solved. The police felt obliged to defend themselves against criticism they had been too slow in investigating the case, giving Justin time to leave the country. Perhaps fearing a law suit Howard County's State Attorney, Marna McLendon, issued a statement: 'Police cannot predict the consequences of people reacting to public disclosure. This [death] does not rest at the feet of the Police Department.'

* * *

Justin's funeral was held on Saturday 9 May. Organised by the Fashanu family it took place at the London City Cemetery and Crematorium in Manor Park, east London. The service was conducted by Pastor Wynne Lewis, described in *The Voice* as a close friend of Justin. After Wynne Lewis died in 2009 a tribute on YouTube called him 'one of the last of the old-school Welsh Pentecostal preachers'. Also contributing to the service was Pastor Maxine Hargreaves. Among the 40 or so people who attended were the footballer, Garth Crooks; boxer, Frank Bruno; and Justin's former fiancée, Julie Arthurton.

In the programme for the funeral service, John wrote: 'My Tribute: Even though we've had our differences like all families, I have always loved you and always will. At least I know for sure that you have now found your eternal peace. I know that Jesus, whom you loved, will welcome you home. Free at last! Your loving brother, John.' The entrance music was *Yes I Will* by the British R&B Gospel Group, Nu Colours. During the service Phillip's son, Andre, and John's daughter, Amal, read from Ecclesiastes 3: 'To every thing there is a season, and a time to every purpose under the heaven.' Justin's sister, Dawn, read a poem. A.J. Ali, and Lonny Wortham from the Bridgeway Community Church, had travelled from the USA to be at the service and spoke. Mourners filed out to the sound of Puff Daddy's *I'll Be Missing You.*

Three further events to commemorate Justin's life were held, illustrating the cultural and geographical divisions in his life. On 17 July a memorial service was held in Norfolk. Organised by Edward and Rachel Jackson it took place in St Mary's Church, Attleborough. Over 150 people attended including John Fashanu and his family; Ronnie Brooks; Justin's boxing coach, Gordon Homes; business manager, Roger Haywood; Canaries teammate, Peter Mendham; school friends and their parents, and teachers. The service was led by the Reverend John Aves, Rector of Attleborough. Edward Jackson directed the Southburgh Choir. His eldest children, Jemima and Simeon, sang the Lloyd Webber setting of *Pie Jesu*. Prayers were read by Rachel Jackson and David Jones, an English teacher from Justin's school, Attleborough High School.

An address was given by the Reverend Canon Derek Price, Rachel Jackson's father. He had been a minister in Norfolk for 30 years before retiring in 1992 and had known Justin since he was a teenager. He began by acknowledging people's fond memories of Justin. He spoke of visiting the Jackson family home where Justin was brought up with 'love, discipline and good food'. He talked about the many tributes which had been sent in and shared extracts from a letter from Jane Meakin, Justin's art teacher from Attleborough High School. She described Justin as being 'exceptionally polite and gentle towards others' and shared a story of him once scribbling her a message on the back of a painting: 'Can you do a little to help me along?' He recalled the last time he had seen Justin, at the funeral for Betty Jackson; how Justin had greeted him with 'a broad smile and friendly hug' and how, 'it was so characteristic that at the tea after the funeral, whilst the adults were talking solemnly, Justin was giggling with the children.'

Derek Price did not shy away from what he called 'his strange life story'. He spoke of everyone having a shadow side to their personality, 'vulnerable secret spots which others do not normally see and which we do not usually choose to reveal'. He suggested: 'Life would be unbearable if we all went around speaking of the ugly bits and pieces in the cellars of our minds.'

Then he launched into an attack on attitudes in the church towards homosexuality: 'Whatever the legal verdict on Justin's suicide I believe the ultimate, original and rock bottom cause was the prejudice and antagonism of the church and society-in-general towards homosexuals, pushing many of them – most of them – into a life of excruciating secrecy, deception and despair. The church down the centuries has always had a morbid fear of the body and all its functions and thus done untold damage to people's minds and spirits by repressing that which is good. And things are not all that much better today.'

He spoke about a TV documentary, *Better Dead than Gay*, which had been shown recently: 'It explored the suicide of a 26-year-old Ipswich man because he could not reconcile being homosexual with being Christian, part of the predicament I suspect Justin found himself in right up to the bitter end. Simon Harvey's story concretely expressed the dilemma faced by many homosexual people, especially those who embrace the Christian faith like Justin did – the struggle to find self-esteem and to love themselves amid such negative, rejecting, critical messages, and the common use by some Christians of their religion to justify their social prejudices, often masked by moral certitude and self-righteousness – together with a one track mind that somehow sees homosexuals as a greater problem to focus on than thousands of fly-blown skeletal men, women and children dying under the Sudan sun or even homelessness and other social problems of our own communities.'

He continued: 'I believe that in God's created scheme of things of infinite variety there are both heterosexuals and homosexuals and every sexual shade in between, and that homosexuality is no more deviation, flaw or falling short than being created left handed, blue eyed or dark haired – not at any rate in the eyes of God, who is not only the God of Adam and Eve but also of David and Jonathan who loved each other…and who kissed, cuddled and wept on one another's shoulders…

'We meet this evening in a Christian building in which rich medieval art conveys the fact that fear and judgement were at the centre of lives in those days. But the very, very centre of our faith is not fear but love; love expressed in forgiveness, and we must not forget that Jesus Christ spoke special words of acceptance and forgiveness to the marginalised in society including not only the social outcasts and cheats but the woman caught in the act of adultery and the woman of the streets whose humble anointing of his feet he received with affection and feminine tenderness. Hypocrisy and greed, of which there is no shortage today, seemed far more soul destroying in Christ's eyes than sexual aberration.

'Forgiveness is not simply forgetting. Forgiveness is remembering all the hurt with love. Justin's much publicised sexual attitudes and activities not only totally mystified us; we must admit frankly that they hurt relatives and friends as well. It is very important that this evening we remember all that hurt with love, just as we hope he remembers with love our part in a society that all too easily treats homosexuals with levity, scorn and abuse.'

Derek Price's criticisms of the church were reported on the front page of the *Eastern Daily Press*. They were all the more newsworthy for being made on the eve of the Lambeth Conference, a meeting of senior figures in the Anglican church from around the world, who were due to debate the contentious issue of the place of lesbians and gay men in the church. Price declined to be drawn into the controversy, saying he had never before had occasion to make public his views on homosexuality and refusing to speculate on how other church officials might react. There was to be no public row. A spokesman for the General Synod, a sort of governing body of the Church of England, would only say: 'It would not be appropriate for us to comment on what is essentially an address at a funeral. Mr Price was undoubtedly trying to set this tragic incident in its context and it would not be right for us to take a view and interfere with his pastoral duties.'

After a divisive and heated debate, the Lambeth Conference passed a resolution saying that homosexual practice (though not necessarily orientation) is 'incompatible with Scripture'. The most graphic illustration of conflict within the church on this matter came in a public confrontation between Bishop Emmanuel Chukwuma of Enugu, Nigeria and the Reverend Richard Kirker of the Lesbian and Gay Christian Movement. It was reconstructed by Stephen Bates for his book, *A Church at War: Anglicans and Homosexuality*: 'Chukwuma announced that Leviticus ordained the death penalty for homosexuals. "Would you be prepared to stone us to death?" asked Kirker, who was handing out leaflets, whereupon the Bishop attempted to lay his hands on top of his head. "In the name of Jesus I deliver him out of homosexuality", he declared as Kirker ducked out of the way. "I pray for God to forgive you, for God to deliver you out of your sinful act, out of your carnality." Kirker civilly replied: "May God bless you, sir, and deliver you from your prejudice against homosexuality." "You have no inheritance in the kingdom of God. You are going to hell. You have made yourself homosexual because of your carnality", the Bishop reposted, sweat streaming down his face and his voice rising. As his wife nearby murmured "Alleluia", Bishop Chukwuma shouted: "We have overcome carnality just as the light will overcome darkness... God did not create you as a homosexual. That is our stand. That is why your church is dying in Europe – because it is condoning immorality. You are killing the church. This is the voice of God talking. Yes I am violent against sin." When a South African bishop intervened, saying Archbishop Tutu supported homosexual inclusiveness, Bishop Chukwuma replied: "Desmond Tutu is spiritually dead", and stalked off.'

And there you have it. The conflict Justin Fashanu was never able to resolve; Chukwuma, a black man from Nigeria and Kirker, a white man born and raised in Nigeria, epitomising another unhealed division in Justin's life, between the black family he was born into who were abandoned by their Nigerian father before Justin's mother abandoned him, and the white family which took him in and raised him.

A week after the memorial service at Attleborough, another event commemorating Justin's life was held as part of London's Pride Arts Festival. It was billed as 'A tribute to the life of Justin Fashanu, Britain's first out gay footballer'. Held in Carlton Hall in Brixton it featured contributions from three black women who were out as lesbians. They were Valerie Mason-John, also known as Queenie, a performer, writer and activist who, like Justin, had been in care; Dorothea Smartt, a poet and live artist; and Linda Bellos, a political activist who had been leader of Lambeth Council in south London. Peter Tatchell spoke about Justin. Barry Laden, writing in *Metropolis*, reported: 'Cuban Red involved the audience with an inspiring African Libation where we stood together, breathed and chanted.' There were, he wrote, 'poignant personal reflections about Justin. Some were from friends. Most were given by those who had never met him but were nevertheless touched by his life'.

The last of the memorial events for Justin was in September. It was held at All Souls Unitarian Church in Washington DC and organised by Charles Briody, a human right activist and Christian. Peter Tatchell spoke about Justin, and Michael Sainte-Andress, a performance artist and Aids activist, read from Justin's chapter in *Stonewall 25*. They were followed by a service which included Holy Communion.

*   *   *

The inquest into the cause of Justin's death was reopened by coroner, Dr Stephen Ming Chan, on 9 September at Poplar Coroner's Court, East London. The chain of events described in chapter 14 was established through interviews with witnesses who were present and statements made to the police by others. In recording a verdict of suicide Dr Chan summed up Justin Fashanu's life: 'All in all a very tragic end for a man who had become a fallen hero but yet, in the eyes of many, a man who succeeded in life against tremendous odds, who appeared to triumph over his disruptive upbringing and much difficulties in life in the face of prejudices against his colour and hostilities against his sexual preference. Sadly in the end he felt overwhelmed by this same pressure not helped by his worries and concerns over an alleged incident in the USA against him. Indeed it is clear from his note he made a declaration of innocence. He expressed his lack of faith in a fair trial. Clearly he did not want to take any more pain or indeed to cause further distress to his family and his loved ones. Sadly he decided that death was to be the only way out for him.'

The headlines following the inquest were made by an exchange between Dr Chan and Detective Constable Andrew Ormiston who had looked into the matter of the arrest warrant:

Chan: 'It has been widely publicised in the media that the deceased was wanted on warrant in the United States of America for an alleged offence involving him against an under-age youth.'

Ormiston: 'That has been reported, yes sir.'

Chan: 'You have liaised with the United States. He wasn't wanted at all. There was no warrant out for him.'

Ormiston: 'I made immediate inquiries. At the time of the incident being identified and being brought to police attention there was no request from any other agency to seek the whereabouts or to arrest Justin Fashanu for any other matters.'

Chan: 'If any inquiry was made then it was to do a run on his record, to check he had any form.'

It was a muddled exchange. DJ was not 'an under-age youth'. By repeating this error Dr Chan gave the impression Justin had committed a criminal offence even if the sex had been consensual. Also the exchange between Cham and Ormiston gave the strong impression that the Howard County Police Department did not have a warrant for Justin's arrest. It was difficult to draw any other conclusion. It appeared to confirm the accusation attributed to the Fashanu family by *The Voice* that Justin had killed himself because of stories in the British media which had no foundation. It offered an explanation as to why the people who had most contact with Justin in the weeks, days and hours before his death, Maria Sol Acuña and Kaveh Abadani, had found him so positive and happy. It then seemed reasonable to assume that Justin's explanation of what had occurred between him and DJ was correct. Perhaps the police had looked into it and taken no further action but somehow the story had been blown up out of all proportion by the British media. This apparent revelation led to a dreadful conclusion: Justin had taken his own life in the entirely mistaken belief that he faced arrest and trial for an alleged sexual assault.

John and Phillip Fashanu, their mother, Pearl, and other members of the family attended the inquest. Speaking immediately after, John latched on to the apparent absence of an arrest warrant, saying: 'I beg everybody, especially the media, to listen to what the coroner had to say. We are very happy that Justin eventually is resting in peace with a clean bill.' Reports of the inquest focused on this aspect. For example the headline in London paper the *Evening Standard* was 'Justin Fashanu "not wanted for sex assault at time of death".' Dominic Kennedy of *The Times* spoke to the Howard County Police Department who confirmed they did have a warrant for Justin's arrest and asserted that once they knew he was in England they would have begun extradition proceedings. But his report did not receive the prominence of the original story.

It remained true that some of the British media's original reporting of the Howard County Police Department's interest in Justin had exaggerated their efforts, claiming Interpol had been alerted and an international police hunt was already underway. If these were the stories Justin came across they may have caused him to panic, fearing imminent arrest. The possibility that, had Justin known he had more time and more options, he may not have taken such drastic action cannot be ruled out.

*   *   *

When Justin Fashanu died it was over seven years after coming out as gay. In that time, as far as anyone could tell, no other professional footballer in the world had followed suit. In every subsequent year in which Justin remained unique in this respect, his significance grew. British professional football was going through a revolution. A sport once almost exclusively the preserve of the white working class changed beyond recognition as talent was recruited from all over the world. Dressing rooms, those traditional sanctums of bonding, banter and shared baths, became places where different languages were spoken and religions observed. So many players were openly Christian that in some clubs a group of them would meet for prayers before running out on the pitch. The position of lesbians and gay men in British society was also changing. The age of consent was eventually equalised at 16 in 2000 and civil partnerships legalised in 2004. Legal protection against workplace harassment and discrimination was introduced. It became easier to be openly gay in many occupations.

Football moved from the margins to became more central in British culture, its multiethnic nature epitomising a modern inclusive society, its family-friendly stadiums attracting a broader range of support. The absence of openly gay players became incongruous, a reminder of the bad old days of menace and violence, when racist and homophobic chants on the terraces and insults on the pitch were tolerated. Organisations, such as Stonewall and Kick it Out, campaigned against homophobia in football. The 10th anniversary of Justin's death was marked by the launch of the Justin Campaign: 'A campaign against homophobia in football that focuses on vindicating the memory of Justin Fashanu.'

Occasionally a professional sportsman came out as gay. Gareth Thomas, a rugby union player who had captained Wales and the British Lions, did so in 2009. In February 2011 the English international, Stephen Davies, became the first openly gay professional cricketer. A steady stream of articles and programmes in the media lamented the lack of similar progress in British football. Inevitably they would refer to Justin Fashanu, often linking his decision to come out with his death, as if the one had led directly to the other. An article in *The Guardian* referred to Fashanu publicly saying he was gay and then being 'hounded until his suicide'. In March 2011 Anton Hysén who played for Utsiktens BK in the fourth tier of the Swedish soccer league spoke publicly about being gay. After more than 20 years there was another openly gay professional footballer.

When Justin was 19 years old he said he wanted to be 'richer and more famous'. The money came and went. The young footballer, who no doubt wanted to be famous for his goals, is famous for just one. His glorious goal against Liverpool was featured, in 2011, on the website bleacherreport.com, as one of the 50 best ever scored in world football. But he always played down its significance. His greatest feat as a footballer was that magnificent 1980–81 season for Norwich City in which he scored 22 goals.

And of course Justin Fashanu is famous for being gay. He did not choose to be gay. He did not choose to come out. His Christian beliefs meant he was never comfortable with his sexual orientation. He did his best to live with the situation he found himself in, showing courage in speaking up for gay people in professional sports and in the black British community. He loved men and found a way of expressing it. He loved people and was loved back. He loved life and lived it to the full. His Christian faith brought him joy as well as anguish. It is equally true that Justin treated people badly, very badly at times. As his football career faltered his craving for wealth and a celebrity lifestyle distorted his priorities and his values. He can be blamed and criticised but the argument with his mother which began this biography, and the reasons behind it, probably explain a great deal about how Justin lived his life.

Justin showed bravery and tenacity in rebuilding his football career after injury with the added burden of homophobia to contend with. In doing so he found comradeship and respect among some of his colleagues at the 11 clubs he turned out for in this second phase of his career. Like any footballer he is fondly remembered by the supporters of teams where he performed well. He was a pioneer and a significant figure in football, in the story of black people in Britain and in gay history.